CW01433113

PASSING
CLOUDS

PASSING CLOUDS

GRAEME LEITH

A Winemaker's Journey

ALLEN & UNWIN

SYDNEY • MELBOURNE • AUCKLAND • LONDON

First published in 2015

Copyright © Graeme Leith 2015

All rights reserved. No part of this book may be reproduced or transmitted in
any form or by any means, electronic or mechanical, including photocopying,
recording or by any information storage and retrieval system, without prior
permission in writing from the publisher. The Australian *Copyright Act 1968*
(the Act) allows a maximum of one chapter or 10 per cent of this book, whichever
is the greater, to be photocopied by any educational institution for its educational
purposes provided that the educational institution (or body that administers it) has
given a remuneration notice to Copyright Agency (Australia) under the Act.

Allen & Unwin
83 Alexander Street
Crows Nest NSW 2065
Australia
Phone: (61 2) 8425 0100

Email: info@allenandunwin.com
Web: www.allenandunwin.com

Cataloguing-in-Publication details are available
from the National Library of Australia
www.trove.nla.gov.au

ISBN 978 1 76011 120 5

Set in 12.5/14.5 pt Minion by Post Pre-press Group, Australia

Printed and bound in Australia by Griffin Press

10 9 8 7 6 5 4 3 2 1

MIX
Paper from
responsible sources
FSC
www.fsc.org   FSC® C009448

The paper in this book is FSC® certified.
FSC® promotes environmentally responsible,
socially beneficial and economically viable
management of the world's forests.

Contents

9 Musk and more

10 Making wine

INTRODUCTION

When I started writing this book, my intention had been to recount my forty-year involvement in the business of making wine, and the knowledge I had accumulated as a grower, maker and seller of wine. This, I hope, has been realised.

However, as my recollections began taking shape for the book, I became aware that so closely aligned were my experiences of life with those of winemaking, it was becoming increasingly difficult to separate the two. In fact, as I proceeded with the memoir, I discovered that there were not two strands of experience at all, but experiences so inextricably entwined that the business and the personal were actually one. So simple, really, and so obvious, when the penny drops.

Confirming my rethinking of the book's shape and purpose, various friends who read early drafts would frequently want to know more about my other experiences: for instance, what drew me to owning a vineyard in the first place, and what my relationships were with the family and friends, the loves and acquaintances, the kindred (and un-kindred) spirits, the neighbours and strangers, who have populated my seventy-three years of life.

And so the memoir grew to accommodate some of the people, occasions, events and highlights—both catastrophic and joyful—of my life before and during the wine days, which continue on.

Eldest son Sebastian is not involved in the winery but enjoys good wine so we often share a glass together when we meet. Nowadays my second son Cameron is Passing Clouds' winemaker, and my third and youngest son Jesse handles sales and cellar door. However, we needed a Superwoman to keep things running smoothly and we found one, a mother of three who owns a property not all that far from our vineyard and winery. Her name is Andrea Brabham and she works with us part-time, doing the books, sharing cellar door sales duties and doing many things that Sue Mackinnon, my then partner, used to do at Kingower—that is, things that the boys can't or won't do, and she does those things calmly and gracefully. There are other various good people contributing to the end result, and my own enthusiasm remains undiminished—the old stock horse still snuffing the battle with delight! We all work together, and I expect to be part of the team until I am removed by whatever it is that the gods have in store for me.

Until then I will look forward to each new vintage with a sense of excitement and the anticipation of another new wine to taste, to savour, to drink, to enjoy, to talk about, and to share with friends—the best thing one can do with a bottle of wine!

Graeme Leith

1

A vintner's boyhood

Grape juice in a goat skin

I don't know exactly when the winemaking bug bit me. I think it was in 1961, in Perugia in Italy where I was doing a three-month course in Italian language. However, I had shown some interest in the fermentation process at a much earlier age when, in contravention of the teachings of the church to which I belonged, I claimed that the wine Jesus drank must have been alcoholic wine and not the preserved grape juice given out at communion at our church.

My proposition was that without the use of preservatives any grape juice bunged into a goat skin was inevitably going to turn into wine. This idea was not supported by my Sunday School teacher who sent me home, after the collection plate had been passed around, to explain my transgression to my teetotal mother.

This teacher had sent me home on a previous occasion when I asked him who had made God. He replied (rather ingenuously, I thought) with a question: 'What came first, the chicken or the egg?'

I had replied: 'That's easy. The chicken, because the book of Genesis tells us that the Lord made the fowls to fly and the fish to swim.'

So I suppose it's not surprising that I grew up to become an atheistic, wine-drinking smartarse.

Years later, when I had concluded that God had not made man in his own image, but rather that *man* had made God in *his* own image, I would presumably have got myself into more trouble, but I'd ceased going to Sunday School by then.

How it was, though, that I presumed that the desert tribes had not learned from the Romans that the addition of elemental sulphur to grape juice could delay or prevent fermentation, I have no idea. For although I'd read quite a lot of the Bible, I had not read any treatises on winemaking and would have been unlikely to find any in our Presbyterian home.

At any rate, our mother was of that church, although to my recollection she never attended. Our father, if he had any religion, never spoke of it. But there was never any alcoholic beverage in the house and I never spoke to him about it as he died of a work-related lung cancer in 1953, at the age of forty-three, when I, aged thirteen, was too young to have heart-to-heart chats with him. But my brother Robin had heard stories of very old whisky bottles being dug up in the vegetable garden, so maybe there had been some excessive drinking in a previous generation of which Dad was aware.

As children, we were opposed to the consumption of alcohol, and if reason needed to be found for that opposition then one had to go no further than the local hotel at six o'clock on a Saturday afternoon and observe the rowdy, drunken, beer-swilling, urinating and occasionally vomiting mess of patrons as they poured as much as possible into themselves before they were kicked out at ten past. Once, emboldened by their apparent inability to pursue us, we gave cheek to some of them from the doorway, and when they came after us, threw wheat on the floor to make them slip, but it was a close shave and we never did it again.

Born in an earlier age

My father's family had come from Scotland and at some stage must have possessed some style and money because once, in a locked storage shed in the backyard among the framed photographs of deceased relatives and the musty mounted antlers of long-dead deer, we found trunks filled with fine and elegant female apparel. There were dresses in silk and satin, silk-covered shoes and silken scarves, much of which was eagerly seized by one of the sons of my parents' visitors. The rest of us boys, destined for a life of heterosexuality, left him to his dressing up and used the silk parasols we had found as parachutes to assist us in landing as we jumped from the shed roof, to the detriment of the parasols and—when our whoops of delight attracted the attention of the elders at the house—ourselves.

I doubt that it ever occurred to us that those gorgeous clothes probably belonged to the wizened old creature slowly dying in the front room—my father's mother, cared for by our mother whose destiny it was to look after five children and a succession of dying family members, her end reward to be a shared ward in a mental institution when dementia prematurely overcame her in her late sixties. She'd given birth to five children—Ian, Graeme (me), Robin and Carolyn in fairly rapid succession then, after a spell of a few years, Gregory. Four boys and one girl—poor Carolyn!

My father's business had been motor body repairs, panel-beating and spray-painting. It was the spray-painting that got him in the end because 'real men' didn't wear protective masks in those days. I clearly remember a mask hanging on a hook above the paint bench, unused over the years, and enveloped in the same crusted patina of paint that ended up killing our dad from the inside.

My father had been born in an earlier age—for him, a time of roaring flaming forges, of bellows and coke, of red-hot horseshoes and the blows of the mighty sledgehammer as it tamed the once adamantine but now malleable metal upon the anvil, for, as a boy, he had been a blacksmith. In later life, one of his greatest joys was to fire up the forge and, with the aid of the tongs, the hammer and the hissing cauldron of water, turn raw pieces of iron into useful things.

During his apprenticeship to his father, Dad had learned coach-building at Melbourne Technical College, a course that embraced blacksmithing, wheelwrighting, woodwork, marbling and graining, signwriting, upholstering and even the application of gold leaf. Thus he could build you a coach and adorn it, for that was the family's work. As their letterhead proclaimed, they were J.B. Leith and Sons, Coachbuilders, located at 231 High Street in Preston, an outer northern suburb of Melbourne.

The next iterations of the letterhead saw the business as 'motor body builders', and later, 'panel beaters and spray painters'. And so the intricate web of pulleys and belts in the rafters above the workshop that drove all the machines below that sawed and stitched, and even the mighty forge, fell mostly into quietude, replaced with the throbbing of the compressor, the banging of the hammers against the metal dollies, and the hiss of the spray guns that were to take our father's life.

Dad had been raised in the old and substantial house over the road from the forge and workshops. The area around Preston was mostly given over to small farms at that time and one of his after-school jobs was to ride any horse that had been left for shoeing back to the farm to which it belonged, and he would then hike home across the paddocks.

My mother had come from her family home in Geelong to Melbourne where, as a seamstress, she reached the pinnacle of her working career, securing the dream job of making costumes for His Majesty's Theatre. As a teenager she had excelled at gymnastics—there were more of her trophies for gymnastics in the crystal cabinet than there were of Dad's for cricket. (In fact, Dad only had one that I recall, which I now have—a silver teapot presented to S.J. Leith, Best Fieldsman 1944. As a twelve-year-old I teased him about it, cynically suggesting that he mustn't have been much good at batting and bowling.)

Mum was an attractive woman, with a lovely face, a good figure and cornflower blue eyes. I had an old photograph of her in her gymslip, which I carried with me in my wallet during my European peregrinations. She and Dad had met at a dance at the Northcote Town Hall. Dad told me that he and his mates would often walk home from Northcote to Preston, having overspent buying milkshakes and chocolates for the girls and lacking the fare for the cable car.

Some memories of my father

My memories of my father are sparse but fond. He loved angling but never had much time to indulge that passion due to the demands of a young family and a small business.

But I have one joyous memory of this. We had driven to
a not-too-distant stream, the King Parrot Creek at Flowerdale,
about 15 miles north-east of Melbourne. An uncle was included
in the trip and he and Dad had contrived to allow Dad to precede
us upstream, so that we could unload and erect the tent and not
tear ahead of him and frighten the fish as young boys inevitably
do. When our onerous task was completed, we raced upstream
to the pool where Dad was fishing and above the streamside
shrubbery could see the beautiful glistening arc of the split
cane rod as it bucked to the weight of a trout. As we approached
closer we could see the trout in the clear water, its speckled form
wondrously camouflaged above the pebbled creek bed, almost
exhausted now. My father's face had a look of unforgettable
rapture—a look I never saw before or have ever seen again on
the face of any man. It will stay in my memory forever.

Sometimes we would go rabbit shooting, too. Our family
had a car but in my early years petrol was rationed and the
'gas producers', which were bolted onto the back of the car
and burned charcoal to produce gas that was then fed into the
carburettor, were ingenious, although not very efficient. Two
or three times we took the 'milk train' up to Whittlesea in the
early mornings and walked around the paddock of a friendly
farmer, having a few shots and bagging a few bunnies for the
table at home where they were known as 'underground mutton'.

The train line was decommissioned in the 1950s and the
track torn up in the 1970s; now they're re-laying it and putting
the stations back. Back then, no doubt, somebody, or somebody's brother-in-law, made some money from the scrap metal.

Some time after our father's death, one of his mates told
me a strange story, probably because he saw it as being to
Dad's credit. He and Dad were shooting rabbits one day and
as they crested a hill they came upon a strange and disturbing
tableau. Two men were laughing at the antics of a rabbit that
was running around in circles, clearly distressed and half mad,
for it had been skinned alive and was released for the entertainment of these sadists. Dad established which one of them had
done it and, with his strong blacksmith's arms, removed the

man's weapon and broke it against the nearest tree. He then ordered the man to strip himself naked and run after the rabbit until he caught it and put it out of its misery. My father was redheaded and had the temper to go with it; his temper must have been fiery hot that day in the sunburned sheep paddocks of Whittlesea.

Dad himself related a story to me once, concerning his early school days during the Depression when there were plenty of men 'on the wallaby' (on the road) with swag on back in the hope of finding work. Some of the school bullies had decided to torment Dad because of his red hair and were pursuing him through the bush, throwing sticks and stones at him. Suddenly, before him, the dishevelled figure of a swagman arose from the leaves and bark beside the track and seized him by the shoulders, halting him abruptly and causing his tormentors to turn tail and disappear back into the bush. 'Why are you running away, son?'

'Aw, well, sometimes they decide to tease me 'cos I've got red hair.'

The swagman drew himself up to his full unkempt height and thrust out his chest beneath his tattered shirt. 'Well, boy, when I was your age I had red hair, and look at me now!'

I often pondered that simple story in bed at night, speaking as it does not only of intolerance and discrimination, but also of poverty, of dignity in adversity, of compassion, all wrapped in a glorious envelope of absurdity.

Warrandyte Flip

The suburbs of my boyhood in the early 1950s—at any rate, Preston, the one we lived in—were little hotbeds of religious intolerance, with the Protestants hating the Catholics and vice versa, the enmities doubtless remnants of the English–Irish disagreements from the old countries. Any encounter between the warring parties of boys was an excuse for verbal abuse at best and, at worst, physical confrontation.

I had joined the Boy Scouts before Dad died. It was a Salvation Army troop, so it was Protestant. The leaders were very good to me at the time of his death and helped me through that. To my astonishment, at the funeral for my ex-wife more than twenty years later, a man emerged from the group of mourners, shook my hand using the 'scouts' grip', reminded me that he was my old scoutmaster from the early 1950s, told me he had read the death and funeral notice in the paper, and had come along to show support—a great and selfless gesture which left me dumbstruck. To my discredit I never contacted Jack Bott to thank him. It would have been easy, too, as there wouldn't have been many by that name in the Melbourne phone book.

Scouting was good for us boys; it provided physical exercise, mental stimulation, a sense of camaraderie, and responsibility as part of a team and as individuals. We had many great adventures. The leaders had bought an old tray truck, a 1929 Chevrolet with a canvas canopy over the tray, and into that we shoved as many wooden benches as were required for the number of scouts to be accommodated. Included were all the canvas tents, the big oval Dixie billies for cooking, the food, and then our personal backpacks for the hiking to come. The old truck would wheeze its way to our projected camping destination, as far away as the Grampians or, one year, Wilsons Promontory—a long enough drive today, but it must have taken eight or nine hours in that old Chevy, with a top speed of 50 miles an hour, stopping before the largest hills so that all of us boys could get out and push.

At our camping sites we'd construct rope bridges, flying foxes, even a Roman catapult, then use these things in mock combat. It's quite possible that scouting has been dumbed down a bit these days; maybe they're not even allowed to cook anymore in case they burn themselves on the campfire!

Back then we shared cooking duties and if anybody showed the skills required, mainly those of campfire management and timing, then they got the chef's job and the other kids got to peel things and scour out the Dixies. I'd had some

experience at cooking when Mum was occasionally confined
to bed—usually preceding childbirth—and I would trot up
and down our long dark hallway between the kitchen and the
bedroom with further instructions for the ginger, the chocolate
or, the ultimate culinary challenge, the steamed fruit pudding!
Steamed cape cod with mashed potato and peas, scrambled
eggs, French toast fried in dripping, pancakes, dumplings
with golden syrup, jellies and even homemade ice-cream, were
produced in this manner by our mother–son partnership; a
strong bond was forged between us which remained for the rest
of our time together.

It must have been due to the skills I'd acquired and the
associated hubris that led me to produce the pancake that
later entered the lore of the scout troop and was referred to
reverently as the 'Warrandyte Flip'. We were camped on a cool
creek there, for it was a hot few days, and we had some supplies
left over at the end of the trip. There was an excess of butter,
self-raising flour, condensed milk, eggs, sugar, quite a lot of
cocoa and some sultanas. I was quartermaster cook on the day
of departure and so was able to allow myself the indulgence
of experimentation and observe the 'waste not, want not'
philosophy instilled into us by parents who'd lived through
the Depression. So I combined the lot into a Dixie, except
the butter, which was used liberally to fry the pancakes in the
huge pans. They were a spectacular success and the memory
of the cocoa–chocolate flavour, the gentle yielding texture of
the sultanas and the buttery velvety mouthfeel is as alive to me
today as is the later love of experimenting with different blends
of grape varieties, fruit from different vineyards, all the variables that make winemaking so fascinating.

The art of selling newspapers

We were living in the old family house in Preston. The house
was an anachronism even then, surrounded as it was by old
ironbark trees and the remnants of an orchard. It was Dad's

turn now to die in the front room, and Mum's unhappy duty to
pave his way to the next life. He didn't know what was wrong
with him until a fortnight before his dreadful death but he
had tried every form of treatment he thought might help—
massage, Chinese herbs, acupuncture . . . I was certainly aware
of the deterioration of his health and there's a small but vivid
illustration of the severity of his illness that's stuck in my mind
ever since.

At the time I was selling newspapers after school at a corner
in Northcote, in close proximity to the tram workshops where
trams were built and repaired by Australians, before somebody
had a better idea. The *Herald* truck dropped off the papers just
before we arrived from school on our bicycles. Our job was to
cut the big bundles open and distribute them to the various
workshops before knock-off time—often a close thing as we
finished school a few miles away at four o'clock and knock-off
time was four-thirty. The men would hurry past the stacks of
*Herald*s, grab one if they wanted it and fling their fourpences
at the honesty box. We'd collect the contents along with any
unsold papers, which we then sold at the tram stop on the
corner.

Often we'd board the tram to make the transactions, and
if paper-buyers took too long fumbling for their change we'd
have to leap out at quite high speeds, or if the speed was too
great, stay on the tram until the next stop. There was a large and
aggressive lad selling papers at the next tram stop who resented
us selling to customers who would otherwise have been his;
he'd give us a thump if we were unable to find an adult to shelter
behind before catching the next tram back to our corner. (Years
later I had a motorcycle for sale and this lad came to my house
as a potential purchaser. He had not become bigger or stronger
in the intervening years, but I had. I had also acquired some
boxing skills at various scout camps. Upon recognising him, I
announced who I was and gave him a belting in the driveway of
my mother's house. Revenge was sweet, indeed.)

When we'd sold all our *Herald*s, or as many as we could,
we'd ride back to Green's Newsagency, count our money and

then ride home, having assuaged our hunger with Wagon Wheels, White Knights or vanilla slices from the milk bar over the road, purchased with any tip money we had earned.

We needed to have the correct sum of money for the papers we'd sold and sometimes had to make that up with our own money. If there was a shortfall before Thursdays (paydays at the workshops), it was always compensated for on Fridays. Saturdays were miserable at 'our corner' as we didn't have much passing trade. The first papers were delivered from the city end of St Georges Road, where the men waiting for their *Sporting Globe* would assemble, and so reached our rivals stationed there before us.

After some time we realised that the papers were delivered earlier to another corner on High Street, parallel to St Georges Road but some distance away, accessible via the tramway bridge known as The Hump over the railway line that ran between the two roads. So we had our Saturday papers delivered there and, after a hair-raising ride over The Hump with the papers wedged between the handlebars, were able to get our papers first and thus snooker the opposition, which pleased them not at all.

My new mate Marshy, who worked with me at the paper corner, was not only a Roman Catholic but also a Preston Tech boy, so he was an alien and an enemy on two counts, for there was enmity, too, between the students of Northcote High and Preston Tech schools. I was apprehensive when we were first paired together by the newsagent, but surprised and pleased to realise that he was human like the rest of us. We were soon great mates, sharing our workload with the corner and the 'round'.

The round involved delivering the newspapers to nearby residences, and on one occasion two pretty sisters—who were waiting, to my surprise, for the delivery outside their house—teased me to the point of mortification. On the day before, a Sunday, I had ridden out with my mate, Bob, in the company of two girls from the same school and we had taken a spell beside a quiet and cool aqueduct to engage in some wondrous albeit fairly innocent petting. My first glimpse and touch of an almost naked female breast had evoked a complimentary but clumsy comment from me which was gleefully repeated verbatim by the pretty sisters.

Maybe I learned something about sisterhood then, or maybe not.

Saturdays at the paper-selling corner were incredibly boring, and one day Marshy brought along an air rifle, which he had cut down with a hacksaw so he could conceal it between a sheaf of newspapers. In repeated acts of mindless vandalism we would shoot out the street light over the road every Saturday, for they'd replace the globe during the week. Once they put a bloke there to observe any wrongdoing, but we twigged and didn't shoot the light out until after he'd gone home.

Anyway, back to Dad. One afternoon he drove back from the city in the big Chev Fleetmaster and spotted me selling papers. His face broke into a huge grin—he was so pleased to see me and obviously proud of me, his second son, selling papers to earn money for a new bike. But as he slowed and pulled into the kerb he scraped the beautiful mudguards of the car against the lamp-post. I was aghast.

'Dad, Dad. You've hit the lamp-post!'

He was still grinning with delight at seeing me. 'Don't worry, son, that's easily fixed.'

But I realised then that there was something wrong with my dad that wasn't going to be easily fixed. Death and his funeral were not far away.

2

Rev heads

Victory enow for me

After Dad died we moved further out to suburban Reservoir, back to the new dream house where my parents had begun their married life together. My mother had left it to nurse her mother-in-law in Dad's old and gloomy family house. It was now a longer haul up the hill from Northcote High School, a couple of miles further from the old house. I had my new bike by then, which had three-speed gears, but it was still hard work, particularly in winter when it was often raining and dark by the time we left the paper shop. The dynamo for the bike lights was an additional drag, so if there were no cars coming (on High Street, Preston, at 6.30 p.m.—those were the days!), I'd flip it off the tyre and put on a bit more speed. It was always good to get home and have a bowl of Scotch broth in front of the slow combustion stove while talking to Mum and the kids about the day's activities.

I was not a good student, unlike my older brother, Ian, who was dux of Northcote High in Fifth and Sixth Form, two years ahead of me. I didn't have his discipline or his ambition. I had jumped a form in primary school, doubtless for being a smartarse, so was always the youngest boy in my year, and can clearly remember in First Form heading off alone in the annual cross-country run for which I had trained fairly hard during lunchtimes and weekends. It was a handicap event and I was the only eleven-year-old in the school. Thus, embarrassingly, I had to set off alone thirty seconds ahead of the next age group. At the finish line an eternity later, the crowd was cheering for the Fifth and Sixth Formers who would be the winners. I came in fifth and that was more than pleasing to me but I was unnoticed by the crowd, even though I fell to the ground exhausted at the finish line. A kindly woman helped me up but the crowd continued to ignore me and cheered those who came in behind. But I didn't care, I had tasted something close to victory: 'twas victory enow for me.

Academically, then, I dragged the chain and could never pass the two different maths subjects, usually getting

51 per cent for one and 49 per cent for the other. I just couldn't get the hang of it, although later in life I had a job that demanded a mathematically dexterous brain, dealing with complex electrical circuitry; even winemaking calls for a bit of sums-in-the-head activity.

English expression and literature were my strong suits, due largely to my voracious appetite for books. Ian and I were reading the William books when our friends were reading Enid Blyton, and Edgar Rice Burroughs and Conan Doyle when others were reading about the air adventures of Biggles. This familiarity with literature coupled with a lively imagination meant 90s were my usual marks for those subjects. I often achieved 90s for French, too, not that I was any good at it but because the class average was abysmal.

One year the class maths genius, to his bewilderment, received 51 per cent for Maths One and 96 per cent for French. I, on the other hand, got 96 per cent for Maths One and 51 per cent for French. When I suggested to the teacher the possibility of a mistake, he told me that was impossible and to go back to my desk. Perhaps that was when I first discovered that all is not right with the world—lesson number whatever . . .

I become a tradesman

Brother Ian was off to university but the academically inferior Graeme was not. Dad had died by then and there wouldn't have been the money in any case, even if I'd had the capacity and the ambition. It was to be a trade for me at the end of Fourth Form. Dad had expressed his ambition for me to become a draftsman and I must have taken that to heart for my skills at trade drawing were sufficient for the teacher to criticise me for using a ruler to do my lettering. I had to do some examples for him to demonstrate that it was, indeed, done freehand.

An uncle, who was advising my mother on my career, asked me which trade I would like to pursue and my response was very positively for carpentry, since by then I had learned, in the company of a school mate, respectable skills in the making of model aeroplanes. We made them in the winter and flew them in the summer. So I knew I liked to work with wood.

In those days an aeroplane kit consisted of the appropriate sheets and blocks of balsa wood and a plan marked with all the various struts and spars, which were traced onto the balsa wood and cut out with a razor blade. All the component pieces were gradually pinned and glued together. When they had properly set and dried, they were carefully assembled and the plane—clad in its diaphanous paper skin, with several coats of 'dope' to toughen it, and rubber bands and the propeller added—was ready to fly.

Our most ambitious plane, which had taken us months to build, was so successful that it flew to an unexpected height and smashed into an overhead high-tension powerline and was thus destroyed. But I've never forgotten the exhilaration as we watched it soar towards the heavens like a caged bird released—until its untimely demise, and I bet that Jim Linton, if he's still alive, hasn't either.

It transpired that there were no carpentry apprenticeships available in our suburb but there was an apprenticeship for an electrical mechanic. I'd never had a great rapport with electricity and didn't like it very much. If the electric lights on my pushbike played up, my mate John would fix them. Anyway, on the morning of 6 January 1955, at the age of fifteen, the first day on which I could legally commence an apprenticeship, I was in the workshop of a local electrical contractor, my new employer, making up 'drops' (those pieces of electrical flex that attach the wires in the ceiling to the suspended light globe beneath) and wondering if brass was a conductor of electricity. However, within months I was confidently wiring up houses; it used to take about a day to wire one up and another day after the house was plastered and painted to 'fit it off' (that is, install the switches, power points and switchboard).

The boss soon realised that he could drop me off at a job with the rolls of cable and the tools. These were all hand tools for there were no electric drills on the site. In fact, there was no electricity on the jobs at all, so we apprentices put on muscle fairly quickly as we laboured with the brace and bit, the stocks and dies to thread the pipes, and the little hand drills for the final small screws to finish the job.

It wasn't long before the boss also realised that I could drive a car, so he bought himself a new Holden and I would set off at age fifteen in the old Holden and do my jobs while he would do his, or other things. I would work like a whirling dervish, have a quick lunch then, for a glorious hour or so, belt that poor Holden around the dirt roads beyond the housing estates where we worked. How I loved that car! It must have cost the boss a few bob in tyres and petrol but he didn't complain. After all, he was paying me three pounds and fifteen shillings a week (for four days' work, the fifth day of the week being spent at trade school), and was getting a house wired and fitted for less than two quid in labour costs.

The boss started wearing his good gold watch and smoking Du Maurier cigarettes, an upmarket brand, but it all came to an end when Mum found out about the driving and dobbed him in to the Apprenticeship Commission. I'm not sure that I ever forgave her for that. Mr Anderson, the gruff but fair inspector of apprenticeships, had to find me another position, for it was decided that my boss had made himself unfit as an employer of apprentices.

So I was off to my next employer, an electrical contractor in Collingwood where they specialised in industrial instal- lations and electric motor repairs. But this was not to be my last term of employment as a 'sparky'—in fact, someone later pointed out that I had set some sort of record for having had more employers over the duration of my apprenticeship than any other apprentice in Melbourne, and they'd had to print an extra page and add it to the indenture document.

The termination of my employment at this firm came about in the following manner. After repairing a motor we would paint it—one colour for the internal windings, visible through the end covers, and another colour for the actual external housing. There was a traditional formula for this, one that I was carefully observing when the very elderly and obviously demented founder of the firm walked past me on the way back to the office with his steaming cup of hot water to assist the digestion of his lunch and told me that I had the colour scheme wrong. This I hotly denied, claiming that only two days ago he had personally explained the different colour combinations to me—namely, that grey motors had red windings and that black motors had grey windings. To the great entertainment of my fellow employees in the workshop, an argument ensued.

Although respected as the firm's founder, Mr F. was not considered to be particularly useful around the place anymore. Sometimes he'd arrive at work and the other people in the office would say, 'You don't look well, Mr F., perhaps you should go home.'

To which he would respond, 'At home they told me to go to work!'

Anyway, as the battle raged, the whole staff was soon in the workshop and the other partner, Mr B., came from the office and poured oil on troubled waters and asked me to apologise to Mr F. But I was not satisfied. I had done exactly as I was told and was to be punished for it. The injustice rankled! So that evening, unseen by my fellow workers, I snuck into a corner of the workshop, found some other tins of paint and gave the motor a bit of creative decoration; some nuts were yellow, some screws blue, and the terminal box bright green. In the morning, when the workshop lights were turned on and the motor was seen in all its psychedelic glory, I was of course sacked and Mr Anderson from the Apprenticeship Commission had to be called again.

He was less sympathetic this time but managed to find me a position with another contractor, and things went well for eighteen months or so until another matter of principle raised its ugly head. This time, when we were doing an electrical installation in a largish factory which built bus and truck bodies, there was a sort of catwalk running around two walls, high above the work area. From there the factory owner observed the activity (or otherwise) around the vehicles below, and one day he spied me talking to the plumbing apprentice and rang my boss to tell him. I was summonsed to the telephone—most unusual for an apprentice—and was told I'd been caught talking and must not do it again.

I protested to my boss that we had, in fact, been discussing work. Both of us needed to get pipes through a very thick brick wall high above the ground, so we were discussing whether to put through a larger shared hole rather than two smaller ones, but my protests seemed to be falling on deaf ears. So I marched up to the office of the illustrious owner, knocked on his glass-panelled door, entered that inner sanctum and explained the truth of the matter to him.

He was apparently unimpressed by my forthrightness because half an hour later my boss arrived. My tools and I were bundled into the ute and we were off back to the workshop. On the way it was pointed out that the owner of the factory was outraged at my audacity in approaching him, would only find satisfaction if I was sacked and, if I were not sacked, various contracts would be altered to my boss's considerable financial disadvantage.

Mr Anderson had to be called one more time. He was gruff and displeased in front of my boss but, when I drove with him later to an interview with my next prospective employer, he was quite friendly, and later I thought that maybe he respected me for taking a moral stand. We were now scraping the bottom of the barrel in terms of employers—it would be highly unlikely that any contractor would employ me—but good old Mr Anderson, God bless him, had got me a job with the Harbour Trust, where he figured I should be able to serve out my final year without mishap.

Old cars, fast bikes and good mates

And he was right! And what a job! It was all about crane maintenance so it became necessary to learn to drive one. I had to learn a completely new set of skills for both the huge jib cranes and the smaller travelling ones in the sheds. They require coordinating three different movements to drop the hook exactly where required—luff, slew and lower on the jib cranes, and travel, traverse and lower on the travelling cranes. It's a lot harder than it looks, requiring the sort of skills needed to pilot a helicopter, and many enjoyable hours were spent doing crane maintenance and 'testing'. Boy-oh-boy, could those things accelerate! One day I begged a crane driver mate to let me ride on the very end of the jib to see what it felt like. This was completely *verboten* of course but he did it to shut me up, and I can attest that the G-forces applied to a human body clinging to the handrail of one of those apparently slow-moving cranes is considerable—in fact, terrifying.

Another job required driving around the wharves in the ladder truck to replace light globes and that, too, was fun for the thrill-seeking petrol-head I'd become. And there was spare time to work on pieces of the car that my mate Rob Hall and I were restoring! I'd take bits to work to file and buff and polish as close to perfection as they were going to get.

Socially, I lived two different lives: one life as the owner and enthusiastic user of a succession of old cars and motorcycles and the paraphernalia and friends who went with them; the other as a member of a church-going group of mainly girls, one of whom I fell seriously in love with. When it came, the parting (largely engineered by her parents, for I was not a good catch) was traumatic—my first and worst broken heart! Strangely, and to my delight, she visited me at my family house a few years ago after almost fifty years without contact.

So in 1957 it was goodbye to the cashmere twinsets, pearls and dances at Heidelberg Town Hall, and on with the leather jacket, motorcycle boots and jeans.

When I began my first-year apprenticeship, I gave half of my wage to Mum as board, leaving me with twenty-seven shillings and sixpence, the exact average amount I had been earning selling newspapers. But, somehow in my second year, I managed to purchase a 1928 Chevrolet. I'd chauffeur my mates around between milk bars, where we'd drink double sarsaparillas, the car fuelled by the petrol they'd acquired by fair means or foul, until the police came around and told my mother that they knew her son had a car and, as he was aged sixteen, not eighteen, he'd better get rid of it.

So I came home one night to be greeted by Mum and my sanctimonious brother, Ian, who smugly informed me of the police visit and the ultimatum. This didn't worry me over-much, though, for a bloke wanted me to swap my Chev for an Ariel 500-twin motorcycle he had. So the following night my mother and brother were alerted to my ownership of a new machine when the house vibrated to the throb of a powerful motorcycle engine coming up the driveway. They must have given up then, for I heard no more about vehicle ownership and the cops didn't trouble me—although they tried to catch an Ariel 500 on a couple of nights, not knowing that it was me. In this they failed, for the Ariel was faster than a Holden police car and more nimble than the Ford V8 Customlines they later started using.

From the beginning of my apprenticeship I was plagued by a lack of money. This was possibly a good thing concerning alcohol, for I couldn't afford to drink and maintain motor-cycles at the same time. Sometimes, late at night, we'd go to my house on the bikes, no doubt annoying the neighbours, and make something to eat. Spaghetti was about as rebellious as we could get and Mum always had some 'Kookaburra' pasta in the cupboard for these nocturnal feasts. I had heard that you could use olive oil to cook onions and things—garlic was unheard of then. I purchased a small bottle from the chemist one day and that night we fried some onions in it and, with the addition of some Kia-Ora tomato sauce and a couple of sausages, it became my first attempt at sugo (bolognese meat and tomato sauce). I was pretty pleased with myself but Mum was concerned the next day when she realised that I'd been cooking with 'medicinal' olive oil.

But far more dangerous than my cooking exploits was my Ariel phase. This was a time of racing at night with my bikie mates on powerful machines at high speeds—until two of those mates hit a truck. One was killed. The other went to hospital with a fractured skull and brain damage, from which he never recovered. We didn't wear helmets in those days, but I doubt that helmets would have saved them; they were going too fast for that.

After the funeral of my friend I thought that my time of racing around on motorcycles had more or less come to an end, but I was still riding my bike to work from Reservoir. Then one morning, barely a month after the crash, I jumped on, kicked it over to start it and grasped the clutch lever with my left hand prior to engaging first gear. But my hand began to shake and wouldn't apply any pressure to the clutch lever, and the more I tried to apply pressure, the more violently my hand shook. I had to abandon the bike and run to the train station to get to work, speculating as to whether it was some sort of delayed shock, or omen—some sort of message from the gods.

In any case, I sold the bike and hung my dead mate's leather jacket on the back of the garage door. His mother had given it to me after the funeral—she, I am sure, not having realised that her son's bloodstains were on the sheepskin lining.

The love of bikes must run in my family. I remember Dad telling us about my uncle Jack being pursued by a policeman, also on a motorcycle, and Jack, not wanting to reveal the whereabouts of his domicile, riding around the block with the policeman in pursuit. It was apparently quite entertaining, for Jack had extinguished the lights on his bike and all that could be seen of him in the darkness was the tip of his exhaust pipe glowing red hot as he roared past for the hundredth time. Mum and Dad put chairs out on the verandah to further enjoy the show, which ended when the policeman ran out of petrol and Jack was able to ride up the rear lane undetected and enter his property via the back gate.

After selling the Ariel, I set about purchasing an old Ford V8, for that is what the rest of my mates were travelling in then. The best thing I could afford was a 1938 model with worn-out piston rings and terrifyingly inefficient mechanical brakes. The only time they worked with reasonable effectiveness was on the first application of the day, so the trick was to delay the first application for as long as possible and enjoy that first good safe stop. Somehow I didn't crash it, and it didn't wear out completely, but it was worthless by the time I'd finished with it.

Shooting for England

My apprenticeship was coming to an end, and although I had promised my mother that I would complete it, I had sworn to myself that I would not work a day longer as an electrician than the allotted five years of the indentured apprenticeship. I'd had enough; I wanted a challenge. A plan was evolving between me and some mates—Rob Hall, Roland Betheras, Michael Buck and Brian Savron—that we'd go to England. In those days England was referred to as the 'Mother Country' and travelling there was a virtual pilgrimage, but to do this I needed money, a lot of money, comparatively quickly. We'd heard a rumour that professional kangaroo shooters were making fabulous money in the desert around Broken Hill in Outback New South Wales, so I decided to go there and check it out. It's a long way from Melbourne to Broken Hill, and it was unthinkable to take the Alvis. Instead I hitch-hiked the 300 miles or so, finally ending up at a roo-shooters' camp on the Darling River where I was able to question them on the viability of a roo-shooting operation.

After the men had gone for their daily sleep—for they shot by spotlight all night—I decided to do a Huckleberry Finn and build a raft to float back down the Darling, which according to my map passed close to the shanty town of Pooncarie. I made a crude raft by lashing together some dry logs with old fencing wire, left behind by successive floods, and set off down river, only to have my craft gradually sink as the timber became waterlogged. By the time I saw the roof of the Pooncarie pub in the distance and abandoned ship, my wallet clamped between my teeth, my torso was the only bit above water level. The patrons at the bar were very surprised to see a wet young man without a vehicle appear from nowhere. One drinker at the bar was headed south to Wentworth on the way to Melbourne so I was able to cadge my first lift for the long trip home.

Two other mates, Michael Hall and Philip Buck, neither of whom were included on the planned England trip, were interested in a roo-shooting adventure so that when I reported back positively it was all go. We borrowed some money from Michael's church credit fund and bought rifles, knives, a rebuilt World War II army jeep, then had a trailer made, which we loaded with bullets and other provisions, and headed off towards Broken Hill. I'd established the location of the most convenient 'chiller', where the butts of the kangaroos were delivered and purchased if they were of good quality, so we camped reasonably close to one and began a new and very challenging slice of life; it was a steep learning curve, becoming nocturnal riflemen/slaughtermen in that inhospitable country. Philip didn't last long; he hadn't realised how much he loved his girlfriend, so he soon returned to her loving arms. Then Michael developed serious back problems, but we mucked along all right for some months, making money but using a lot, mainly on fuel and vehicle maintenance.

When in Broken Hill, I would stay Friday nights in a hotel, The Globe, which was frequented by middle-aged ladies of the night who saw me as a novelty, calling me 'Professor', insisting I drink with them and buying me beers. Their pimps had no time for me, for when they came in with a job offer the girls would often say, 'Bugger off, it's Friday night and we're talking to the Prof.' Whenever one of the girls did speak to me alone, they all made the point that they had once been truly loved; it was important for me to know that their lives had not always been like this, that there had been better times, more dignified times, that had preceded the pimping and prostitution. Perhaps to them I was the son they'd lost, or had never had.

Back then, out bush, the time was fast approaching for my departure to England, but the desert held me in thrall. I didn't want to leave. One day I collected a card from the post office from my best friend Rob Hall, asking what the hell I was doing. We were due to sail in two months and why hadn't they heard from me?

It had rained in Broken Hill, Tibooburra and Silverton; everything had turned into a sea of mud, and roo shooting became impossible for a week or two. So I retired to a camp-site close to Broken Hill, which meant I could go to the pub sometimes and have a beer with some of my new Broken Hill mates. A few days later the police began enquiring about an incident—a marksman had shot out the 'POLICE' light in front of the Broken Hill Police Station, and someone claimed the marksman was chauffeured by a young bearded man in a jeep, who apparently looked a lot like me, as the Johnny Cash song goes. So after a chat with the constabulary, I left. Despite being in a four-wheel drive, I only just made it through to Wentworth, with the sides of the road littered with, at first, two-wheel drives and, later, four-wheel drives that had slid off the road into the muddy roadside ditches.

We hadn't made a lot of money, but we'd matured an awful lot and grown physically and mentally a lot stronger in a few short months.

Then it was time for another project.

Beloved Alvis

Rob Hall and I had bought an Alvis, a 1924 vintage car in a state of advanced decrepitude, although still being used as a daily commuter. Its owner agreed to part with it for the sum of forty pounds, about two weeks' wages for a tradesman.

It was a four-door open tourer and although it looked dowdy with the roof up, we knew what it would look like refurbished and with the hood down, so we spent many evenings in a shed we had borrowed from Rob's uncle—polishing, cleaning, filling, patching, rubbing back and finally spray-painting. My work experience with my dad at the panel-beating shop was invaluable in the restoration of this lovely old vehicle.

At the time I was in my fifth year of apprenticeship at the Harbour Trust, and had access to a workshop and a job allowing me plenty of spare time at work, so I spent many hours polishing brass headlamps and filing down the windscreen pillars prior to re-chrome plating, until between Rob and me we had the thing sparkling like a jewel. It had an exhaust note that made our blood race more than any musical instrument we'd ever heard, except perhaps the voice of Mahalia Jackson. The night we finished it, we drove it out of the shed beneath a street light, its German silver radiator sparkling, its brass head-lamps glowing, reflected in the shining plum brown duco, and to the beat of the exhaust going 'pom-pom-pom' we danced with joy and triumph in that deserted Reservoir street.

We loved that car, and as Rob and I were close friends we were able to share it, often going out as a foursome with any girls we had been able to attract. We would go to the dance at Powerhouse in our corduroys and desert boots (brothel creepers, as they were called for some reason), or to one of the little jazz clubs, or maybe take some girls home and after an extended kiss and cuddle, for that was all you got or expected in those days, return to Reservoir along an almost deserted St Kilda Road with the top down and the exhaust burbling away beneath the roadside trees. That was paradise enough for us.

Rob had had exclusive use of it while I was away for the months of kangaroo shooting, so when I returned from the killing fields of Broken Hill and Silverton it was my turn with the car. I made the most of it, which included briefly squiring a young lady around. I'd suggested lunch and she had agreed, insisting that I pick her up in the Alvis. I learned only later (aboard the *Castel Felice* on my way to England), that almost every girl in the building was watching from above, having been made aware that Jenny, or whatever her name was, was being collected from the street below ten minutes before the normal lunchtime in an open vintage car. They no doubt assumed that a wealthy and idle young man drove the car. Idle I was, indeed, at that time, but not wealthy, for I'd just a few days previously had my employment terminated.

I had realised that I would have to get a job because there were a few weeks to go before our departure for England. Money was running out and we were trying to sell the Alvis, even though that wasn't going to fetch much anyway, for vintage cars didn't attract the huge sums they do today. So I did something that I'd never had to do before and went to the employment office to ask them for a job—but not as an electrician.

There were only two jobs going, both breaking rocks at quarries, one at Heidelberg and one at Coburg. I asked which one might be preferable and the man behind the counter said: 'The hammers at the Coburg quarry weigh sixteen pounds and at the Heidelberg quarry they weigh fourteen pounds.' So I duly reported for work at the Heidelberg quarry at 7.30 the next morning and signed on.

I jumped into the truck with the other men and down we went to the floor of the quarry to be greeted by very large rectangular metal bins and vast quantities of huge chunks of basalt. During the night these massive rocks had been liberated from the precipitous cliffs by the ministrations of the 'powder monkey', the explosives expert, after the rock-breakers had done their work on the previous day's crop.

The idea was that we were to break the rocks into pieces small enough for the rock-crushing machine to handle. They showed me how to hit the rock on the correct side, so that it would split with the grain, for if you hit it against the grain the hammer would just bounce up and down and wear you out. The reward was five pounds a day for six bins, and five shillings for each bin after that. If you couldn't fill six bins a day you got the sack, and while I was there I saw several men come and go without achieving the desired target.

Having worked in the desert for so long, gutting, skinning and throwing kangaroo carcasses around, I was pretty fit and muscular, so I set to the task with gusto, managing eight bins that first day. The truck came to collect us at lunchtime and I headed off to find a milk bar, noticing that the other men, mostly short, stocky and broad-shouldered Italians, had extracted from their lunchboxes their salami sandwiches and enormous quantities of fruit. Few words were spoken as they got on with the job of fuelling up and when I returned from the milk bar, to my amazement, they were all asleep with their heads on the table. I, too, slept well that night, barely able to stay awake until I'd cooked and eaten some dinner. That became the pattern for the next week.

The 'gun' rock-breaker was a fairly short but enormously strong, barrel-chested Mediterranean who filled a dozen bins every day. He was the only one allowed to work overtime so he would come in on Saturday mornings and fill half a dozen bins before lunch. Being of a naturally competitive nature, I decided to attempt to increase my output by an additional bin each day in order to eventually draw level with his tally, but this was easier said than done, and it was many days and a couple of weekends until I considered myself within striking distance of my goal.

The day on which I was going to go for my twelve bins dawned clear; it was going to be very hot on the floor of the quarry where the sun's heat was magnified and reflected from the basalt walls. We started work smashing the rocks and flinging the spalls into the yawning mouths of the bins. I was matching him bin for bin but it was harder for me; his body seemed specially designed and built for the job, and he worked with a metronomic efficiency I could not match.

It was not yet lunchtime and we had filled six bins each but the heat was becoming difficult to bear. My God, I was glad to see that truck coming down the hill to pick us up for lunch.

After lunch we returned to the fray. I kept up with him but it was even harder now. I would give my all to a bin and on completing it, I would look up and over to where he toiled to see him seamlessly move on to his next bin. It was halfway through the third bin that the lights went out for me and I awoke on the floor of the office with my pay envelope in my hand. My employers were not happy—they didn't need a stupid twenty-year-old fainting on the job.

However, things went to plan for the five of us adventurers about to see the other side of the world: Roland, Robert, Michael,

Brian and me. We had our bookings for the ship and its departure date was rapidly approaching. Rob Hall and I reluctantly
parted with our beloved Alvis, selling it to someone who would
care for it and who, I believe, still owns it. He collected it on
the night of a going-away party a friend had thrown for us.
We stood on the balcony of the terrace house and miserably
watched it motor out of our lives. (It didn't bring any bad luck
to the buyer, for he was a member of a singing group who were
soon to become world famous.)

Using the funds so obtained we bought some new clothes
in preparation for our grand journey and were soon sardined
into our five-bunk cabin on the *Castel Felice*, the 'Castle of
Happiness'.

3

England and Italy

Castel Felice, the Castle of Happiness

So that is how five of us mates, not yet twenty-one years of age, arrived in England in October 1960 after a lengthy journey at sea aboard the *Castel Felice*.

The voyage was occasionally dull, but generally pretty interesting. And it was cheap, for the shipping company made their money transporting migrants from England, for which the Australian government paid full price, allowing them to run the return journey with cheapskate Aussies wanting to go to the Mother Country. I'd made good money kangaroo shooting but there wasn't much left by the time I boarded the boat. When onboard we seemed to spend quite a bit of time in the ship's middle bar, and there were various ports along the way that could burn up a few bob, too. At Port Said my funds were so low I didn't even leave the ship.

However, I found that I was able to subsidise my journey to some extent by shooting clay birds over the side of the boat. I had never used a shotgun before but because of my experience with a rifle I achieved some success with the clay birds, and was able to bet on myself to make some money—until people realised that I was quite good at it and wouldn't take me on. One of the other boys was quite good at 'sculling' beers and he, likewise, took a modest amount from our adversaries who, for some reason, seemed to be Western Australians.

There were some lively New Zealand girls on board and one morning we found a note slipped under the door of our cabin on 'D' deck, inviting us to a wine and cheese party at their cabin on the (in every way) more elevated 'B' deck. The party was a great success and spilled out into the corridor, or whatever they're called on ships. Much cheese was consumed, and wine flowed from the pretty little flasks of Chianti which were, and possibly still are, wrapped in raffia and generally more distinguished than their contents. So I don't think that the wine bug bit me there. No amorous relationships developed between any of us, but we'd made some new friends and that made the journey more pleasant.

But I did embark on a caring and close relationship with a girl. She was a kind and beautiful person and we became great friends and lovers. It could later have become more than a shipboard romance, but due to my peregrinations we soon lost touch. I used to wonder . . . She gave me a carton of duty-free Pall Mall cigarettes before we parted, knowing that my supplies were exhausted. Seeing the price of tobacco in England, I immediately stopped smoking and sold the carton to a tobacconist in London for a good price.

On the payroll in London

On our first night in London we had hoped to stay with friends of a friend but only one of us was welcome, so the rest of us slept under Hammersmith Bridge, me in my suit and the others in their overcoats. From there we gravitated to Earls Court, sharing a room with six others, including a Ceylonese with a close-to-death cough, an experience I wouldn't recommend to anybody.

Once, maybe a year later, after a hotel bar closed, I went into a toilet below the pub. The entrance faced the street and to my surprise there were no lights on, but I had a feeling there were people there—in fact, I heard someone clearing his throat and it made my skin crawl. I struck a match and saw men standing with their arms draped over a rope that was slung across the room. I later discovered that they paid half a crown per night for that accommodation, and maybe that was when another warning—that all was not right with the world—stirred in my soul. A stockbroker could make enough money with one phone call to house them all for a year. That was as close as they were going to get to sleep that night and a bed in a room with six others would have been luxury indeed for them.

Rob Hall had been thoughtful enough to bring some money with him to England, enabling him to take a small flat. He generously allowed me to share it with him so all I had to do then was find a job, and to that end I donned my suit and made my way to the nearest job centre, where I was informed that

the only work available was a labourer's job at Kew Gardens.
I made my way on foot to their unexpected magnificence, a
crystal palace rising from the mist, and followed directions to
the furnace rooms.

They were replacing some old coal-fired boilers with oil-
fired ones and above the subterranean works were workmen
and trucks and bricks and things. As I approached, resplendent
in my suit, a man approached me and doffed his cap, saying,
'Can I help you, sir?'

I took the small green card that the labour exchange had
given me from my pocket and presented it to him.

His eyes went a strange angry milky colour and he carefully replaced his hat on his head.

'Yes,' he said. 'You can start work at eight o'clock tomorrow
morning.'

'Thank you,' I said, holding out my hand. 'My name is
Graeme, what's yours?'

'My name,' he ground out between clenched teeth, 'is
Foreman.'

Now that I had a job I cheerfully walked the five miles or
so back to the flat. My problem for the next week was going to
be how to feed myself and get to work.

'Foreman' was ready for me and told me to wheelbarrow
about a thousand bricks down a plank laid over the stone stairs
to furnace number one. Men were breaking up concrete and
doing other things in preparation for removing the boiler. After
some hours I reported to him that I had finished the job and
he, observing the completed task, stated baldly, 'I've changed
my mind, I want them in furnace number two now.' Which
meant, of course, wheeling them back up the plank. It took me
quite a long time to complete the task cheerfully and report to
'Mr Foreman', as I had taken to addressing him. This was an
impertinence for which I knew he wouldn't sack me—he was
having too much fun.

As I was the last man on the payroll, it was my job to make
the tea and this gave me the chance to go through people's
lunch packets and steal something from their sandwiches.

My scruples evaporated in the face of such a ravenous hunger, but I did repack the lunches neatly. At lunchtime I went for a stroll through the glasshouses above and there, to my delight, discovered an orange tree with fruit on it. I was to visit that tree often over the next few days. At the end of the week there was not an orange left on it. And there were dark mutterings about the sandwiches, but Friday was payday.

A couple of days earlier I had used a bit of wire to pick the cheap, ineffective locks on the 'coin in the slot' gas and electricity meters around the flats, so I was now travelling to work on the bus and buying the odd pork pie. If Rob was home, I could usually bludge a meal from him that night but if he was not there it was too bad. I remember once washing some potato peelings I found in the kitchen bin then boiling them and eating them with salt and pepper; they were good.

Landladies

The flat was in Putney, but we'd met some girls who lived at Hampstead and, on visiting them, found that suburb much more to our liking. The sands of time were running out in any case for Rob's flat, which had just been completed when we moved in. It had been built into the ceiling space of an existing house, was very attractively painted, and had new, slightly off-white carpets on the floors.

Rob, the artist, stayed at home painting all day and needed to have a heater running, for the weather had turned chilly. The flat had its own electricity meter that, it was easily established, was set at the outrageous tariff of one shilling per kilowatt-hour—more than twice what was charged for the electricity coming into the house. I had no qualms about changing the wiring to bypass the meter, for I owed Rob a favour for the meals he had shouted me. He promised to put an occasional shilling in the meter so that when the shit hit the fan, there would be some money in there and we could escape blame in the ensuing confusion.

But alas, it was not to be. One night I rounded the corner to the flat to see an electrician's van parked outside, and inside a distraught landlady berating the electrician as he tried to examine the meter to the flat below ours, tenanted by our friend, Don, one of the Western Australians we'd met on the boat. I sprinted upstairs to be greeted by an agitated Rob, who explained that Mrs Codrington-Ball had received a colossal power bill and there weren't nearly enough shillings in the meters to cover it, much less the 100 per cent mark-up.

Time was of the essence, for the electrician was to check our meter at any minute. Not having a screwdriver, I grabbed a kitchen knife, which I had used to perform the initial illegal deed, and, standing on the kitchen chair Rob had thoughtfully placed below the meter, proceeded to disconnect the wire and replace it into its proper, metered terminal. During the transfer of the wire, there had to be a moment of darkness and the light from the match held in Rob's trembling fingers must have been inadequate, for the knife slipped as I was tightening the screw, shorting out on a neighbouring terminal, dramatically melting the end of the landlady's kitchen knife and plunging the entire house into darkness.

It appeared from the sounds below that the electrician was getting the blame so I replaced the cover on the meter, and Rob and I descended the stairs by candlelight, as any two concerned tenants would, to see what had gone wrong. The power was reinstalled and the landlady went down to her quarters, presumably for a large sherry or two. The electrician was to return the next day to try to sort out the mess and we went down to Don's flat to have a couple of beers with him and meet his 'bird', as prearranged.

During the boat trip to England, Don had made no secret of the fact that he was a virgin and didn't intend to remain in that unfortunate condition, so many pounds had been spent at two or three ports along the way on women who were supposed to provide the service Don was seeking. Somehow this ended up with the women or their pimps pocketing the money and not providing the service. But a couple of times he had taken out a London lass who was pretty keen to marry into an Australian sheep station. With some justification, Don felt that perhaps, at last, his hour had come. So we met Don's girl, heard her charming Cockney accent and observed her blonde hair, her tip-tilted nose, her pert breasts and her long, shiny patent leather boots. We also met her neurotic little white poodle. It seemed so simple. We would go upstairs to our flat and Don would entertain and possibly go to bed with his new young love.

But landladies were custodians of morality then and when the poodle started barking frantically at his mistress, who was engaged in some unexpectedly violent and noisy wrestling activity with a strange man on a bed, Mrs Codrington-Ball rapidly ascended the staircase to find out what was going on. There was quite a commotion for a while which resulted in girl and dog departing into the night, and Rob and I speculating as to whether or not the union had been consummated before the moment of coitus interruptus.

The next day was to be the moment of truth with the electrician, and there was another factor to be addressed. Painters, in their obsession with their work, can be a little absent-minded, a little careless of the sensibilities and sensitivities of other, more pedestrian folk, and Rob was no exception. He had failed to notice that in his constant toing and froing from canvas to a point where a better perspective could be obtained, some drops of oil paint had inadvertently fallen from his brush onto the 'off-white' carpet, which, despite the application of turpentine, had not been successfully removed. The carpet was a little more 'off white' than it had been.

If Mrs Codrington-Ball came up with the electrician, as she was bound to do, it was inevitable she would observe this and there would be consequences, so I was not unhappy to be going to work. If the electrician noticed that one of the terminals on the meter showed signs of partial meltdown, that would further complicate things. And it did!

So a short time later we found ourselves in a rooming house in the less salubrious suburb of Kilburn, where the residents, on seeing us (or perhaps anybody) in the hallway, would retreat into their rooms like startled rabbits, or crayfish backing into crevices in the rocks. We were probably noisier than anyone they'd been used to. The two girls would sometimes come around—Lois, a New Zealander, and a rather assertive American girl, with whom we would discuss philosophy into the night, until my head spun, for I had only completed Fourth Form, *sans* philosophy, a long time ago.

Turning twenty-one!

It was around New Year and my work had shut down for the holidays. I could have worked a few more days before my twenty-first birthday on 5 January 1961 but I considered it essential to leave my job and take the outstanding wages to buy the necessary ingredients for a party, which I did, and great and magnificent were the purchases. The five assembled guests were all to be spoiled rotten. I bought a heap of vegetables and a gigantic loin of pork, little bottles of Mackerson's stout, plenty of cider, a bottle of cheap spumante for the toast and specially selected cigarettes for each of the guests—Lucky Strikes for the American girl, Benson & Hedges for Michael, Passing Clouds in their delightful pink packet for Rob, a little packet of Old Holborn for Lois, who used to roll her own, and for me a half-ounce of Fribourg & Treyer 'Negrohead' pipe tobacco.

It was a truly wonderful party and we all stayed in the bedsitter as planned. It was pretty cold outside, but in the morning we were all feeling the deleterious effects of an unaccustomed excess of pork, alcohol and tobacco—and perhaps insufficient fresh air.

It was a Saturday and we sat around discussing the future, mine in particular, for I had spent all my money on the party. I had to get a real job, and quickly. It transpired that it was possible to get work as an electronics technician at a paperprocessing plant in Kent and, as I had taken electronics as a final year apprenticeship subject, I felt I might have enough knowledge to bluff my way into a job. But first I had to get a union ticket and some tools.

Lois generously offered to lend me some money to get me started. To my surprise the local trade union branch accepted me as a member and I was ready for a job interview, which again to my surprise I passed. I was soon on a train to new digs at the Isle of Sheppey Hotel and Country Club from which I would travel daily to my job on the mainland, over the bridge. It only took an hour or two for my co-workers to establish that I was not a qualified electronics technician and must have got the job under false pretences but, as we'd all had a few beers at the bar the night before I started work, we were already good mates and they covered for me.

There was plenty of work I could do, however, as long as they kept me away from the really technical stuff, and at the end of the week I had a pay packet containing about five times what I'd received for my weekly efforts at Kew Gardens. I went to the room I shared with Johnno, shut the door, placed all the bank notes on the bed then exultantly threw them up into the air like Scrooge McDuck.

The hours were long, usually seventy per week, for the owners were keen to get this particular paper-processing machine on which we worked into action and making money. But they didn't mind paying the overtime required, and we still had time to have a few drinks after dinner. The Isle was more or less a holiday resort for London's East Enders, but it was winter—which is why we found ourselves in motel-type accommodation at budget rates.

Some of the people running the local businesses seemed to have a theatrical background; hanging behind the bar were photographs of the hotel manager with Gracie Fields on the island of Capri. It was all rather like a deserted fairground under a mantle of slightly camp melancholy. But on Saturdays some East Enders would come up, we'd have dancing, the manager would sing 'Give me the moonlight, give me the girl, and leave the rest to me!' and we'd all have a good time. Particularly if there were some girls from London, usually the daughters of 'barrow boys' who didn't always notice that their daughters were missing, although one did once and came after me with a 'shooter', which put some extra pep into the evening's activities.

An additional bonus was that you could keep an eye on the poker machines ringing the bar and get a fair idea of which one was ready to pay out. If your timing was right, pumping in some coins inevitably resulted in a jackpot, so that was a bonus. The other bonus was that your bedroom was on the premises. Some of the boys established liaisons with some of the female staff, as did my roommate Johnno with the very large and not particularly attractive cook. He had a little van with a mattress and some blankets in the back—their mobile love nest. With the radio playing and the motor occasionally started to run the heater, it served its purpose well and, being windowless, also preserved the anonymity of the couple on the mattress.

On the nights of these trysts Johnno usually came home quite late, but once he was particularly late and woke me when he turned on the light. He was ashen faced and looked as if he'd aged considerably since I had last seen him, earlier in the night. I assumed that he'd had a car accident and asked him what had happened. He told me that after their lovemaking they were unable to locate the condom that had been used and searched the van fruitlessly, to conclude that it must be in the one place they were unable to search. It would have to be found by people more qualified than them.

And so it came to pass that Johnno was forced to sit, late at night, in the hospital waiting room while every nurse in the hospital paired up with a friend and giggled their way through the room while glancing sideways at Johnno. No doubt it haunts him still, if he's still alive.

Compromise or cowardice?

Michael Buck, one of our original *Castel Felice* adventurers, and I had heard about the Italian language course at Perugia University, the 'Universita per Stranieri' and had

made enquiries. It transpired that no fees would be charged
for foreigners (*stranieri*), for the Italian government was
subsidising them in the interest of promoting an awareness
of Italian culture and language. This suited us very well;
we found the idea of attending this ancient institution and
learning the Italian language in the company of other students
from around the world very appealing, so we applied by mail
and were accepted.

Michael was working at a bulb farm on Tresco, one of the
Scilly Isles group just west of Cornwall, and the plan was that
I would ride my Lambretta to Italy while he would travel by
other means and meet me at Perugia. But the best laid plans
of mice and men found me in receipt of a telegram informing
me that Mike was unable to join me in Italy. It transpired that
he had suffered a slight misadventure on the Isle of Tresco.
One of his jobs on the island was to perform the mail delivery
run on a tractor, for there were no proper roads along the
mail route. Now Michael was a very personable young man
and very good-looking; in fact he had once been a model for a
hairdressing product called Brylcreem back in Melbourne. No
doubt the people (mainly women) to whom Mike delivered the
mail looked forward to his daily attendance on them and were
saddened to learn of his impending departure. On what was to
be his last daily delivery they were there, outside their doors,
with a small glass of celebratory elderberry wine, a ubiquitous
homemade product that is more alcoholic than its appearance
suggests. Michael drank several of these toasts along the mail
run and the alcohol must have affected his reflexes or his judge-
ment, for he ran the tractor into a substantial stone wall and
did it considerable damage, for which the owner insisted he
pay, so his Perugia money was gone.

I'm sure that I would have had an even better time in
Perugia with Mike's company; however, the story had a
romantic ending, for an extremely attractive young Rhodesian
lady, Jane, had come to work as receptionist at the Tresco hotel.
They fell in love, later married, and their three daughters and
my two children spent many good times together at Daylesford

and later at the vineyard at Kingower. The girls and their children still come to stay; in fact their youngest daughter, Vanessa, has worked with me over many vintages at Kingower.

With sad goodbyes I finished up at the plant in Kent when the overtime ran out, as I was on a mission to make as much money as possible before going to Perugia in September. A job with lots of overtime had been advertised by a contractor doing electrical work at the Atomic Weapons Research Establishment at Aldermaston in Berkshire. I had to go to London to apply for the job. I stayed with Lois for a few days and paid her back the money I owed her. I also bought an almost new 175cc Lambretta motor scooter while I waited for my security pass to be granted.

During the interview I asked if they were sure they had obtained all the information possible on me from Australia; the interviewer detected a note of supercilious sarcasm in my voice and, referring to his file, said, 'Did you enjoy your time at Sixth Preston Boy Scouts, where after twenty months you were promoted to assistant patrol leader?' That wiped the smirk from my face.

I was, however, granted the security pass and soon headed off to Berkshire with all my worldly possessions strapped onto the pack-rack of my Lambretta. I sought board and lodgings at Reading, since it seemed to be the closest large town to Aldermaston, but it wasn't, and finally I gained lodgings at nearby Thatcham.

The next morning I was due to start and duly rocked up to the main gate, which anti-nuclear protesters were picketing. There were hundreds of mainly scruffy but obviously sincere people lining the road into the plant and hurling abuse at any vehicle about to enter, their worst excesses censured by police. As I was mounted on my Lambretta, bearded and wearing a corduroy cap, they must have thought I was one of them, for I passed unhindered through the phalanx. But when I produced my papers and handed them to the security guard at the gate, all hell broke loose and I got more of a bollocking than the truck drivers, since in my gear I looked like a traitor. Which I knew I was, having not so long ago in Australia argued that the world was endangered by nuclear activity and that for the first time in human history we were likely to destroy ourselves and the product of millions of years of evolution. Compromise or cowardice?

The work there suited me well. It was twelve-hour days, seven days a week, in a fascinating windowless building that reminded me of a giant 1940s Australian Arnott's biscuit tin. All the interior floors were suspended from the roof, and in the event of an explosion the roof was supposed to lift so the sides would not blow out and damage the surrounding buildings— an admirable and arguably slightly eccentric bit of British engineering.

The object of the exercise was to use an intricate system of conveyor belts to place equipment that had become contaminated with radiation inside various large triple-glazed boxes containing robot-operated workshop machinery, which could work on them.

It taught me much that I was able to draw on many years later, on other jobs involving conveyor systems. Unfortunately we weren't allowed out of this hermetically sealed prison, and for three weeks I did not see proper daylight, as we went to work and came home in the gloom of morning or evening.

One day I pleaded a dental appointment, got a pass out and was soon zooming along the country lanes between the hedgerows in the sunshine, seeing and smelling the golden flowers of England's early spring—I've never forgotten that ride! It reminded me of the Oscar Wilde poem 'Symphony in Yellow', about the gorgeous yellows and golds of the English countryside and I luxuriated in it before returning to the 'biscuit tin'.

When the overtime ran out at Aldermaston, I managed to get a job down the road a bit at Harwell, where they were building some sort of particle accelerator. It was a 'Euratom' project, and both the site and the labour were England's contribution to the scheme. The deadline was quickly drawing near and they were throwing money at it. Those of us chasing overtime would leave our job at an hour's notice and appear

at the next one. So on the day of the Harwell job appearing
in the newspaper, three motorcycles and a Lambretta left
Aldermaston for Harwell; the four of us started our working
day at one place and finished it in another.

At Harwell I had my first experience with the 'ghoster', a
shift that required you to start work at 8 a.m. and work right
through until 4.30 p.m. the next day—very demanding, but
you got triple time for the last eight hours. Apprentices were
not supposed to work such shifts and at about 5 a.m. one
morning I watched one young lad, carrying a bundle of conduit
on his shoulder, simply buckle at the knees and go to sleep on
the concrete floor.

(Many years later when I had a team working under me at
the Longford gas plant in Victoria, I was aware of the dramatic
loss of efficiency that occurred when people were overtired. I
would not let any man in my team work more than a twelve-
hour shift. Later still, at the winery at Passing Clouds, I often
insisted that people went home for a sleep even if they didn't
want to—cock-ups and accidents happen when people are
worn out.)

One day I was riding to work at Harwell on the Lambretta,
having had some performance-enhancing work done, and was
keen to see how fast it would go. I was crouched over at full
throttle with my eyes about six inches from the speedometer
when I felt as if I were being watched. Despite the unlikelihood
of that, I looked to my right and observed a police motorcycle alongside; the rider seemed to be looking at me with
some amusement. When we stopped he took off his helmet,
dismounted and approached.

'Good morning, sir.'

'Good morning, officer.'

A smile played about his lips as he cast his eye over the bike,
obviously observing the AUS plate below the rear numberplate.
'Didn't quite get to seventy, did it?' he said.

'How close, according to your speedo?'

'Sixty-eight, but you're supposed to be going no faster than
fifty.'

I hung my head in shame while he inspected my licence. He handed it back with the rebuke, 'Fifty, Aussie.'

'Yes, sir!' I replied, at which he replaced his helmet, remounted, gunned his Triumph 500 Tiger and let me hear what a real motorbike sounded like when it took off.

Riding to Italy

My trusty little two-stroke steed had carried me everywhere at a maximum speed of 68 miles per hour, so it seemed logical to take it to Perugia, which didn't seem far; just across France, through Switzerland, and a little bit of northern Italy. So I put it on the ferry and across the Channel we went.

One of my workmates had a Swiss wife who suggested a little *pensione* where I could stay, so I rang them and booked in for a couple of days to rest after finishing work, packing up and so on. Riding through France took me a little longer than I expected but when I arrived I was enthusiastically greeted, given a good meal and shown to my bed on which I had a wonderful sleep. The next morning I awoke, had breakfast in view of the snow-capped mountains and listened to the peaceful chiming of cowbells, knowing I had done the right thing by breaking my journey in this bucolic paradise.

By evening, however, I was stir-crazy and didn't want to hear another cowbell or see another snow-capped mountain for the rest of my life, so I told my hostess I was cutting my holiday short and would be leaving the next morning. I aimed the trusty Lambretta towards the St Gothard Pass, beyond which lay Italy—that land of food, wine, romance and all things beautiful to me, and the inspiration for two of my favourite Shakespearean plays, *Romeo and Juliet* and *The Merchant of Venice*. It takes quite a while to ride through Switzerland—it has so many winding roads—and I didn't know as I roared through the bends of the St Gothard Pass that it was usually snow-covered at that time of year and that only an extraordinary dry spell had allowed me to travel it at all on a motorcycle.

Over the border everything changed; the towns were perfumed with the aromas of food, coffee, wine and tobacco. There was music from the small cafes; the motor cars changed in style, the functional designs of Opel and Mercedes giving way to the cheeky good looks of Fiat 500s, 600s, 1100s, to the sporty elegance of Alfa Romeos, Lancias and the occasional Ferrari and Maserati. Here was a country to love!

I took a room at Verona for the night, after a near-miss with some Alfas and Ferraris travelling very fast in the opposite direction, their lights so bright that my Lambretta light was no match for them and I had to pull off to the side of the road. Instinctively I chose the left-hand side—the wrong side of the road in Europe—creating such confusion for these rich Italian youths having a 'burn' and speeding along nose to tail that one or two of them must have applied the brakes a little too enthusiastically and some of them ran into each other, causing considerable panel damage. I had turned my scooter around and was close enough to hear them yelling at each other when I realised that I could contribute little to the discussion. I turned the Lambretta around again and roared on towards Verona at 68 miles per hour, occasionally looking back over my shoulder. After a good night's sleep, punctuated by mild nightmares with a soundtrack of torn and rent Ferrari and Alfa Romeo mudguards, I rode on the next day through Emilia Romagna and Umbria to Perugia, where my friend Brian Savron had booked me a room above a bar overlooking the busy piazza.

From Preston to Perugia

Although I had no knowledge of the Italian language, I was determined to make a good showing and, while in Switzerland, had learned what seemed an easy phrase. If I were asked what I wanted for breakfast, I thought I would order a glass of milk, 'Un bicchiere di latte', and practised the pronunciation with the aid of my Teach Yourself Italian book. In the morning I went down to the cafe and confidently made my request; but any panache I may have had was shattered when the waiter responded, *'Calda o freddo?'* ('Hot or cold?'). I had no idea what he meant so I gibbered in English and bad French and had to swallow my embarrassment. I enrolled in my language course that day and began a magical twelve weeks of learning, of new friendships, seeing the treasures of Assisi, Florence, Gubbio, even once as far away as Rome.

It was a far cry from roo shooting eighteen months before, eating roast mutton and vegetables from the camp oven buried beneath the ashes of the fire and washed down with billy tea. Once a week I would go to the nearest town, Broken Hill, service the jeep and usually get a couple of new tyres, for they were often spiked in that country. I would have a meal at a Greek place where I was introduced to the wonder and delight of stuffed capsicums, cabbage and tomatoes, a little red wine and delicious cakes which had been sent up from Adelaide. The proprietor, his wife and I soon came to an arrangement; they loved to eat rabbit, but only three-quarter grown ones. It was easy to pick up a pair during the night's roo shooting and exchange them for the full Greek meal, a situation that I found to be entirely in my favour.

At that time I introduced myself to Wynn's flagon wine, so the meals became a little more refined and varied, as wine went into the camp oven with the meat and vegetables and a couple of Vegemite jarsfull accompanied the meal. Sometimes, if we were really hungry when shooting, we'd roast a rabbit skewered on a piece of wire over the fire, and this was good with Bonox or tea. That Greek experience was my first taste of a cultural change, although my friend Brian Savron's family lived (to us Aussies) an exotic life in Gertrude Street, Fitzroy—a life that included pasta and wine, black coffee and grappa, and the exciting sounds of a foreign tongue.

Perugia was a very different world indeed. Students of many different nationalities were studying there with different degrees of application. For example, there were Yemenites who, it seemed, were from important families who could have posed a threat to their sheik, so they'd been granted scholarships to

Perugia University and not encouraged to return home except for holidays. Basically they were in exile with a lot of disposable income, much of which they used patronising nightclubs. I once watched them play a very unpleasant game that seemed to involve getting the youngest member of their clique drunk, knotting their headdresses, wetting them and then thumping the little guy on the head with them. When I asked them to stop, they did so reluctantly but were not happy with me. That didn't matter, they didn't really go to classes anyway and I saw little of them after we stopped nightclubbing.

There were Americans, some of whom had jobs at the American embassy in Rome. Somebody had decided it would be a good idea if they went to Perugia and learned Italian. They went to Perugia but they did not learn any Italian. However, they were attracted to the nightclub scene and would 'shout' the odd impoverished Australian to a night out—specifically in my case because I had an attractive girlfriend. They would drink quite a lot of bourbon, tearfully fish photos of their loved ones out of their wallets, then drive back to town at high speed in the big Buick, leaning on the horn as they approached intersections. On the last trip I chose to take with them the driver exclaimed, 'That's diplomatic immunity for ya!'

Other Americans were there on Fulbright Scholarships. I envied them, for they had the wherewithal to complete a nine-month course with enough money to take holidays between semesters. There were also a few Americans who were just parking, leading one of the English wags to comment that the Americans were all either Fulbrights or half-brights.

I can recall only two English students, both males, delightful in their different ways. We became friends, and the three of us—Charles, Misha and me—used to make 8 mm films together. We certainly had some good settings, and once filmed a Roman orgy scene on the balcony of the Arco Etrusco, the Etruscan arch near the university. One of the boys, Misha, who intended to become a filmmaker, had a room there, in the actual arch. It seemed incredible to this rude colonial, and still does, that you can rent a room in a building of such antiquity made by people whose very language was extinct in the reign of the studious Emperor Claudius, who had learned it from surviving writings. I seem to recall that he taught it to his consort Messalina, an ex-prostitute and noted scallywag who disgraced herself and the emperor in some way or another with a squadron of centurions on their night off—or on . . .

There were some Greeks too, all keen to learn the language, and fun loving with it. We became friends and communicated in tortured Italian, they calling me *'Amico de Grasso'* (roughly, 'Friend of Grease'). Domenic the Scot was there. His employers had sent him to learn some Italian, but would have been disappointed upon his return. No Germans, but some Swiss who, although they studied conscientiously, stayed together as a clique and never spoke to Italians. They probably had a good theoretical knowledge but couldn't speak one comprehensible word of the language after twelve weeks, so were failed.

There were three other Australians, all female—one was Gill Smith, a highly intelligent and independent girl who learned much; she later married Brian Savron, one of the original five. We are still friends, fifty years later. The other two were both bright and cheerful, rebuffing, with good-natured Aussie humour, the often-unsubtle advances of the local Casanovas.

An ethereal wine

There was a Dutch girl whose mother was half Italian. This girl, whose nickname was Vosje, or 'Little Fox', spoke fluent French as well as English and German. English-speaking people couldn't pronounce her name properly and usually called her 'Vosh' instead of 'Vossjeh'. So rebellious and charming was she that I fell completely in love with her. She returned my affections and after classes we spent many happy hours touring nearby villages on the Lambretta, having sunset picnics in roadside copses, looking over hills and valleys in the soft glow of autumnal light, over the very plains that had been battlefields when the men of Assisi fought the soldiers of Perugia.

One day, when we were looking for a filming site in a grassy field, Misha and Charles stumbled across an overgrown well. An inscription was chiselled into the stone but they could not read it, as it was in neither Italian nor Latin. Vosje, having knowledge of ancient Greek (perhaps a legacy of her expensive Dutch education), was able to interpret it as 'fresh water'.

As students we soon found the *Mensa Populare*, a dining room run by the Communist party to give working people a good lunch at a fair price. It was humble, but located in an exquisite, recently re-excavated and renovated Roman cellar with vaulted ceilings of ancient bricks without mortar courses. The menu was simple and delicious. One day there'd be pasta with bolognese sauce, a piece of either cheese or fruit and, if you chose, a 'quarto' of either red or white wine which came in a charming little quarter-litre glass flask. The next day maybe there'd be minestrone with freshly baked bread and a green salad.

There were occasional variations as something came onto the market at a good price, none of it cafeteria style, and didn't I feel so European taking the food and wine to our table! For dinners we had a fair choice: pizzas were very cheap and made on square trays, the pizza then sub-divided into smaller squares, the cheapest being, I think, *Rosemaria*, just a sprinkling of rosemary leaves on the pizza base.

There were plenty of other cheap places to eat, and we found a little trattoria, slightly more expensive than some, but boasting an array of traditional dishes we had never encountered before. They served wine straight from the barrel, and wine the like of which I had never tasted. It was a glorious full red colour, concentrated, with an array of flavours—berries and fruits and liquorice and earth that was stunning and unexpected to me, who had only had wine that tasted like wine.

It became a regular Thursday evening meal and we loved it. But one night, after ordering and having our carafe of wine brought to the table, we took our gloriously anticipated sniff and taste and were shocked to find that this one was different and profoundly ordinary. Bewildered, we asked the proprietor for our usual wine, and he informed us that the barrel was finished; we were now drinking a different barrel from another vineyard, another winemaker.

Questioning revealed that the new wine actually came from the winery and vineyard next door to our favourite, so the following Sunday saw me and Vosje on the Lambretta, heading up to the hills behind Perugia. As we approached, we could see that the road was stained red from the juice of the grapes that had leaked through the floors of the wooden carts, for the vintage had not long been over. We were like hounds following a blood trail. At the vineyard we asked the mystified owners if we could buy some of their bottled wine. But the proprietors of this mixed farm told us that they only bottled wine for the family, the rest being sold by the barrel. Still, they sold us a few bottles. Leaving the group that had now gathered to observe these peculiar strangers, we returned triumphant to Perugia with as many bottles as we were able to purchase and stuff into our pockets. That proved to be the basis for a riotously successful party on the ancient balcony of the Arco Etrusco.

But it continued to vex me, that question . . . How could this wine be so good and the one next door so ordinary?

That puzzle remained dormant in my brain for a long time and, even now, is only partly resolved. For wine during fermentation is a living thing and a series of barrels filled with the same wine will produce different results after the maturation. There are still some things about wine that science cannot properly explain; there is no universal formula for making the best wine possible from the available grapes: we come close, but the variables, the permutations and combinations of fruit ripeness in terms of flavour, the total acid, sugar, tannins, pH and, ultimately, alcohol are endless, and fashions change.

It was many, many years later that I looked at Hugh Johnson and Jancis Robinson's *The World Atlas of Wine* and learned that the tiny pocket of vines above Perugia produces excellent wines using grape varieties of which I, of course, hadn't heard; and if we were drinking Sangiovese, Cilliegiolo, Sagrantino, Trebbiano or Grechetto, or a combination of these, I will never know. But I wonder if the men who dug the well and capped it with the inscribed stone were the same men who brought the Grechetto vine cuttings from ancient Greece to the hills above Perugia.

All too soon it was time to leave Perugia. It had been snowing heavily and it appeared that I was stuck there unless I sent the Lambretta to England by train, which is eventually what I arranged. On the night before our planned departure we were having drinks at a little bar cafe with some of the gang, including a few of the American boys, with whom I had always for some reason been competitive.

Vosje and I had been down to that particular bar before and knew some prostitutes who worked from there. Vosje was fascinated by them, as she was by courtesans generally. (Her favourite author was Colette—she loved the illicit erotica Colette sometimes wrote about—and the short stories of Anaïs Nin.) At that earlier meeting, when we first met the ladies, they invited us for a meal a couple of nights later and I asked them what we would eat. 'We're eating *cazzo impera*,' the spokeslady responded, but when we arrived on the correct day and at the correct time, they weren't there. It was the day after, when I learned the translation of *cazzo impera* was 'erect penis', that I realised we'd been sent up gloriously by these ladies of the night, these *puttana*.

Anyway, as our last night in Perugia progressed it seemed to be an increasingly good idea to pull a 'No Parking' sign out of the ground and place it over the lance of the bronze soldier on horseback whose statue was in the square in front of us. This was achieved with some difficulty, due to it being 3 a.m. and snowing, but it was achieved.

Unfortunately the statue was that of Giuseppe Garibaldi, saviour of Italy and the Italians. Later that morning, on their way to work, many Perugini didn't find it funny to see Garibaldi holding a 'No Parking' sign, and a hornet's nest was stirred up. After all, it was virtual sacrilege and some witnesses from the bar said that the man who climbed up onto the statue with the sign looked a lot like me.

So we left, after I told my landlord and landlady that we were going to Rome. However, we hadn't left yet and I went down to the *circolo*, the large circular dining and meeting room in the university, to say goodbye to our friends. While we were talking, two young Carabinieri (military policemen) came in, recognised the man they were looking for and arrested me.

My mind worked fairly quickly as they escorted me along the corridor towards the entrance to the university. I was desperate and could only envisage a long jail sentence in a cell with poor food, no wine and without a girl to keep me company; but a thought sprang to mind—a long shot, but worth a try.

The male toilets were on the left-hand side of the corridor and served by one doorway, but I knew there was a small ventilation window in there, high up, above the hand basins, but possibly accessible for a fit and desperate young man. On the negative side, it was about 3 metres above the road; on the positive side, there was about a metre of snow banked up against the wall. I had seen it there fifteen minutes before when Vosje and I walked up the Via del Fico, having left our luggage at the railway station on the Firenze side of the platform. So I pleaded with the two young officers that I needed to go to the toilet and they, believing there was no escape, stood on each side of the doorway and let me go about my business. As the walls were thick, I was able to leap up and perch upon the sill while I opened the window and soon thumped onto the snowdrift below. I was extremely lucky, but later felt sorry for the two young officers who had let me escape, if of course they owned up to it. Vosje walked down to the station and was delighted to find me hiding in the luggage room.

As we left on the train for Florence, as disguised as we could make ourselves from the contents of our suitcases, we could see many Carabinieri, frighteningly close, on the Rome platform opposite.

Joining up with Vosje

That wine at Perugia was the last ethereal wine I tasted for an awfully long time, for after returning to England I was joined by Vosje and we lived in a bedsitter in Hampstead. I worked as a bricklayer's labourer and she read and walked and talked, occasionally picking up stray hippies whom she wanted me to meet. One night I came home from work to find the walls of our room newly ornamented with appalling murals done in charcoal and the bereted and moustachioed perpetrator happily sitting on the end of our bed, for Vosje had asked him to stay until I came home, knowing that I would love to meet him!

Some nights we drank at a pub in the High Street, The Pilgrims Arms, patronised by lots of struggling artists and poets—some struggling so hard that they apparently couldn't afford paint or paper. But cider was cheap and talk was cheaper so it was a cheerful place to be; the conversation was often so animated that we referred to it as 'The Gesticulating Arms'.

Saturdays we would go to the market and I would cook on our single gas ring, then after our meal I'd go to the pub and buy a little 'pig' of cider, attach it to the carrier rack on the Lambretta and we'd share the cost with friends and all have a party in our bedsitter. Vosje was very popular because of her charm, looks and sense of fun, and we were never short of party guests, particularly male ones.

For recreation I was rewriting *The Rape of Lucrece*, putting it into a form more acceptable than the original opaque Shakespearean version, but mercifully the manuscript was lost—or used to wrap rubbish.

For in England we had discovered calamari and also cos lettuce; we bought the calamari whole, cleaned it and sliced it, wrapping the remains in many layers of newspaper—or useless manuscripts—before putting them into the bin. The cos lettuce was a delight, crisp and crunchy with olive oil and vinegar but no wine—anything affordable was undrinkable. We had pasta, too, but, having had proper bolognese sauce in Italy, it was pathetic to try to substitute it with minced meat.

A leg of lamb cost as much as a decent wristwatch so we ate frugally, although once or twice I bought a small piece of eye fillet, locked the door, and we cooked and ate it guiltily but blissfully.

It was to be in Holland where I next ate well. After some time Vosje went back to complete her studies there and I would go across some weekends to stay with her and her parents. I was introduced to the new sensations of Indonesian food—satays and sambal, nasi goreng, cap cay and lumpia—from little restaurants dotted around Amsterdam.

I was making comparatively good money in England, working long hours commissioning the electrics and electronics back at Aldermaston and Harwell, so I could afford a couple of really good restaurants in Amsterdam. What a revelation that was. I had never had food of such quality or presented so well, and I became, after just a few visits, a worshipper at the shrine of pinot noir, since the Burgundians sold much wine to the Dutch at that time. The South African wine was generally appalling, apparently being made from grapes chosen more for their resistance to powdery mildew than for their capacity to make good wine. To hear the name of the variety pinotage still makes me shudder slightly. With Vosje's parents I was also introduced to the joys of Dutch food—cold meats and cheeses, baby carrots and peas. Her father was a member of a socio-economic group that could afford to buy their edams and goudas quite fresh from the maker, then have them cured in a special storeroom with other people's cheeses until they were considered mature enough to eat.

The smoked horseflesh, a luncheon delicacy, offended my scruples, as had the fresh horsemeat displayed in the horsemeat shops in Italy. But it certainly had a wonderful texture, and really tasted more of smoke than anything else. Evening meals were hearty but elegant, and almost always included baby carrots sautéed in butter as well as potato and green peas or beans.

The Bols Genever, though, I could not stand; it absolutely offended my young palate, and when offered one at the yacht club restaurant by my future father-in-law, I only just managed to get it down. He enquired as to whether I liked it or not and when I responded politely that I did, immediately signalled to the waiter for another, which I discreetly managed to pour into my shoe, for had I drunk it my lunch would have been ruined and possibly also that of some fellow diners. I managed to do this by using the old trick of pointing to something, in this case yachts, to distract the eyes of my table companions.

Sometimes Vosje and I would borrow the family car and go to the yacht club where I learned to sail her small yacht, experiencing the exhilaration of being powered and empowered by the wind.

But Vosje had another agenda of which I was unaware. She wanted to thumb her nose at the stuffed shirts from the yacht club and one day encouraged me to leave the sails down and gun the boat around with the outboard motor, which I cheerfully did, finding it great fun and not knowing that it was absolutely forbidden. But she knew; she was cutting her ties with what she considered to have been her excessively disciplined childhood, and was using me as the knife.

She made another cut a couple of days later. Vosje was a member of an exclusive rowing club and therefore had access to the club's rowing sculls. I had learned to row at lakes Jubilee and Daylesford as a child and had refined those skills with the Richmond Rowing Club on the Yarra River before I went kangaroo shooting, so I knew how to handle the craft. We often rowed up and down the conventional course but, one afternoon, with me rowing and Vosje as cox, she directed us away from the course and into the canals. I became uneasy as people were pointing at us and staring but, despite my protestations, she declared it okay. But it was just as 'unconventional' as the motorised yacht had been.

Many serious words were spoken after Mr Fros received the phone calls. I didn't speak much Dutch then, but I got the gist. I was due to fly home to Australia within a few days and Vosje planned to follow by ship some time later. Thus she had rebelled with both barrels; she was unrepentant *and* she was going to Australia! Her parents may not have been pleased for their only daughter to be going to the other side of the world with a young man of unknown origins and expectations, but possibly less displeased after the boating incidents.

I was worried at the time that Mr Fros might have had another phone call from the police, for Vosje and I had used the family car for a day trip to Dusseldorf in Germany. It was intriguing there to observe the long queues outside the cinemas, for the American-made film about the Normandy invasion, *The Longest Day*, was screening. Apparently the film portrayed the Germans unflatteringly and there was some resentment towards English-speaking people. So when Vosje and I went to a nearby cafe and spoke in English, some young males hectored me and a fight ensued, resulting in the family car being escorted to the border by two police cars, one behind and one in front. My passport was stamped with a very long German word that Vosje interpreted as 'Not wanted to be seen in this country again'. or words to that effect.

If Mynheer Fros ever did get a phone call about that incident, he kept it to himself.

4

Return to Australia

The Little Fox hits Melbourne

Ever rebellious and unconventional, Vosje came to Melbourne, and we married in September 1963. We lived in a little two-storey bungalow that I had quickly built at the back of my mother's house in Reservoir, had our two children, Ondine and Sebastian, and saved to buy a first house.

I should never have expected Vosje to live like a caged bird in the northern suburbs of Melbourne, and both of us being so stubborn did not help. We disagreed about how we should plan our lives. I was convinced that we should be patient, allow me a few years to buy a first house in the inner suburbs of Carlton or Fitzroy, then renovate, rent out and buy the next one. But Vosje was too impatient for that. She wanted us to rent in one of those suburbs now and get the hell out of Reservoir. Houses in those suburbs were about $10,000 then, or about five times the price of a new Volkswagen, for instance, but it was to be many years before I was to have a house there, for the marriage didn't survive, and there was no Plan B.

The parting, when it came, was quick, dramatic and painful. For a time, my mother looked after Sebastian, who was little more than a baby in 1967, until Vosje sorted out some accommodation. However, Vosje and I shared a lot of love and good times to the end of the marriage, and even after, which may have been to our discredit in the eyes of some, had they known.

During those few sweet years of marriage we used to stay at my family's cottage at Daylesford in Central Victoria, sometimes buying a bottle to take from Jimmy Watson's Wine Bar. Jules, behind the bar, once thought I was taking the mickey when I asked him if the bottle of Rutherglen red would travel to Daylesford, but I wasn't; I was really earnest and naive. At Daylesford we had good times, occasionally eating trout that I would catch as a result of my new sport, my new passion—fly-fishing.

There was a tradition at Daylesford: the fly-fishermen would meet at the Victoria Hotel on Saturday mornings to have a few beers and discuss the afternoon's angling prospects while the wives did the shopping. These little meetings were held in the public bar, where no women were allowed, so everybody there was surprised when Vosje walked in, sat down beside me, and asked me to get her an Advocaat and cherry brandy. I obliged, and Vosje became the first female ever to have a drink in the public bar of the Victoria Hotel in Daylesford. She was like that!

Before Sebastian was born we carted Ondine everywhere in a basket strapped into the back seat of our Fiat 500. On Saturdays we would go to the Victoria Market to buy the week's fruit and vegetables, then we'd meet friends at a little restaurant, Gregory's, in Carlton, for an Italian meal. In later years, with two children, we would go to Brian and Gill's place in Parkville to cook some of the produce we'd purchased that morning. Gill was the Australian girl we'd befriended in Perugia; she met Brian when he visited me there. When they married later in Adelaide, Vosje and I drove to the wedding in the Fiat Cinquecento, arriving late.

Anyway, they were great lunches and would go for hours— fried sardines, garfish, calamari and a few bottles of wine that Brian used to procure from his Italian friends. We talked about winemaking, and finally borrowed some equipment, bought some boxes of grapes from the market and started to make wine, fermenting it in a bathtub.

All looked good until it finished fermenting, then it became quite oxidised, aldehydic and generally *off*. We knew nothing about sulphur additions, pH values or anything much, really, but an imaginative mate thought we could go to somebody's uncle's place in Fitzroy where there was an illegal still from which we could make grappa from our spoiled wine.

So off we went into the night with our wine in all manner of containers and eighteen empty bottles for the grappa. But the first distillation produced more than two dozen bottles, and the uncle didn't want us attracting attention by leaving and re-entering the property by the side lane. It was decided a second distillation was required to reduce the volume of grappa. This was done, leaving us with a little more than a dozen bottles of perfectly good rocket fuel—my first foray into the world of winemaking!

One bottle, I remember, was put to good use when a boastful Australian girl was showing off her handsome Italian boyfriend. The other girls had had enough of her, so it was suggested that Italian men couldn't handle their drink. She took the bait, and the handsome Italian, for whom I felt very sorry, dutifully downed about three shot glasses before he collapsed and was carried out to a car. The others were very happy for they never saw the girl (or her boyfriend) again. I don't know what happened to the rest of it—I guess Brian added a shot of it to his coffee each morning until it was gone. I never drank the stuff, so lost interest in it. Lost interest in winemaking, too, for some years.

Later, a medico friend told me that many Italian men in Melbourne were mysteriously becoming ill and occasionally dying. Researchers found that the illness was due to lead poisoning and, later again, that the lead was being leached from lead-based enamel in the bathtubs in which the wine was made. Sad irony, indeed, for it was suspected that many wealthy and influential early Romans died from lead poisoning due to the insertion of lead pellets in wine to give it a softer mouthfeel. The poor people couldn't afford the lead and so didn't die at the same rate as their 'superiors'. A friend speculates that it caused the fall of the Roman Empire: good wine, bad wine—it was always there in the back of my mind.

Retreat to Tasmania

After Vosje and I split up, I found it too painful to be in Melbourne, knowing that my children were close by but that I could only occasionally see them, be with them and hold them and, feeling that they had adequate substitutes for me, I made other plans.

Michael Buck and I sold off our small garage-door business, which had provided us with an income for the previous three years. The decision to sell up must have pleased him, as I'd become something of a loose cannon after my break-up with Vosje and both of us had more or less ruined our backs carrying heavy garage doors around building sites.

So, in early 1968, I took a job at a construction site in north-western Tasmania, at Port Latta between Burnie and Smithton, in view of 'The Nut' at Stanley. After spending a couple of months in the single men's quarters at Port Latta, I rented a little shack at Cowrie Point, a rocky outcrop above the beach with the whole of Bass Strait before me. The work was demanding enough, the hours very long, but there were girls at the township of Burnie. Saturday nights saw a procession of cars from Port Latta to Burnie, but a combination of fatigue, alcohol and challenging winding country roads usually meant that they didn't all make it home, and there were unfortunately some funerals to attend on Wednesdays or Thursdays—after which, of course, everybody went to the pub and got drunk and drove home.

The food in the dining room was not at all bad and every effort was made to keep the men content; plenty of steak and chips but very little greenery. Sunday nights saw a choice of salad, a huge coleslaw sort of thing, or curry and rice. The local doctor found that men were coming to him with problems which he assumed to be diet related, for the symptoms could be removed after a course of vitamin supplements. Talking to him one night, we established that generally his patients were the ones who had the curry and rice, and not the salad. Presumably they didn't have fruit juice in the morning, either.

After I moved into my rented shack, I was able to get organised and do some fishing. Angling had always been a passion of mine. As a child, when we went camping next to a small stream near Daylesford, I would not take my eye from the float for the entire day. Mum would bring my lunch of camp pie, tomato and lettuce and place it close to my elbow. I would thank her and eat without looking at the plate as I watched that float and waited for a bite. Anyway, a more sophisticated form of angling, fly-fishing for trout, had become the sport I loved, so I came to terrorise the trout of the Duck, Detention and Black rivers.

I also discovered the mud oyster. These could be found on the sides or undersides of rocks in the estuaries, so if low tide coincided with some spare time from work it was well worth-while turning over a few rocks. The oysters could be huge, and one I found under a particularly large rock had a shell that was almost the size of the steering wheel of my car. I can still remember the extraordinary sensation of swallowing it, the size of a dozen normal oysters.

There were other delights at the seaside, too. I was once talking to a girl with whom I was falling in love as we walked along the beach near my shack. I was telling her about John Steinbeck's first published literary work, *The Log of the Sea of Cortez*, when I made the unfortunate Freudian slip of saying 'marine orgasms' instead of 'marine organisms', but it turned out all right in the end.

I had brought with me a small dinghy I'd built in Melbourne, so I bought a craypot and was soon sitting on my balcony, with a glass of home brew to hand, looking at the buoy on my craypot bobbing in the waves and wondering if I had captured one yet. Scale fish could be caught with rod and line on the rocks beside the shack, silver grunter being the preferred species; and occasionally a school of black-back salmon would provide good sport on the fly, although they weren't very good eating. They could be frozen in the 'Silent Knight' kerosene refrigerator that was not supposed to be a freezer but was, and the salmon provided excellent bait for the craypot. There were abalone on the rocks there, too, which could be relieved of their boredom with the aid of a large flat knife, goggles and snorkel so, given time, it was possible to assemble a meal of the very finest quality and freshness imaginable. If my girlfriend was visiting from university in Hobart, we would sometimes share this bounty and a bottle of wine while overlooking Bass Strait.

Later on I bought a lovely little yacht, a Rainbow, which consisted of a planing hull, a mast and a lot of sail for its size.

Myrtle went like the wind and almost as fast. On a sunny day, when I was not on shift, I used to surf it on the waves in front of the 'pellet plant' where we worked to torment my workmates, who could watch me from the windows of that dark satanic mill.

I can't recall if there was any Tasmanian wine then. Graeme Wiltshire hadn't got Heemskerk going, nor had the Alcorsos started at Moorilla, and it was long before Andrew Pirie came over from Riverina College, and later Andrew Hood, who also lectured there. And, of course, it would have been a very long time since the infamous failed experiment on Maria Island, when bunches of grapes were tied to unproductive vines to fool investors. It was an old-fashioned scam. The grower had realised that the climate was too cold to ripen grapes but needed the investors' money. So he imported grapes from the mainland and attached them to some vines in a small area where he led them to inspect the 'crop'.

And so I used to drink some Tahbilk Marsanne and occasional mainland rieslings. Vosje would come over with the children sometimes, or friends from Melbourne would visit, and the challenge was always to assemble as many of those fishy ingredients as I could before their arrival.

At that time I met Estelle, who worked in the office at Port Latta. She was a bit of a tomboy whose family lived in Stanley and sometimes had roast wallaby for Sunday lunch. So we caught a wallaby and I was introduced to that delight—it was cooked as you would a leg of lamb and some of the meat was saved for wallaby patties.

Over a couple of years I was given several families' secret recipes for wallaby patties. I gradually came to realise that they were all the same—wallaby, bacon, breadcrumbs, flour, onion and egg. It was Estelle who also introduced me to whitebait patties. We would net the whitebait from the estuary with dip nets, and occasionally a trout could be seen slashing at their shoals as they plucked up their courage and charged, seeking safety in numbers as they ran the trout gauntlet to get upstream to their breeding grounds. This meant that the fly rod usually accompanied us on the whitebait run. When the season was right, Estelle also showed me where and how to catch the giant Tasmanian freshwater crayfish. I'll never forget her excitement when I landed my first primeval monster from the deep.

Unfortunately, I then made the mistake of putting it in the front luggage compartment of the new Volkswagen. It escaped from the hessian bag in which I had (inadequately) secured it and backed down a crevice between the petrol tank and the mudguard, necessitating removal of the bonnet with a spanner and an interesting tug-of-war with an enormously strong opponent.

Estelle had a beautiful Arabian mare and would sometimes borrow another horse for me, and we'd gallop them along the hard sand beaches at low tide, a wonderful experience. Estelle appeared at the vineyard tasting room last year and we had a good reminisce about these old times from forty-five years ago.

As a fly-fisher, I was inevitably drawn to the Highland Lakes—only a two-and-a-half-hour drive from the beach at Cowrie Point to the Tasmanian equivalent of the Scottish Highlands, above the snowline in tundra country. Among those windswept tarns I succumbed to the lure of 'the uncertain trout' and would bolt from whatever shift I was on to camp and hike and fish for a couple of days—a habit I've never broken. It is country that gets into you, perhaps particularly if you have Scottish blood in your veins. But almost everybody who came up there with me has returned, and most of us still do. The trout there are some of the best in the world, often hugely challenging to catch and always spectacular to eat. Their flesh varies in colour according to the lake they come from, reflecting variations in diet, becoming more orange as the amount of crustaceans and mayflies in their diet increases.

The most striking colour I've ever seen was in a fish from Lake Baily, where their diet consists almost solely of water snails, mayfly and anthropods. I approached the lake on foot one day to see an angler about a kilometre away cleaning a fish. As he, John Philbrick, opened up the fish there was an explosion of Day-glo orange against the dull grey of the tundra as the sunlight caught the flesh.

A group of four or five of us, varying every year except for me, the common denominator, used to fly to Launceston after Christmas then take a taxi direct to those lonely lakes and tarns of the Tasmanian Central Highlands plateau. The first driver we engaged for this unusual fare was not comfortable as he drove his Fairlane on the unmade road that sneaks alongside the Liaweenee Canal leading up to Lake Augusta. As we unloaded our gear below the majestic but forbidding Wild Dog Tier, he commented that it looked like a moonscape and that he couldn't wait to get out of there. It was only after the payment of a hefty deposit that he agreed to return in ten days' time to collect us. And off we went with our Volkorn bread and smoked bacon, rolled oats, dried peas and instant mashed potato in our hiking packs. Ten days later the taxi driver was amazed to see us emerge from the swirling mist and set ravenously upon the chocolate bars we had asked him to buy for us.

Bass Strait deckhand

I had long nurtured a desire to work on a fishing boat, having seen them moored to the wharf at Stanley, and having talked to the deckhands and skippers in the pub there. Towards the end of my last employment in Tasmania, I found I could do just that, for the skipper of a cray boat had come to Stanley searching for a deckhand. So I was soon sailing out on the *Amelia,* a lovely old double-ended carvel-built thirty-footer which had been registered at St Helens on the east coast of Tasmania.

The skipper was a taciturn and well-educated Dutchman by the name of Jack Meyer. As we motored out to the fishing grounds, he explained the drill and showed me how to bait the craypots, a procedure with which I was familiar. Using his echo sounder he was able to read the sea floor below and when he found a suitable rock formation, he would call for me to drop a pot, and overboard it would go with its attached marker buoy. And so we would continue until all the twenty or so pots had been released. After that we would clean and wash the deck then have lunch—for him a frozen steak put straight onto the frying pan which, amazingly, cooked properly, and for me a couple of small cray tails done quickly in the pressure cooker, some bread, salad and a half bottle of Australian chablis. It was fun for me to practise my rusty Dutch with him, he being surprised to have an Australian-born Dutch-speaking deckhand. After lunch and a lie-down we would then return to collect the pots.

On my first trip the wind came up and it became quite rough out there, making it difficult to winch the pots onboard. After we had recovered about fifteen pots and dropped the crays they contained into the seawater hold of the boat, I pulled up one pot containing not crays but a Bass Strait crab, a giant of a crustacean with one small claw and the other a monstrous threatening thing about as thick as my arm. Jack had not told me about them, so I looked to him in the wheelhouse for guidance. The boat was pitching and rolling, I was drenched with spray every time we hit a wave and the wind was blowing hard so communication was difficult. He was indicating that I should put my bare hand into the pot and pull the creature out. I must have appeared reluctant to do so for, keeping one hand on the wheel, he leaned out of the wheelhouse and yelled: 'Put your hand into the big claw and pull it out! It's just like a suitcase handle. It can't hurt you, it can't close that claw!' Then followed perhaps the most challenging few seconds of my life until that time. But he was right; they can't close that big claw enough to slice your hand in two.

The other drop-offs were comparatively uneventful after that and we returned to the Stanley co-op with a good load of lobster in the seawater hold. But it was a Saturday and the co-op was closed. Jack wanted to return to St Helens before the weather got worse and sell the catch there instead. He would pay me cash for my share of the estimated value and if more was owing he would send me a cheque for the balance. We parted on those terms; he sailed off to St Helens while I got into my car and went back to my shack, hoping to find a girl waiting there. Some days later I received a hefty cheque in the mail, for he had underestimated the weight of the catch.

A few days later I went to the pub to see if I could get a job on a shark boat, for I wanted to continue my experiences at sea. There *was* a job available, on the *Tingarra*, a fifty-foot steel-hulled shark boat, which was leaving as soon as the weather cleared—and they could use another deckhand! The skipper had already hired an inexperienced hand, but was soon satisfied that I could do the job, given my experience at crayfishing. I neglected to tell him that I'd only done one trip.

The weather seemed fine to me, but the skipper and his mate were apparently enjoying a few days on land after their last trip, which had apparently been rough. The idea seemed to be that you stayed in the pub until you tired of it and then set off no matter what the weather. So I had to hang around the pub for a couple of days until the skipper was ready to leave; my shack was only 10 miles away so it wasn't hard for me to stay in touch.

One morning the skipper decided he'd had enough and we set off into a howling gale, the weather so bad that the other inexperienced man succumbed to seasickness of such virulence that we put him off at an island with a sleeping bag, some water and food, promising to pick him up after the trip, and we bashed through the waves to the fishing grounds.

The weather subsided enough to bait up the longlines and we were ready to fish. The job of baiting up hundreds of hooks with smelly salmon on a heaving boat, with a hangover and the smell of diesel in my nostrils, trying to fight off seasickness, was not pleasant. We fed out the longlines from the baskets in which they were coiled and sailed back to the beginning of the drop and, as on the cray boat, we cleaned the decks, had something to eat and a lie-down, then began retrieving the lines and their catch of sharks with the aid of a rotating winch. This was quite a tricky job, avoiding the bare hooks, then bleeding and gutting the sharks and flinging them into the freezer.

I was glad when, after two days and nights, it was over and we could sail back to retrieve our little seasick Robinson Crusoe from his island. He was still green around the gills when we collected him and not happy to be boarding the boat, but his alternatives were limited. Worse was to come for him, however, for the wind blew up again and we had to seek refuge in a cove on the mainland. It was a troubled night, but in the morning the wind subsided and we cleaned up the boat, throwing the offal and unused bait over the side, preparatory to departure. A weak sun began to shine and I decided to have a quick swim, but just as I was about to launch myself into the water, I saw, lying under the boat, the unmistakeable shape of a gigantic shark. That was the end of swimming for the day—I was to remain filthy.

We headed back to Stanley and the skipper decided that I should drive the boat while he and the first mate got out some large bottles of beer and started drinking them. I had noticed that the skipper had a very long belt around his waist and I was now about to find out its purpose: with one end embracing his waist, and the other wrapped around the large metal stanchion in the wheelhouse, he was able to urge me to put on more speed. The two big Perkins diesel engines responded to the throttles and the big steel-hulled boat crashed through the waves and swamped the decks and the windscreen, while I clutched the wheel for dear life and the skipper drank more beer and urged me on. It was an exciting ride, but I was very glad to see the huge shape of The Nut at Stanley loom up through the spray and rain, and could back off the throttles.

Bloody workplace

In many ways reluctantly, for there were several loves to leave in Tasmania, I moved on to my next job at Longford, near Sale in eastern Victoria, to work on the installation of a new section of the Esso gas plant. I was still supporting the family, so I needed the extra money construction work gave me, for my lifestyle wasn't cheap. There were not many wine and food adventures there, but I did have the opportunity to buy the entire stock of a pub cellar that had been flooded. There were hundreds of bottles, from chiantis to Hunter Valley semillons to South Australian reds, and I got them for a song as most had lost their labels (although it was not difficult to identify the chiantis after experiencing them on the *Castel Felice*).

Vosje was then, in 1969, living with her new partner, Rod Parker, and our children, Ondine and Sebastian, at 453 Canning Street in North Carlton. Rod was in the process of purchasing the house from the Richardson family, a large and lively clutch of music- and food-loving vegetarians who always had pots of delicious things simmering on their slow combustion stove to the accompaniment of taped classical music.

The Richardsons had a young friend named Vicki Barclay, who then became a friend of Rod and Vosje. She was a gregarious and fun-loving girl who would sometimes babysit Ondine and Sebastian. I came to know her quite well—so well that I fell in love with her and, despite the difference of ten years in our ages, we got on like a house on fire. Over the following years we had good times and holidays. Once she came on a fly-fishing hike over Wild Dog Tier in Tasmania, where we were trapped by a blizzard for some days as we were about to break camp, our supplies being almost exhausted. Four of us males and Vicki had to hike out of that unforgiving country for many hours, with empty bellies, in the snow and rain. Not surprisingly, Vicki succumbed to hypothermia, and the rest of us were very close to doing the same. We had a hire-car parked on the bleak shore of Lake Augusta, and had it not been there the outcome would have been fatal for some of us.

There were warmer times, too, of course, and every weekend I would return from Longford to Drummond Street in Carlton, and we'd eat at home at Vicki's flat, or we'd go to Jimmy Watson's in Lygon Street, or Dennis Conroy's Borbles restaurant in Elgin Street; veal zingara smothered with roasted capsicums was a favourite.

I was pleased when my mate from the Tasmanian days, Rod Williams, arrived in Sale with his wife Cheryl so that he could join the team at Longford, for we needed a skilled electronics technician. But in August 1970 at Longford things were about to change catastrophically. Tragedy struck in the form of a gas explosion.

I saw it happen. Rod was shutting down a valve that had become live due to a failure in the safety system during maintenance shutdown. Heroically, he stayed to shut it down manually when he could have run. But a huge area was flooded with gas, which exploded.

At the time I was in the control room, and all of us there, hearing the huge hissing roar of escaping gas and knowing the possible result, were transfixed with fear. We could see the distant figures of the men below us, and we actually watched Rod turning the metal wheel to close the valve until it became silent, after which he, too, began to run. There were several men running on that concrete plain when some spark ignited the gas and acres of concrete became a giant fireball, obliterating the fleeing overalled figures. The large metal pipes in their racks beside the control room crashed and banged, bouncing around like boiling spaghetti in a pot. Then we, too, were rushing through the smoke to our wounded workmates. As the smoke cleared we found their blackened forms, some writhing in pain.

I travelled with Rod in the ambulance to Sale Hospital. His face and hands were burnt black and his overalls were burnt through to the skin in places, but he insisted on riding in the front of the ambulance between the driver and me. He was in frightful pain but kept talking—I think to keep our spirits up as much as his own. I stayed at the hospital until after his treatment, spoke to him in his state of morphine-induced lucidity, and even spoke to the doctor in charge of his treatment, congratulating him on Rod having pulled through. I was devastated when the doctor said: 'We haven't really saved him, Graeme. We'll probably lose him tonight.' And we did.

Rod had survived the Vietnam War but in the end a bloody workplace got him. He was a wild but compassionate man who told me that during Vietnam he and his mates in the helicopter gunship were not happy with what they were instructed to do. They suspected that the people they were supposed to be shooting were guilty of nothing except having been born there. So they would take the chopper into the jungle, shoot some bullets into the trees below and hover about for a while—some would smoke a joint—then they'd go back to base and write false reports on their number of 'kills'.

It was I who had recommended Rod for the job in the first place, knowing his work from Tasmania. So I had to live with the fact that I had inadvertently caused his death. I was left grieving—and angry and dismayed by the subsequent legal proceedings and findings. What's worse, the disaster was to be replicated many years later, in September 1998, when there was another explosion. Two people were killed and eight injured.

Carlton Dark and meeting Sue Mackinnon

I chose to leave Longford in any case, and ended up establishing an electrical contracting business. This became known as the infamous Carlton Lighting—or 'Carlton Dark' as David Brown used to call it, for we were often working in just that.

I set up the business largely because I wanted to be with Vicki, and also closer to my children, who had settled with Vosje and Rod in Steiglitz, a small town in the Brisbane Ranges, about 90 kilometres west of Melbourne. Rod ran the Moreland High School education and holiday camp there. Strangely, perhaps, now that they were living in the country an hour from Melbourne, it seemed possible to see them with less heartache than before. When they'd lived just a couple of blocks from me, I'd been frustrated almost to the point of madness that I could be so near literally, and yet so far from them. It was somehow easier with them being geographically further away—although I was still anguished that I couldn't be with them. I loved them so much and missed them every day, and was taunted by the irony that Vosje's partner, Rod Parker, would probably have been delighted at times if Graeme Leith had taken his bloody kids away and, a little later, his bloody wife, too!

Vosje had introduced me to John Timlin, who was converting an old Carlton factory into a theatre, The Pram Factory, and needed some serious wiring done. It was to be a base for the grandly titled Australian Performing Group—basically a fairly scruffy troupe of unemployed actors with big heads. I'm still friendly with a couple of them today. John was organising the conversion from factory to theatre, dealing with building inspectors, tradesmen, bureaucrats, scriptwriters, producers and actors, and generally keeping the whole show on the rails. With a bit of creative thinking and a studied analysis of the relevant regulations, we were able to set up the electrics for a fraction of the original prohibitively expensive quote they'd received. I'd applied for an electrical contractor's licence, bought an old van and some tools and equipment, was granted the licence, and Carlton Lighting was up and running.

One night I was finishing off a dimmer board for The Pram Factory in the dining room of Vicki's flat, just as the audience was filing into the theatre over the road. By the time we carried it over to the theatre, five minutes before the play was due to start, The Pram's lighting man, Ian Mackenzie, had torn out a generous crop of his hair.

A lot of house renovation was being done in Carlton then: the suburb was becoming gentrified, as I had earlier predicted. The price of houses had risen dramatically so I now worked on them as a tradesman contractor, rather than owning two or three of them as an entrepreneur—my marital separation had taken care of that, one way or another. I'd assembled a little crew of employees and the business ran successfully, so a few years of happy contracting followed.

After several years Vicki and I went our separate ways, although we were still friends—in fact, over the years, as our birthdays were one day and ten years apart, we'd send birthday telegrams and cards to each other. (She and her husband Graeme are devotees of Passing Clouds wine.) I then happily shared my life with Gail Morton for a couple of years, living at 453 Canning Street for some time. (I had come to an arrangement with Rod Parker, and was now the occupant of the ex-Richardson house.) But when she headed off adventuring overseas, I was on the loose again.

I met Sue Mackinnon at a mutual friend's place, and after a couple of false starts on my part, Sue and I took up life together.

I loved her intelligence, her wit, her love of literature and her general lack of reverence for things normally revered, which we shared. We seemed to have read and admired much of the same literature, so were always making literary allusions. It was a lot of fun for us both, although often a mystery to my children. Later, when my daughter Ondine started reading Shakespeare at school, or other books from our shelves at home, she began to understand, to her surprise and delight, the code we used, and she joined in. From The Bard to Oscar Wilde, from James Thurber to Donleavy, it was all grist to our mill.

We had fun with words and, sometimes, other people. Once we had a pretentious visitor who loved to use big words, and I put him down by referring to Sue's 'infracaninophilic tendencies', using the word as if it was completely familiar to us. We had in fact only recently and joyfully discovered it a few weeks prior, in the introduction to a book on Conan-Doyle. In this case it worked a treat at quieting the pretentious sod; we enjoyed the thought of him scrambling for his dictionary when he got home.

Sue had a deteriorating muscular disease that plagued her throughout her late teens and adult life. There was no knowing when the deterioration would plateau or whether it would continue and Sue had to live with that uncertainty, which she did with extraordinary courage.

The electrical contracting was beginning to bore me so I began acting at nights at Carlton's iconic La Mama theatre under Betty Burstall, who seemed annoyed that I could act all right without having had any formal training. I performed in four plays there over a couple of years. La Mama was an exciting place to be and the playwrights, actors and other people who made that sweet unique little theatre work became my friends.

Sue was then working for *The Melbourne Times* newspaper, which had morphed from *The Carlton News*, so we were able to get the play reviews prior to printing. They were not always good, as some of the plays were distinguished more by their controversial elements than their quality. The reviewer, John Smythe, was fond of a joke, so a review of Roger Pulver's play

Ice was headlined as 'Pulverised Ice', and Barry Dickins's *Ghost in the Alley* was hailed as 'What the Dickins?'. And they were only two of the plays I was in.

When we were doing *Ice*, Sue asked her sister Jill, who was visiting Melbourne, if she'd like to go to the theatre and see me in a play. Jill's first sighting of her sister's boyfriend was naked in front of about fifty people, which was usually about La Mama's capacity, depending on how much space the play occupied.

Barry Dickins often acted in his own plays and, as the writer, he felt at liberty to alter the script at any time he chose; he would sometimes launch into a stream-of-consciousness monologue only vaguely related to the script the other actors had industriously memorised, so when delivered the learned lines often seemed strangely irrelevant. But perhaps it didn't matter at La Mama—certainly from the standpoint of eternity, not at all. The last and probably the best play I acted in was Louis Nowra's first play, I think, *Kiss the One-Eyed Priest*. It seemed outrageous at the time, dealing as it did with exploitation of an individual for the sake of television sensationalism, of necrophilia and police dishonesty, but twenty years later seemed quite prescient.

I would have liked to have done more acting but the opportunity wasn't there. I had burned my bridges (again) by leaving Melbourne and since then my acting career has been restricted to some melodramas in various country towns, and campfire or after-dinner recitations of *The Green Eye of the Little Yellow God*, *Albert and the Lion*, *The Shooting of Dan McGrew*, *Gunga Din*, and so on. About twelve years ago an actress had to pull out of a melodrama, *The Drunkard's Dilemma or Her Honour for Sixpence*, at a church concert at Daylesford. My youngest son Jesse was the only person I could think of who could learn the words in time, so he was roped in, reluctantly, to play the heroine, with me as the drunken uncle. He did it brilliantly—it was a hilarious performance.

5

The vision splendid

'Coming out' in '73

The spirit is restless. Some men have always wanted to plant vineyards; fewer women, as they are usually more conservative and sensible. But since Old Testament times and before, men have wanted to plant vineyards and my appetite was becoming whetted.

My friends Roger Milner, David Brown, David Reimers and Robert Roles had all worked at Reynella in the Southern Vales, near Adelaide, for varying lengths of time. They were oenophiles all, lived communally at a house over there known as 'Four Winds', and didn't mind spending money on good bottles of wine. They drove old Peugeots and Renaults, loved their food, wine and good fun. (Incidentally, the old Peugeots and Renaults always carried the best wine buyers to the cellar door in those days.) Over time they introduced me to grape varieties and styles that I never knew existed—their gods were winemakers and their holy grail was great wine. I really don't recall how we all came to be friends; I certainly wasn't the glue that held them together. Maybe I was more like a strip of sticky flypaper that trapped a few of them when they were trying to fly past.

Sue Mackinnon and I shared many good meals with David and Ann Brown at their place, or at mine at 453 Canning Street, almost over the road from Ferranato's where we bought most of our Italian smallgoods and wine. Sometimes we'd go to Osicka's Vineyard near Graytown, an old goldmining ghost town north of Melbourne, and buy some bottles of wine and a 20-litre container of bulk red to take back to Carlton for bottling, marvelling at the sheer power and colour of the wine and always wondering where the strong eucalypt character came from. This flavour would diminish with time in the bottles. There was a rumour that during the war a man had been selling wine barrels made from mountain ash eucalypt, but whether that was the origin of the eucalypt flavour, or whether it was due to the proximity of the eucalypt forest to the vineyard, I still don't know. I have had my own experiences with eucalypt flavour in wine at Passing Clouds over the years, but more of that later.

We would sometimes eat at Jimmy Watson's Wine Bar, where you bought your steak and bottle of wine and then went out to the back courtyard and cooked your own meat on their barbecue. David Brown and I worked together for a time and would have a counter lunch at the Lincoln Hotel or the Evelyn Hotel sometimes—in fact, most times during the week, because, well, you did have to eat, didn't you? For our Friday lunches we'd go to the Railway Hotel in Nicholson Street in North Fitzroy where the best value for quality traditional Italian pub food was served, and probably still is. And then there were lunches or dinners at the Clare Castle Hotel in Carlton. Fulvio was the maître d' there and I have never before or since seen a man who performed that role with more skill; his ability to sense the needs of a customer were intuitive and profound. Much later I observed those same qualities in Simon at the All Nations in Richmond. To my delight, many years later Simon turned up at Daylesford where he and his wife Vanessa bought and ran the Farmers Arms.

We were renovating houses at the time, but these establishments didn't mind our work clothes at lunchtime. They had not become gentrified, and I'm sure that you can still get fed at the Railway if you're neither a retired Italian businessman nor an artisan in dapper clothing.

It was during one of the lunches at the Railway that, momentously, I announced I wanted to establish a vineyard and become a winemaker. Present at that lunch were Stuart Mair (who later set up Coal Valley vineyard near Yallourn) and David Reimers (who was about to plant vines on his family property in Central Victoria). I had 'come out'.

The lie of the land

The Reimers' property was at Kingower, a hamlet in the dry area north-west of Bendigo in Central Victoria, on old gold diggings,

where goldminers had dug the soil more than 120 years ago.
They were treading in the footsteps of their German ancestors,
who had grown grapes and made wine there many years before.
David and his brother Alvin had by then planted some cabernet
sauvignon.

David encouraged us to look at those plantings at Kingower,
already named Blanche Barkly after a huge gold nugget found
there during the gold rush, in turn named after the daughter of
the Victorian governor at the time. So one weekend Sue and I
travelled to Heathcote, west through Bendigo and then through
Inglewood and on to Kingower and Avoca.

As we drove along the dusty unmade road from Inglewood
to Kingower and observed the sparse and hungry roadside
forest of box and ironbark, I remarked to Sue: 'The only
thing you'll grow here is bloody old!' But as we approached
Kingower, as we came into that little valley, we could see fig
trees, peppercorns—a general greening in this otherwise dry
place. We later learned that the valley had once embraced the
lives of 6000 goldminers, but was home now to only a few
families, who were, as it transpired, to become our friends and
neighbours.

It had been a good wet year and David and Alvin's rootlings
were doing well, sprawling over a metre along the ground in
their first year. The soil was impressive; it was a sandy loam
mixed with some clay, ironstone and quartz amalgamated by
the industry of the diggers in the gold rush as they turned over
every bit of soil in their search for gold. What fortunes were
made there, how many hopes and dreams were dashed? Forty
years on, walking today in the silent bush behind the original
Passing Clouds vineyard, looking over the endless diggers' holes
now filled with the debris of generations of trees, of ironbark,
box and occasional red gums on the deepest soil, it is still easy
to imagine hundreds of men spread over the rapidly denuding
landscape toiling for gold.

Downstream from Blanche Barkly (if that is the appropriate direction to give for a creek that only runs a few days a
year and has not run at all for the last ten years), past another

rammed-earth house and behind the Gilmores' old pub, was another property. It had been recently deserted by its occupants, Lily and Ruby Taig, who had died and moved on to a less troubled place. The house was a sad-looking affair, with two rammed-earth rooms near the road and, on the creek side, a slab hut with a one-fire stove and chimney.

In the old days they built the kitchens separately from the living quarters so that if the kitchen burned, the bedrooms would survive. Over the years the space between the two had been filled in with stud walls and a good effective fireplace, but the windows were very small and too high to look out of. The verandahs around the house had been largely filled in with flywire then covered with tarpaulins, for the Taig sisters were apparently worried about 'Peeping Toms'.

However, the soil was good on the 15 acres of flats before the contour rose and the ground became tough and useless for anything but ironbark and box trees. The creek had obviously meandered over the flat for hundreds of thousands of years, because there were water-worn stones in the soil far away from the current creek bed. One paddock had been cleared and grew excellent grass. There were still trees and traces of Tom Taig's original vineyard, from which, according to his son Gordon, younger brother of the now deceased Lily and Ruby, he produced 'three bunches to a kerosene tin'. But the rest of the flat land, still covered with diggers' holes, had regenerated with red or white gums, the pestilential boxthorn and Chinese tree of heaven. Occasional peppercorn trees, *Schinus molle*, had survived, as had a scattering of castor oil plants and wild tobacco, doubtless a legacy of the Chinese who followed the gold trail and often gained sustenance from the land which the white diggers had abandoned.

When David Reimers rang me to say that the Taigs' place was up for sale, I drove around to find Sue at her house, 28 Carlton Street, and said that, if it was all right with her, we would go to an auction the next day and buy ourselves a vineyard site. She agreed, for we were partners and kindred spirits, and we were looking forward to sharing this grand project.

We both embraced the idea of braving the elements, facing the challenge of the land and pursuing the holy grail of making 'the best wine in the world'.

We did the two-and-a-half-hour trip in her Mini to the auction, held in the Lions Park at nearby Inglewood. I was sweating, Sue's knees knocking during the bidding, then the auctioneer's gavel fell for the last time and *it was ours!*

After the auction Gordon Taig drove out to the house with us, showed us around, loaded his ute with some furniture and mementos, and shared a bottle of bubbly that we'd kept cold for the occasion. For better or for worse, as of September 1973, Sue and I were the new owners of the Taigs' place. We didn't know then that we were hatching a dragon that we would have to keep feeding for the rest of its life.

There had to be a party, of course, and a couple of weeks later a disparate and eclectic group of our friends assembled at Kingower and had just that, with singing, bush poetry and plenty of wine, although I forget what we ate.

The Kingower project begins

Some people said we paid too much for Kingower and I defended myself by saying that it was only the price of a second-hand Commodore car. Certainly, over the years, it has produced many millions of dollars' worth of wine, providing much income to the government as taxes, and much to the purveyors of corks, barrels, bottles, labels, capsules, insurance, fuel, winemaking equipment and materials, not to mention corrugated iron and steel tubing, with a little bit left over for us as wages.

It was too late in the year to buy any grapevine rootlings. In fact, being September, a little too late, by conventional wisdom, to plant them at all that season. But we were champing at the bit, and some luck came our way.

At the time, I was doing some wiring at Lazar's restaurant in King Street. The restaurant had an ensemble of instrumentalists who played baroque music from the 'gods' to entertain the diners. They were, I think, asking for more money, so Tom Lazar sacked them, a practice to which he was not unaccustomed. He decided to install a discotheque, which, of course, had to be the best in the Southern Hemisphere. It was duly designed by experts—and me—and I built it. The DJ could sit in front of a console designed like a piano keyboard and by pushing keys make all manner of good things happen. Colour wheels played huge oil-flowing designs on the walls, coloured spots were synchronised to the music, strobes lit up statues, black lights lit up people's white shirts, teeth and dandruff to give a different look, bubbles fell from above, and at floor level 'smoke', as carbon dioxide gas, could be made to emerge from hidden vents, the combination of which made it slippery for the male 'go-go' dancer, Robin Hardiman, who slipped and fell on opening night.

Tom insisted that we have dinner at Lazar's every night for the first week, and one way or another we became friends. A few years earlier he had set up the Virgin Hills vineyard near Kyneton and bought a large bluestone mansion there, and for his mother a bluestone cottage over the road. They had finished planting there for the year and he had some spare rootlings that I could have.

We couldn't wait for the weekend so the night following Tom's offer we left Melbourne after work. David and Anne Brown, Sue and I drove to Kingower in my little work van, collecting the rootlings from Mrs Lazar on the way. Armed with picks and shovels, hammers, pegs and string, we arrived at Kingower and in the lights of the van we dug the holes, planted the vines, had something to eat and drink then returned to Melbourne to be ready for work the next day. I forget what we drank that night but knowing Dave Brown it would have been good, and suitably ceremonial. Five hours' driving, three hours' work and, after eating and packing up, back in Melbourne by about 1.30 a.m.

And so our vineyard had begun, on the site of the original Tom Taig vineyard.

Some years later, when renovating the house, we found a cancelled bankbook that had slid down between the slabs in the lining of the kitchen. It was dated, I think, 1912, in the name of Tom Taig, and showed that he had deposited about one pound a week at the Mildura branch. We assumed he'd worked up there, pruning, and had returned with some Gordo cuttings of the vines that produced the legendary bunches of three to a kerosene tin—fresh grapes in the Depression times would have been a wonderful luxury in the Australian bush.

It is strange to recall how parsimonious we were in 1973–74, and how naive. If you were to set up a vineyard now, you'd be jotting down the following costs: tractor $30,000; spray unit $20,000; cultivator $10,000; vines $30,000; posts and wires $60,000; and so on. But we had no business plan at that stage, and no budget. However, we needed something to hold the water for the vines, so we bought a brand-new Furphy tank from the makers in Shepparton. We were enormously proud of it, its end plates proclaiming in Pitman shorthand and English: 'Good better best, Never let it rest, Til your good is better, And your better, best.' It bore the name 'James Furphy and Sons, Shepparton' and, perhaps incongruously, a stork carrying a baby. The ends are cast iron, the tank is the same as those used in the North African deserts of World War I, when parched soldiers would gather around them to drink, fill their water bottles and gossip—hence 'furphy', a rumour.

(I recently installed the faithful Furphy as a water feature in the dam at Musk, our new headquarters and vineyard, near Daylesford. And so the Furphy lives on!)

From the electrical contracting business I had a spare, ancient van and that was brought up and pressed into service. It became the water tanker from then on, with the Furphy inside, filled from a motorised pump at the dam. There were gum trees overhanging the vineyard so we purchased a chainsaw to deal with them and to cut firewood for winter, some of which we used ourselves and some which we sold to the Evelyn Hotel in North Fitzroy for the fireplace. To achieve that we would fill the trailer with wood and tow it back to Melbourne behind the Volkswagen throughout the winter.

We had to prepare the vineyard for the new planting the following year, 1974, so a tractor was needed. We called into Sheppard's, the Massey Ferguson dealers at Kyneton, and were soon the proud owners of a 1954 grey Ferguson TEF 25, the last of the grey diesels, and surely the best mechanical purchase I have ever made, for today it is still going strong and ticks over like a clock. Its initial purchase price was $2000 and it hasn't depreciated at all—we'd get more than $4000 for it now! It's been back to Brian and Dennis at Sheppard's twice; once it required a new clutch plate and, at the end of vintage recently, a leak developed in a hose feeding fuel to the injectors. Brian and Dennis found a brand new one in the old stock, still marked seventeen shillings and sixpence! They charged me $20 for it! Is there no end to man's greed and avarice, I thought, as I paid them. (We speculated that had it been a bottle of Grange and appreciated at the same rate, it would be worth quite a lot more than $20.)

Trucking then was not as it is today, so Sir Samuel Ferguson Bart, as Sue later nicknamed the tractor, came up on a train from Kyneton to Inglewood where we collected him. I proudly drove him the 7 miles to Kingower, Sue following me in the Mini. We had to purchase a disc cultivator (although why we bought a second-hand one I'll never know, for it never worked very well), and a ripper to break up the soil along the vine rows. We calculated that we had to dig about 10,000 holes so, having learned from the experience of the second-hand discs, I bought a brand-new post-hole digger to fit behind the tractor. Now everything for the vineyard was ready to go.

A simple blend

The original 'Tom Lazar' planting consisted of some shiraz vines and some cabernet sauvignon. These had grown well, so more vines were ordered.

The proportions of cabernet to shiraz were to be simple—
40 per cent cabernet sauvignon and 60 per cent shiraz, for that
was the blend we planned to make. The shiraz cabernet had
worked so well for Penfolds, for Reynella, and lately for Wolf
Blass, although cabernet was always considered the premier
variety and shiraz the inferior. On the Wolf Blass labels, for
instance, where the blend was disclosed, cabernet sauvignon
was in large letters while the shiraz was in smaller letters below
it, even though the shiraz component was greater.

Stuart Anderson of Balgownie was growing both varieties
but kept them separate; John Middleton in the Yarra Valley
only used cabernet; and Baily Carrodus, also in the Yarra
Valley, had his own formulas—idiosyncratic, of course. It
was considered quite brave of Ron Laughton of Jasper Hill to
come out years later and declare himself to be a shiraz man; yet
people considered the Grange Hermitage to be the finest dry
red in Australia, apparently without realising that it was at least
90 per cent shiraz, and often more.

We expounded on the virtues of cabernet but drank Wynn's
Ovens Valley Shiraz when we could. However, because we had
a soft spot for the Reynella Bin 2, to which the 'Four Winds'
gang had introduced us, we ordered 250 vines of grenache, that
being a component of the Bin 2.

We also ordered a few pinot noir, although I don't know
why because Kingower is far too hot for pinot. Ignorance, I
guess. It should be remembered that there was virtually no
pinot growing in Victoria back then and, although there were
many pinot lovers about, I doubt that they drank Australian
stuff—if any was available.

We worked on the soil around the house, preparing it for a
vegetable garden and, before long, and after the frosts, we had
tomatoes, capsicums, aubergine, cucumbers and pumpkins
growing, as well as all the herbs that might be needed. There
was always sufficient water in the house's two modest rainwater
tanks and the garden thrived, although we soon learned that
tending it during the day in 38-degree heat was not a good
idea—it tended to induce dizzy spells, our bodies not being

conditioned to such temperatures. A timer and some trickle irrigation pipes gave the garden a mid-week drink when we were not there, but every weekend Sue and I were there without fail, occasionally with my children, Ondine and Sebastian, and often with friends who would come up from Melbourne to be part of it all.

In those days of the 1970s, irrigation was a dirty word to us; irrigated wines were often green-tasting and of low quality. This was before Max Loder at Riverina College, and perhaps others, began building trellises to hold many wires to lift and open the canopy and allow the desired ratio of sunshine and shade to be applied to the ripening bunches.

Back then, grapes were generally grown on a single wire and consequently would develop the umbrella-like canopy, shading the fruit and thus often giving a green capsicum flavour to cabernet sauvignon and a green tomato flavour to the shiraz. The dense canopies also meant that it was difficult for the sprays used to prevent powdery and downy mildews to easily penetrate through the leaves and canes. We wanted none of that. We wanted unirrigated grapes grown according to organic principles.

Marking out, planting, weeding

The proposed vineyard area was marked out after much discussion on planting distances. *General Viticulture* by A.J. Winkler, the American viticulturist, became our bible. Among other things in it, I marvelled at the Carpenteria Vine in California that produced 12 tons of fruit and covered more than an acre of ground. It stuck in my mind then that it was buds per acre that was relevant, not necessarily vines per acre. (This was a conviction that led to our later Musk vineyard spacings being possibly the widest in Victoria at 4 metres by 4 metres.)

Eventually, spacings of 3.6 metres by 1.8 metres were decided upon for Kingower, although the first 'Tom Lazar' plantings had been 2.7 metres by 1.8 metres. Over the years it has become apparent that the wider spacing is better, allowing us to later put in a 'T' trellis for better penetration of light and air.

Marking out the vineyard was not too big a problem. It had to be accurate so I used wires to avoid stretch and accumulation of error, which could occur with string lines. One wire had knobs soldered onto it every 12 feet and the other, longer wire had knobs every 6 feet. If we'd used paint instead to mark where the holes should be dug, the mud would have obscured it.

My younger brother Greg came up to stay. We marked out the whole grid, indicating where the holes should be dug with whitewash made from lime, for I would never have countenanced the use of 'plastic' paint on our pure, pristine vineyard. The idea was that the wire would be laid aside while the holes were dug, then replaced and the rootlings planted, the soil filled in and later watered in with the water truck, more to drive out air than to provide moisture, for the soil was still damp.

It worked beautifully on the small shiraz paddock. The intention was to plant more shiraz the following year, but to plant the whole cabernet complement that year on the ground that had already been cleared and needed only cultivation. We had just finished the shiraz and set up our wires on the prepared soil of the cabernet block when it began to rain.

It began to rain seriously, and wouldn't stop. Greg and I ground our teeth in frustration, and it didn't stop. We went away for days on end, and it didn't stop.

As the weather began to warm, the vines, packed with sawdust inside large plastic bags sitting in very large cardboard boxes, were sprouting roots. Meanwhile the whole cabernet vineyard was a sea of jelly-like mud that wobbled to and fro if we tried to drive a tractor up it. Reluctantly, we planted the vines in the mud after the rain had ceased for a few days, but it was hard going and the little soldered knobs were invaluable.

Virtually nothing had been done to the house; we devoted our all to the garden and vineyard. We had somewhere to sleep, eat, sit and talk, then on our return to Melbourne we could have a luxurious hot shower. With summer almost upon us, and the weeds sprouting along the vine rows, it was essential to terminate their existence before they stole the soil's valu-able moisture. Not wanting to use herbicide near our precious vines, I was out there from morning until night with a shovel, chipping weeds out in the sun, happy as a sand boy (and doing my skin damage which still appears to irritate me to this day). Before I had chipped the whole 5 miles of vine rows, it had rained again and regenerated the grass, so I had to do it all over again—like painting the Sydney Harbour Bridge but not as much fun.

We decided we had to mechanise, so we borrowed a 'silly plough' from the Reimers. It was supposed to be a horse-drawn implement with two handles which allowed the blade on the ground to be manipulated to dodge in and out around the vines, ideally digging slightly into the soil and then turning the grass over, roots and all.

There was a snap-lock mechanism on the towing cable attached to the horse or, in our case, tractor, so that if some-thing immovable (like a post or a large vine) was hooked by the plough blade, it would release with a sudden snap like an oversized rat trap going off. Occasionally, if the grass had been allowed to grow long and the vine had a bend near ground level invisible to the operator, then the thing could hook up, but generally it was surprisingly efficient and, after the second plantings were completed in 1975, it was possible to 'silly plough' the whole vineyard in a couple of days, with a few days more for cleaning up with a shovel. By the time the whole vineyard was completely planted, there were 7 miles (or 11 kilometres) of row, which is exactly the distance between Inglewood and Kingower. This meant going up one side of the row and back down the other, therefore double the distance.

At walking pace you could do it in a theoretical time of one day but, with other complications, turning around, swearing at or resetting the snap-lock and so on, two days was a good rate of progress. At one stage Sue had decided to complete her librarian qualifications, and would be driving the tractor while her mind was elsewhere, learning by rote as she recited things to herself. This sometimes meant she didn't hear the exhaust note change as the silly plough got hooked behind something it shouldn't have, sometimes not hearing the snap of the lock on the plough or the curses of the operator, but would blissfully keep driving, reciting whatever it is that librarians learn, dragging the cable behind her, leaving the now supine silly plough and the agitated operator in her wake.

Before that time had arrived, however, the remaining potential vineyard had to be cleared. Thus, after much work with chainsaw, chain and tractor, the local bulldozer man, Bob Raven, was called in to grub out the stumps and level the land, filling in the old diggers' holes. Many of the felled trees became end posts for the trellises. The idea was to have intermediate posts of 4–5 inch treated pine alternated with steel posts. The trellis wire was stapled to the wooden posts and attached by wires to the metal ones, so that the wires could be tightened annually to prevent sagging. This was done by the addition of a Hayes strainer in every wire, a device like a fishing reel with a ratchet, operated with a special tool or handle.

This work was all to be done after the vines had sprawled for a year or two. After all, the viticulturist who established Chateau Tahbilk had written in the mid-1800s: 'In this country where drought occurs regularly each summer, it is important to let the vine spread for the first two years so that it gains maximum vigour, to train it up in its third year.' Or words to that effect.

The watering truck, now named Gunga Din, was put to use throughout the summer. The Furphy tank holds, for some reason, 160 gallons, and at half a gallon per vine could water about 320 vines. With a long enough hose I could water sixteen vines at every stop.

Later, when we were living there, a man came down and introduced himself as the local agriculture inspector. He was a charming fellow, and we proudly showed him our vegetables, particularly some potatoes that were throwing out tiny tomato-like things above ground among the leaves. He explained that the tomato, the potato and the aubergine were all deadly nightshades, and that these vestigial fruits did sometimes naturally

occur in potatoes. Then he said, 'I've been watching you. I sometimes have my lunchtime sandwich in the car on the hill there
and watch you watering. You've got a Furphy tank that holds 160
gallons.' He continued with the mathematics and concluded, 'At
three minutes per vine, plus refilling the tank, isn't that six weeks
to water the vineyard? Summer will be over by then!'

I replied, 'The answer is simple, but mightn't readily occur
to a public servant—I work eighty hours a week!'

We all laughed and he went on his way, but after that he
would sometimes call in and have his sandwich with us.

How easily things grew then

In 1975 we had to think seriously about where we were going
to live—Kingower, where there was so much work to do, or
Melbourne. If Kingower, it would mean closing down the electrical contracting business, Sue leaving work in Melbourne,
and ensuring that my children, Ondine and Sebastian, now
aged eleven and nine, wouldn't need me in Melbourne.

At that time, their mother Vosje was still living with her
partner Rod Parker in Steiglitz. I went to see them to ask if their
relationship was secure and permanent, and to think about it
for a week, for Sue and I were about to embark on a project that
would keep us poor for many years to come.

A week later we talked; their relationship was fine and
enduring. So Sue and I put things in motion to clear the decks
and go to Kingower to live, which we did the following year.

In the meantime, the 'Back to Kingower' weekend was held
in 1975 and was a lot of fun, with a procession of floats repre-
senting woodcutting, winemaking, eucalyptus distilling and,
in our case, Kingower Pumpkin Power, our Suzuki jeep filled
with children and huge pumpkins and squash we had grown.
Ondine and Sebastian came up for it and had a great time with
the neighbouring kids.

We had replanted the vegetable garden for the coming
summer crop, having taken off crops of peas and beans,

silverbeet and spinach from the previous autumn and winter plantings. Our first spring plantings had been wonderfully productive, and we were as boring as new parents showing off a baby as we distributed some of our precious produce to friends in Melbourne.

How easily things grew then, before the drought or climate change, or whatever it is. Our garden had been producing beautifully and I'd established another one on the other side of the house near the front shiraz paddock which, because of the soil type, the level beds and the trench irrigation set-up, only had to be watered once a week, provided the seedlings were mulched when young.

We were giving away stacks of vegetables both locally and in Melbourne and were actually selling pumpkins to the organic fruit and vegetable shop in Nicholson Street, North Carlton. When we moved to Kingower, many of the regular customers were upset, even annoyed, that they couldn't get their 'Sugra' pumpkins, as Shirley Hudson described them in the shop. They were very good, due to the limited irrigation and the good soil, no doubt. They had firm flesh but intense flavour and of course great colour.

So 1975 came and went. I think that might have been the year Phil Leamon made his first wine from Big Hill at Bendigo, and maybe Stuart Anderson's first one from Maiden Gully. We, of course, had some years to go.

The birth of Passing Clouds

After Sue and I moved to Kingower in 1976, the rain slowly ceased—we would have prayed for rain, had we been praying people. But the bountiful wet years had gone and as we searched the skies for clouds the name 'Passing Clouds' was born—or, more accurately, borrowed.

It began as a joke but ended up being serious. Sometimes when it looked as if a storm was building up, the clouds would bank up and approach Kingower from the north-west, then they would part and one lot would go to Wedderburn, 20 kilometres north, and the other lot to Derby near Marong, 25 kilometres south. It appeared that Melville's Caves, a nearby large rock extrusion, was sending up a thermal, sufficiently strong to split the cloud. So that became the name of the vineyard, despite the fact there used to be a cigarette brand called 'Passing Clouds', made by WD & HO Wills—the very ones I had bought for Rob Hall for my twenty-first birthday party all those years ago in London. That's what it had to be: *Passing Clouds*!

Most of the winter of 1976 was spent trellising and training. The trellising had to be built and the vines trained up on a string to the wire, having first been pruned back to two buds on the little trunk, still not much bigger than, say, a little finger. A truckload of metal star posts was delivered and another one of treated pine posts. We were starting to spend serious money now, but what did that matter? We were going to make good wine. We could not know how good, but we were tantalised by the prospect of making something as good as or, we dared think, even better than Balgownie or Chateau Leamon. The Reimers' Blanche Barkly vineyard was producing wine and it was a sensation. It was virtually next-door to our property, and some of their vines were planted on their ancestor's original vineyard site.

Friends and family sometimes came up to help us—Vicki's brother Maurice, my brother Greg, and David Brown, who came once for a 'health week' (which it wasn't). One day, while toiling with me in the vineyard, putting up end posts which weighed about 150 kilos each, aided by what he called 'Mr Crow's infernal invention' (the crowbar), in 41-degree heat, David was moved to say, 'I don't mind work, but why does it have to be so bloody hard?'

But we got it done, and the vision splendid began to appear as the vines, with our encouragement, crept up to the wire on the strings of baling twine. We then nipped out the two top buds with our fingers and trained two new buds along the wire, tying down where necessary. The vines were dormant until about September, when they woke in the warming soil and their roots commenced to grow and expand on last year's hard-won territory. They were then reinvigorated and built tremendous pressure in the sap in the spring, enough to force the hardened, overwintered buds to swell and burst into leaf.

So in late September we would observe the woolly bud stage turn to advanced woolly bud, then finally, budburst, as the tiny leaves unfurled and timorously entered their new world—one that can be unkind, for the risk of frost is omnipresent still, and can burn their tender foliage to a crisp.

6

Living life to the lees

Acquiring ancient skills

It is the viticulturist's job to see the vines through what is going to be a perilous journey from the early, delicate stage to growing leaves and canes, as well as clusters of flowers that become bunches of grapes. They must be succoured through the rigours of the growing season—frost, hail and wind, searing heat and, often, drought. They must grow in good health and their carer must ensure that the twin evils of powdery and downy mildews do not strike them down. This would rob the vines of their hard-won crop, which the winemaker inherits from the viticulturist. If the fruit is good, the wine should be good.

There are other diseases and pests encountered along the way, such as a soft little grub that sleeps all day, coiled like a watch spring in the loose soil at the base of the vine, to emerge at night and chew through the growing shoots until they fall as if cut—hence 'cut worm'. I used to pay the kids five cents each for the ones they'd dig from the soil around the vine's base and then put into a tobacco tin for later tallying and payment. There are snails, too, but these are never much of a problem at Kingower, it being so dry. Earwigs can be a problem, though, and also the light brown apple moth and the ubiquitous vine moth caterpillar. These did threaten us, but we were not prepared to spray any toxins on the vines. Elemental copper for downy mildew and sulphur for powdery mildew we considered okay, being naturally occurring substances. But never toxins—poisons—that would kill other beneficial creatures, such as wasps, bees and ladybirds that feed on the erinose or blister mite, and perhaps even our friends, the birds. Imagine poisoning wagtails, superb blue wrens or magpies!

One doesn't see many blue wrens in the established irrigated winegrowing areas, but at Passing Clouds, with the kitchen door open, two or three are often hopping around the floor. I'm not sure they get much to eat; I think they just like being there.

So, for us, spraying toxins was clearly unthinkable; nature must find a balance. And it did, for the magpies cleaned up

the vine moth caterpillars as they appeared. We noted that
the vines in the vineyard had very few, and if a vine was identified as having even one, the giveaway being chewed leaves,
then the caterpillar was allowed to continue its work, but a
visit later in the day would invariably reveal the caterpillar
gone.

However, the vines around the house, where magpies did
not patrol, were infested with caterpillars and they had to be
constantly picked off by hand and put into the chook bucket.
Later a spray product called Dipel was introduced. The caterpillar ingests a deadly bacteria that destroys its gut, killing it,
but without rendering it poisonous to its predators.

However, the biggest menace to the vines during those
critical years was frost. The closer the vines are to the ground,
the more vulnerable they are to frost because the coldest air
collects at ground level, and is particularly damaging when, like
water, it pools in hollows and depressions. It is surprising how
many vineyards are planted in frost pockets, possibly because
the moistest, most fertile parts of the vineyard are in those very
places. The cold air will flow away to lower elevations if it is
able to.

There was much to impede the flow of cold air at our
vineyard—the creek banks were a mass of felled trees piled up
by the bulldozer or towed there with the Ferguson and chain,
left to dry and become firewood. Moist, compact dark soil
sloping to a lower run-off point is ideal; dry, grassy flats with
an impeded run-off are not. That's what we had, an impeded
run-off, a tangle of dead trees on the edges of the dry creek bed.

There are ways of combating frost. One is to create a local
inversion layer of smoke by burning, or preferably smouldering,
hay bales, or burning oil in smudge pots, now illegal in most
places. This inversion layer is really a low airborne barrier of
minute carbon particles, which prevents the coldest air from
reaching the ground.

There are wind machines available, too, and even helicopters are used by wealthy vignerons at times. This is to agitate
the air and combine the warmer with the freezing so that the

temperature stays above −1 or −2 degrees Celsius, at which point the vines become damaged. Water sprays can be used, the water freezing on the vines at 0 degrees, thus preventing cold air of a lower temperature contacting the leaves. But these things require money and huge amounts of water, neither of which we had.

So we would burn fires all night when we expected a frost, going from one side of the vineyard to the other to tend them and keep the smoke and heat going. We would compare notes after dawn with the Reimers from Blanche Barkly—father Tom and sons David and Alvin—and it became a tradition to share a bottle of vintage port in the early morning light before going to bed.

Later on we bought a dinky little frost alarm that sat out on the verandah and was connected with a wire to an alarm on the bedside table—when it rang, you got up!

Later again, when I was living in Daylesford, my Kingower neighbour, Geoff Graham, who had a vineyard up the road and whose grapes we have used for many years, would ring when conditions were set up for a frost—that is, car windows frosting before midnight, clear sky, no wind. I'd answer the phone and Geoff would say, 'Looks like she's on, Leithy,' and I would leave the warm marital bed and drive the 100 kilometres through the beautiful, starry, icy night to light and tend the hay bales. It happened less and less as the years went by and the slopes to the creek were made smoother and freer flowing. But it still happens; we consider Melbourne Cup Day as the end of the frost season, and that is when we plant our frost-tender tomatoes, capsicums and aubergines.

Creative pursuits

The best laid plans of mice and men often go astray. After ten years of partnership, during which their daughter Abigail was born, Vosje and Rod parted company in 1975. Vosje returned to 453 Canning Street.

Barely a year later, Vosje felt she could not look after the children. Abigail, aged six, went to live with her father in Steiglitz. Ondine, twelve, and Sebastian, ten, came to live with Sue and me at Kingower.

This was a less than ideal situation, for they would have to live in a house without running hot water, not even a flushing toilet, and would have to be separated from their mother, their sister, their Melbourne friends and, in Ondine's case, her beloved Princes Hill school. There would be no difficulty with them continuing their relationship with Rod, for he and I were friendly and would facilitate meetings, but there was always the tyranny of distance. In fact, we had become closer, for we shared a problem in common—Vosje—whose eccentricities were becoming less amusing as time went by. It was obvious that she had alcohol-related problems and, I later learned, Ondine had taken responsibilities that should not have been hers to bear.

For Sue, the arrival of the children would mean having to be a surrogate mother of somebody else's pre-teenagers, something that she had never contemplated. However, we couldn't leave the vineyard as Sue's Carlton house had been rented by that stage, and she was now working at a newspaper in Bendigo.

It turned out to be easier than I'd expected. Sue drove daily to work in Bendigo so she could drop the kids off at their new school in Inglewood. The move from Melbourne was somewhat softened because they would be with me, their father. We had great times together as well as periods of friction, but the good times easily outweighed the bad.

As the children had already made friends with the local kids during their visits to Kingower over the years, they had instant mates. It wasn't long before they were sharing projects, the most notable one being the restoration of an old hut in the bush where they would go camping, cooking their own meals and generally being quite autonomous.

It was becoming apparent that Ondine was a girl of exceptional capacity. Years later, fellow vigneron and her teacher at Inglewood school, David Reimers, wrote: 'She was humble about her natural, lively intelligence, and eager to learn. Oni was like a breath of fresh air in an otherwise stagnant country school.' Sue and I were able to supply much fodder for her voracious brain. Thus plenty of carrot was on hand and not much stick was needed, so ambitious was she to succeed.

Sebastian was such a bright spark, so aware of what was going on, that Sue and I had concluded that he was probably going to become prime minister one day. Although less academically inclined than his sister, Sebastian had plenty of friends, his footy and his cricket, and therefore much to do. We set up a CB radio near his bed so he could hear the truckies talking to each other at night, and he soon knew their codes.

Plans were in train to 'borrow' a horse for Seb. Sue's brother Hamish had bought some smaller, more agile polo ponies, so one of his horses, 'Jester', became redundant. We were all so very pleased to have him in our lives and Ondine, perhaps to her surprise, fell in love with him. From then on her mate Karina would often come up on weekends and the two girls would ride him and groom him almost to death. But before all that we had to build him a little stable and yard. Sebastian had to play football the day before Jester was due to arrive so Ondine and I were working on the new horse accommodations. She was moved to comment: 'Isn't it interesting, Poon, that if you see a Disney film and the kid gets a horse, there's already a stable and yard there for it. You would never see them having to actually build it!' Ondine's name for me seemed to appear from nowhere. I once asked her where it came from and she professed not to know, but her friend Karen Gilmore still calls me that almost thirty years later.

After school and work we often used to make our own entertainment at Kingower, particularly on weekends. Adults and children would get together for campfire concerts with music from David and Alvin and whoever was up from Melbourne and could play an instrument. 'Poon' would recite and the kids would put together sketches, often satirising television commercials.

Ross and Dorothy Reading, tired of selling books on counterculture and not being able to practise organic and sustainable living in the suburbs, had planted almond trees at nearby Rheola, so our friends and neighbours from Carlton became friends and neighbours at Kingower.

There was a theatrical group at nearby Wedderburn and we used to perform melodramas at the various town halls in the district, always being careful to use a couple of actors from neighbouring towns in the interest of bucolic harmony—and swelling the audience numbers. As I'd been acting at La Mama over the years while working in Melbourne, and Ross Reading had directed a play or two there, things became a little more ambitious after Ross's arrival, but the golden rule regarding audiences was broken and we once took a whole truckload of props to Charlton and played Alan Ayckbourn's *Gosforth's Fete* to about five people, for we didn't have a Charlton actor in the cast. Ross had a bit to learn about living in the bush!

Ross also produced a couple of theatrical events at the neighbouring Rheola Hall, in cooperation with Drummond Jewitt. One I remember was entitled the *Mallee Whirlpool*, a play on words related to our geographical situation and the brand of a popular washing machine. He also set the poem 'We'll all be rooned, said Harahan' onto the stage. He chose a local, 'Jungle Jim' Poynton, who spoke with a classic slow Aussie drawl, to deliver the punchline. When Jungle Jim asked Ross how he should act, Ross went pale. 'Don't act, James, don't act!'

Those shows staged at Rheola were generally successful and rivalled the local 'black and white minstrel shows' at nearby Arnold for popularity. Full of wisecracks and slapstick, minstrel shows used a formula that must have been imported by some of the American goldminers who came in after the gold rushes quietened down in America—think of all those 'California Gullies' in the area, and even the 'Jim Crow Creek' at Daylesford. There were certain set passages and procedures in these shows, one where 'Mister Johnson' would conduct a dialogue with another man wearing blackface, allowing them to make commentary on local characters and events. This would lead to the singing of verses satirising such events. I got a gong once after having reversed my brakeless forklift into the creek—another trip I'll never forget! There was also a drag component where very large ungainly farmers would dress in tutus and dance to the music of *Swan Lake* played on a fiddle.

There was no set date or year for these minstrel shows, but they were always put on during a drought when people were bored and frustrated and had nothing to do. They were a rare cultural phenomenon for Australia, probably gone forever, such innocent and creative fun succumbing to television and changing lifestyles.

Sue and I were more or less marking time as the vines grew over the years. I was doing an odd job here and there—I still had my electrical contractor's licence and wired a few houses. (Today I think the greatest luxury in my life is ringing the electrician!)

During this time we wrote articles for *This Australia* magazine, and we co-authored *The Grassroots Vegie Growers Companion,* dog-eared copies of which were still in public libraries many years later; incredibly, to me, cheques for lending rights were posted to us annually.

Sue wrote the copy for Derek Stone's lovely coffee-table book *Life on the Australian Goldfields.* Writers are frequently confronted by that long journey from the kitchen table to the typewriter and will often procrastinate to delay it. Sue was no exception. We decided that discipline could be enforced by me locking her in the tasting room with her reference material and her typewriter, but no telephone, so while she was writing I'd do just that, between the hours of ten and twelve-thirty every day.

It worked brilliantly! I wrote *Establishing Your Own Vineyard* using the nom de plume Grenville Nash, for I was terrified of anybody knowing that I had the presumption to be writing a book on the subject, because at that stage, I was studying part-time at what was then Riverina College of Advanced Education. My lecturer in viticulture was Max Loder, who was planning to write a book upon his retirement. The publisher, Thomas Nelson, was doing a series of four books for hobby farmers and Dorothy Reading had got the gig for the 'Chook Book'.

I'd had a children's book, *Annie the Anaconda*, published by Greenhouse, and the publisher, Sally Milner, insisted I was qualified enough to do the vineyard book and, if I didn't, it would be done by some pen-for-hire with possibly less knowledge of the subject than me. The identity of Grenville Nash (Grenache), as with that of my other nom de plume, sometime food critic for *The Melbourne Times*, Ezekial Kearney (yes, zucchini!), remained undiscovered for years, if anybody cared. I discovered the self-discipline required to complete these short works due to my fear of Sue locking *me* in the tasting room!

Sue's mother, 'Poggy', would sometimes come to stay, and although she was used to a better standard of living, she didn't seem to mind the primitive living conditions that were imposed upon her at Kingower. She always had her bottle of Scotch in her suitcase and her carton of Benson & Hedges handy. She behaved like an outrageous snob and played the 'Grand Dame' to the hilt with the theatricality of an actress, but I sometimes thought she was a bit tongue in cheek; I didn't find her snobbish at all, apart from the superficial.

Once she was staying with Sue while I took Ondine and Sebastian camping and fishing to Eucumbene in the Snowy Mountains. On the way back the 'Golden Holden' finally died and stranded us by the side of the road about 80 kilometres away from home. I walked to the closest house and they generously allowed me to use their phone. I rang Sue and explained that we wouldn't be home that night, but would try to organise things for the morning. Poggy realised what was happening, got on the phone to me and said, 'Don't you worry, dear boy, is there a tow rope here, does Susie know where it is? I'll find out from Susie exactly where you are and come across in the morning and tow you back.'

The next morning Poggy turned up in her medium-sized Renault and towed us back to Kingower, skirting the Bendigo traffic. Every, say, 15 kilometres or so there'd be a few puffs of smoke emitted from the driver's side window as she fired up another B&H. If she was a snob she was a remarkably down to earth one; I think she took herself less seriously than some other members of her family, as did Sue. A couple of times, when we were living in Sue's house, at 28 Carlton Street, on some pretext or another she would ask me to meet her at the exclusive Alexandra Club where she was staying. I was to meet a couple of other 'old girls' and tell them some jokes.

Once, at a party at a property in the Western District, Ondine was wearing a very pretty dress and Poggy and a female friend asked her where she had bought it.

Oni replied, 'I got it from the Op Shop. I've washed it twice but I can't seem to get the "old lady" smell out of it.'

The two charming old ladies looked at each other and smiled. I was standing nearby and overheard the conversation. I was discomfited by Ondine's innocent candour, but Poggy's friend, Mrs Rymill, said to Ondine, 'Yes, dear, we know exactly what you mean!' The local children were awed but not overawed by Poggy, who would lock horns over a Scotch in a friendly manner with John Sendy, our Communist neighbour. So there were some fun and games along the way that led us inexorably to the production of our first barrel of wine in 1979.

Family relations

In the meantime, Ondine had taken herself back to Melbourne, had in fact 'run away from home'. Although initially annoyed and angry, I had accepted it as inevitable and probably ultimately for the best because, despite her attachment to her friends, particularly Karen Gilmore, at Kingower and Inglewood, she was never going to have the intellectual and social challenges she needed. So at the age of fifteen she was reunited with her beloved school at Princes Hill and her old schoolmates. She was boarding with our mutual friend Ann Polis and her daughter Mary in North Fitzroy, not too far away from her school.

However, none of us knew the difficulties and traumas she was about to face, for Vosje had fallen into an abusive relationship and was being bashed by her then boyfriend. Ondine had chosen not to tell me of Vosje's predicament for reasons of her own. I am sure now that she wanted to spare me the worry, knowing I'd had a bit of that with Vosje over the years, and she hoped that she could separate Vosje from a physically abusive partner, and the scourge of drunkenness. This was too big a challenge for a fifteen-year-old girl, although she tried—how she tried—to rescue her mother, then and over the following years.

I had no idea what was going on, but once when visiting Vosje, who was accompanied by the boyfriend, Clarrie, I commented on her obvious injuries. She insisted a fall from her bicycle had been the cause. This was clearly not the case, and I insisted that whoever had done this to her should be reported to the police and hopefully sent to jail for a very long time. Vosje stuck to her story, and it was some time later that I realised the perpetrator had been walking along beside us, saying nothing.

He later made the mistake of threatening Ondine. On a previous occasion Ondine had rung the police, knowing that her mother was being bashed in the house, but when the police went there they could hear or see nothing. Some weeks later she went to her mum's house again, realised that again she was being bullied and bashed, and went to the police station around the corner, which was unattended. She returned to the house and yelled through the door to Clarrie to let her mother go, and that's when Clarrie made his mistake. He said to Ondine: 'If you don't clear off, you'll get the same.'

Ondine had enough coins in her pocket to call me at Kingower from the phone box outside the police station in Amess Street. She was terribly distressed. 'What can I do, Poon? What can I do?'

'Go to Karina's,' I said. 'I'll fix it.'

My big Honda was full of petrol, as always. I put on my jacket and helmet and rode the 200 kilometres to Melbourne powered by rage and adrenalin, every nerve and muscle in my body tensed. I don't know if any police pursued me; I didn't see any. A couple of times I snatched a glimpse of the speedo—I was doing up to 180 kays. There's not much separating life and death at such speeds but it didn't matter, Ondine needed me.

Roaring along, I searched my mind for the quote from Edgar Allan Poe's story *The Cask of Amontillado*: 'A wrong is unredressed when retribution overtakes its redresser. It is equally unredressed when the avenger fails to make himself felt as such to him who has done the wrong.'

By the time I reached Carlton, my plan was formed. This Clarrie had put it around that he was some sort of karate expert so I had decided on the way down that my tactic should be based on surprise. To paraphrase Poe, I wanted that bastard punished; I didn't want him to punish me. The door, I knew, was not very substantial and it yielded easily to my adrenalin-fuelled shoulder. The lock broke, and I used my strategy of surprise to good advantage and didn't stop hitting him until he was pulped, leaving him no time to employ any possible karate tactics. I then threw him out the door onto the footpath below.

Vosje was a mess. I left her there while I went around the corner to the public phone box to ring Ondine and let her know that her mother was safe and that she could sleep tight, Clarrie was no longer a threat. It had been a nerve-wracking ordeal; my hands were shaking so violently it was difficult to dial the numbers. I had hardly been back at the house for ten minutes, coping with Vosje's tearful mea culpas, when to my amazement Clarrie knocked on the remains of the door—could I throw his cigarettes out? Extraordinarily I felt sorry for the pathetic little bastard, his power gone, his woman, too, *and* his cigarettes! But I suspected a trick and threw him down the steps again without a cigarette to keep him company. Predictably, Vosje wanted me to sleep with her and comfort her. By this stage I was a bit fragile, too. I told her to go to sleep and spent an uncomfortable night on her sofa.

The next day Sue and I discussed the matter and we decided to shout Vosje a trip to Holland and worry later about where the money would come from. (Sue contributed to my ex-wife's holiday!) But Vosje didn't stay there long; middle-class Holland still didn't suit her. She missed her children, and Ondine, I know, missed her mother, so the Little Fox was soon back—and back to her old tricks.

Our first vintage—Easter 1980

I had managed to buy a barrel of Reynella Vintage Reserve claret so that after the wine was matured and bottled I could use the barrel containing its all-important malo-lactic bacillus bacteria, and when the first grapes were picked and crushed in our tiny crusher and pressed in a tiny press (which at that time seemed quite large), the resulting 1979 wine was magnificent.

In 1975 I had been fortunate in being able to work the vintage at Brand's Laira winery at Coonawarra in South Australia. While there, working with Eric, Jim and Bill, I'd learned some rudimentary winemaking, but not much wine-making intervention was required because the grapes were in such good balance. However, I'd left before learning anything about the care of wine in barrel so, due to too many enthusi-astic tastings and insufficient sulphur, I allowed the wine to go off. It seemed to be fading fast and a friend of my friends Mike and Jane Buck—one Steve Goodwin, who was a chemist with Vickers Gin and Tulloch wines—examined it under a micro-scope and declared it to be invaded by acetobacter and a host of other bacteria that shouldn't be there, and I should either learn what I was supposed to be doing or give up.

So I enrolled at Riverina College at Wagga Wagga in New South Wales and, by doing the new short courses in wine-making they'd recently instituted under wine whizkid Brian Crozer, recently returned from the acclaimed wine-oriented University of California at Davis, and the lecturers, whom I irreverently referred to as the 'Andrew Sisters'—Markides, Hood and Burke—I learned enough to allow me to approach next year's 1980 vintage with some confidence, albeit with unformed skills.

We were expecting a crop of about 10 tons, so we had to extend the two-car corrugated iron garage, buy a settling tank and acquire a couple of open fermenters. We used ex-milk vats; these were plentiful as they had been made redundant by the use of refrigerated milk tankers. With the insulation removed, they were ideal for the job, since stainless-steel vats shed their heat from fermentation, so necessary in a hot climate. They enabled us to avoid refrigeration as they were small and had a large surface area compared to their volume.

Thus, with our trailer for picking buckets behind the Ferguson, the crusher and the settling tank clean and ready to go, and the press waxed to prevent wine getting into the grain of the wood and possibly causing contamination and therefore spoilage problems further down the track, we were quite ready for 1980 and what was to be our first commercial vintage.

The vines were healthy, the fruit was good, the friends who wanted to pick were alerted—their only reward to be a swim in the dam after work, great food, decent wine, the camaraderie that comes from being part of a hardworking and successful team, and hopefully that hard-to-define satisfaction that comes to so many of us when we have been involved in the process of winemaking.

The weekend was chosen and away we went. It was Easter so there was no shortage of pickers and food preparers. It soon became apparent that some people loved picking, mostly females, for they are more nimble-fingered and generally don't find it monotonous; after all, women have a long history of working, relating, chatting and gossiping at the same time. Others, usually males, could not stand picking so they were put on duty to collect the bins and load them onto the trailer or, later, to work in the winery, crushing, loading stalks onto the other trailer, and cleaning up.

The shiraz ripened first, so it was picked that weekend; the following weekend was to be the cabernet. My job was to drive the tractor; that way I could communicate with everybody—pickers, bucket picker-uppers, winery workers and lunch-preparers. It also gave me the responsibility of avoiding children and dogs, a potentially perilous mix with a tractor.

It all went well. We had vats of beautifully crushed grapes and I was free to make up the yeast culture, a procedure I had learnt from Professor Andrew Markides in the laboratories of Riverina College. Hydrogen sulphide, H_2S, was at that time the greatest potential hazard for winemakers—it occurs naturally in fermentations but its production is exaggerated in must (crushed grapes) when there is a deficiency of nitrogen. In later years in most wine areas it became almost mandatory to add diammonium phosphate to the ferment to provide nitrogen and, later again, specific nutrients to feed the exponentially expanding millions and billions of yeast cells.

I sometimes wondered how it was discovered that the addition of nitrogen to the must would prevent the production of H_2S. Perhaps some little boys were caught and chastised for piddling into a vat of fermenting wine that was later found to be clean and free of H_2S—the nitrogen in the urine had done its job! However it happened, little seems to have been known about it then, and H_2S was accepted as a necessary component of wine. Perhaps it was a component of the 'sweaty saddle' character of some Hunter Valley wines, particularly shiraz, and it was certainly present, often to an alarming extent, in French pinot noir, in Burgundies. If the ferment has been allowed to reach completion without the addition of nutrients, including nitrogen, and some H_2S is present, then the solution is to add tiny amounts of copper, as cupric sulphate, or to expose the wine to some elemental copper. Suspending a copper plate or some copper wire in the container would often rectify the problem.

In France, bronze fittings containing copper were widely used. Copper funnels were also used to top up the wine in the barrels, so the H_2S was inadvertently removed from the wine. As the traditional hoses and other winery fittings were slowly replaced with plastic and stainless steel, copper and bronze were phased out. There was nothing to remove the H_2S and more and more was retained over the years—so gradually that the winemakers never noticed it. But others did.

I once ordered a bottle of muscadet in a Melbourne restaurant and was told by the owner, a noted Francophile, that he had something better for me, a French pinot that he insisted on opening. I had done some work at Riverina College by then, and we had all become well aware of the taste of H_2S. It was present in this wine, unpleasantly so, and I told him.

'I have just the thing for you, then,' he said and opened another, more expensive bottle. This tasted of H_2S also, and I told him so, to which he replied, 'Don't you know that all Burgundies should taste a little like the smell of shit?'

I told him I didn't care for it and that I wanted the bottle of muscadet I'd ordered.

Andrew Markides of Riverina College had taught us, among other things, yeast propagation, and I turned to him for a yeast culture that was not a big H_2S producer. The appropriate one was '729a', and he posted me a small glass vial of it. Inside it was a few match-head-sized dots of a creamy substance sitting on an agar base.

Everything had to be scrupulously hygienic; some grape juice was sterilised in the pressure cooker and allowed to cool to 40 degrees Celsius. A tool made from a 4-inch nail and the tungsten filament of a light globe was flamed to sterilise it, so it cooled immediately, being such fine wire. The hand that held this scraping tool was used to twist off the cap and remove the scrapings, replace the cap immediately and add this tiny blob of yeast to the must. A fish tank air pump was brought into play and, through a sterile hose and cotton wool filters, bubbled air through the must to accelerate the production of yeast cells. This was left bubbling on the kitchen table overnight and, in the morning, would be obviously working hard and producing enough yeast cells to be added to a larger quantity of sterilised juice before being introduced to our vats of must now waiting for inoculation.

Some sulphur had been added at crushing to knock out the wild yeasts, but that would have dissipated overnight and the 729a would dominate the fermentation. I was certainly not going to leave it to 'wild' or naturally occurring yeast cells on the grapes—you don't know what you're getting with them, as some people learned to their cost in the early days in the Yarra Valley. These days most wild yeast has spread onto the grape skins from the culture used in the winery over the years, anyway, and in France naturally occurring yeasts seem to work just fine, as they often do in Australia.

But, in the event of a failure, winemakers are naturally not going to put on the back label: 'This wine was spoiled by the unfortunate domination of an undesirable yeast strain.' No, they're more likely to flog it off as a cleanskin! Fermentation is slower, too, if a yeast culture is not added. This can create space problems in the winery if fermenters are tied up for too long.

As our pickers were volunteers, the picking was done on weekends. So the Saturday picking would be crushed into the fermenter vat and left overnight, because the sulphur, having done its job knocking out the wild yeasts, would dissipate overnight and the yeast culture would be introduced in the morning. The Sunday picking would be treated similarly, with the yeast being added on Monday morning. Given a fermentation time of about five days, the fermenters could be emptied into the press in time for the next weekend's pick— hot bedding, as I used to call it. And so it worked well for us. We pumped the new free-run wine out into the 1000-gallon tank I'd bought second-hand at a clearing sale, and bucketed the skins into the press.

What joy, what exhilaration, what a sense of achievement as the dark ruby liquid poured out of the press into the press tray! To taste it was, for me, to be almost transported to heaven.

So all was pressed or being pressed. The cabernet would be picked the following weekend. The vats were clean and sparkling ready for the next batch. We didn't have a pressure pump then so the cleaning was done with a watering can and brush. But we were better off than the Laughtons at Jasper Hill for they had no mains electricity and had to use a generator!

I hadn't known about the lead time required for ordering barrels, so I had to wait some weeks for them and therefore had insufficient containers for the wine. We solved this by putting the lids on the vats and sealing all the gaps with silicone, leaving only an airlock that we could remove when topping up the wine with CO_2. I fretted in case the flavour of the silicone would taint the wine, but it didn't.

Conventional winemaking wisdom had it that after the new-made wine was settled in a holding tank it would then be transferred to barrel in as clarified a state as was possible. But there was an alternative—to transfer it directly to barrel without settling so that the wine would mature for some time in the barrel on its own sediment, or lees. So a few barrels were made this way for later comparison and then blended.

In 2012 we drank a bottle of that 1980 wine—one of a couple of dozen that had been re-corked in the early 1990s. Although it had aged, it was a beautiful wine in the classical Central Victorian mould—my first vintage, thirty-three years before our 2012 release.

But there were times during those years when I didn't know if I was going to make it, much less the wine.

The 1980 vintage quantity had been insufficient to enter in the Royal Melbourne Agricultural Society wine show, so I would have to wait another year or two, for higher yields, to have Passing Clouds judged beside its contemporaries. The American oak barrels were made by Schahingers, the coopers in Adelaide. I ordered them 'no toast', figuring there was no point in having new barrels then burning the insides of them. I didn't know then that untoasted barrels were inclined to show a 'pencil shavings' character in the wine, thus in future years I ordered partial or full toast, depending on the wine to be put into them. The toasting released different and usually better flavours.

We had picked some pinot, too, but as I hadn't ordered a barrel for it, it was resting in a food-grade plastic cherry barrel under CO_2. We then ordered a 225-litre barrique of French oak for it. I was going to Adelaide for a wine sales tasting and arranged to pick up the barrel in my old 504 Peugeot. It wouldn't fit in the boot so I said to the boys at the coopers, 'This is a French car, it will fit in the back seat,' which it did, with millimetres to spare as it went through the back door of the car.

So the pinot was put into the new French oak barrel, looking and tasting good, exhibiting a density of colour not usually seen in pinots. The temperature had run up quite high during fermentation, but I'd read somewhere that the Burgundians like a high but short peak in temperature near the end of ferment. It reached 29 degrees Celsius at 5 degrees baumé, so I wasn't too concerned, and it had obviously done wonders for the colour extraction. It was almost 14 degrees baumé when picked so the resultant high alcohol would have aided extraction, too. (Baumé refers to the sugar level—the higher the baumé, the higher the sugar. See the glossary.)

The next year, 1981, promised about 20 tons or about 12,000 bottles, a predicted return of $120,000 gross which, after purchase of bottles, corks, labels, packaging, bottling costs and general expenses, including barrels, was close to our predicted income and should allow us a wage. At that stage we were living on rent from Sue's house and her wage, my year being taken up with pruning, winemaking, maintaining the trellis and the property in general—and building a tasting room.

Birth of the tasting room

We had chosen a site across the creek from the house for a tasting room, but first a breakaway creek bed had to be filled in with a bulldozer, a flat area created for the car park below the tasting room, and a couple more trees removed. There was an old community hall at Logan 20-odd kilometres away for which the local populace could not afford to pay insurance and electricity bills. It was for sale and I got it at a very reasonable price, as few people wanted such quantities of second-hand building materials.

Of course we had to have a party to celebrate its demolition and I remember that it was a great party, with lots of dancing on the hardwood floor, polished smooth by so many village dances over the years.

The old building was lined with Baltic pine boards, the outside was rough-sawn grey box weatherboards, and the floor itself was four-inch by three-quarter-inch grey box, one of the world's hardest timbers, not tongue and grooved, but butted together. Two friends from Melbourne, Bob Clegg and Marty Rogers, were keen to have some of that flooring so a deal was struck—we three would dismantle it, take all the building timber to Passing Clouds, their share would be the floor, less a little bit for me to use as the tasting room bar, and Lindsay Brownbill would lend us his farm truck for the transport. A couple of weekends later it was all done, the site cleared and Bob and Marty took their flooring to Melbourne. (Marty's floor-sanding man found it the hardest wood he'd ever had to work and had to raise the price to compensate for the extra time and sandpaper used.)

I had submitted a plan for the tasting room and the building inspector, Stuart Miller, while inspecting the site for adequate termite protection, mentioned that someone was demolishing a shopfront in the main street of Inglewood which had dimensions almost identical to those of my proposed tasting room. Stuart was very keen to see this piece of 1860s craftsmanship preserved, knowing it was destined for the tip. I met the demolisher, Les Miller, who owned the shop, which he was clearing away in order to build a house on the site. The whole front had been covered with corrugated iron, crudely hammered into the woodwork of the frame with roofing nails, but the wood had not been badly split. Of course, some of the panes of glass in the multi-paned front window were broken.

It had been a funeral parlour, so double French doors allowed the coffins to be brought in and out, and there was another door that led to an office. It was a ghastly green and had many coats of paint underneath that, but it would be salvageable and the absolute bees-knees for the tasting room.

I said to Les, 'How much do you want for the shopfront?'

'How much are you offering?' Les responded.

It flashed through my mind that I could get this for $50! 'One hundred dollars,' I replied.

Les looked at me incredulously. 'You fair dinkum?'

'Yep.'

Enthusiastically he shook my hand. 'Done!' he said.

'Okay,' I said, 'and if you want to take the corrugated iron off it, do so carefully and ring me, and I'll dismantle and collect it.'

And that's when I became the laughing stock of Inglewood. 'That winery bloke from Kingower paid a hundred bucks for Lessy Miller's old shopfront, ha-ha!'

Anyway, I hired a car trailer, put the whole thing on it and took it back to join the growing pile of second-hand timber and tin that was going to become the Passing Clouds tasting room.

We had to change the interior design slightly but that didn't matter at all; in fact, the extra setback in one wall gave the place more character. Stuart the building inspector was most helpful and he became, and still is, a friend. With his help I ordered roof trusses and radiata pine for the walls. The idea was to build a brand new frame and roof, then line it with the old Baltic pine boards and clad it with the old grey box weatherboards, topping the lot with the gloriously aged grey corrugated iron, thus adding, as my friend Bob Stinson said, 'that veneer of antiquity'.

A grey nomad named Frank had been staying in the bush in a caravan. His dog had knocked the heater over and his caravan had burned to the axles, so he camped with us for a couple of weeks. It turned out that he was a retired carpenter, so he got another caravan and lived on our property, working with us for a few weeks until the frame and trusses were up. Between Philip Adam (friend, farmer, self-taught carpenter, sculptor and later grape-grower) and us, it didn't take long. Then a local lad, Shane Walker, and I lined and clad it. I'd cut a large useless old rainwater tank into half lengthwise and propped it up on some concrete blocks. A bag of caustic soda and a few hundred gallons of water later, with a big fire under it, we had a huge caustic soda bath which effectively removed all the layers of paint from the old shopfront and exposed the beautiful old timber beneath. Soon it was washed off, put in place, broken panes of glass replaced and, with the timber oiled, it almost looked as if it had been there since 1864, although the sign on the glass window above the door says: *Leith and Mackinnon; Vignerons; 1974.*

For weeks after we would often see cars belonging to Inglewood people sneaking along the road near the entrance, hiding behind trees, to gain a peek at Les Miller's old shopfront. Ha-ha, one up to me!

The Passing Clouds tasting room was completed in 1982 just in time for the release of the 1980 wine. It was necessary to have this facility to gain a tasting room licence, and this necessitated septic tanks, rainwater tanks, electricity, plumbing, toilets and so on, which were all passed at the final inspection. All that remained was for us to apply to the licensing court. Judge Camford at the Liquor Control Court duly approved our application in 1982 and we were ready to trade.

The 'boutique bubble'

The year 1981, to be our second proper vintage, had produced an Indian summer. Baumés rocketed up and when the hydrometer was reading 14 degrees, I began to panic. The picking was planned for the following weekend but perhaps I couldn't wait that long, so I rang around—and couldn't get pickers. Some Bendigo friends, whom I'd telephoned, had organised to go to the Avoca races but they called back later and said they'd cancel their social race day and pick for us instead. That's friendship.

So instead of eating good food and drinking champagne at Avoca, my friends toiled in the Kingower sun. Thanks John, Greg and co.! You know who you are.

The 1981 therefore became a huge wine, concentrated and brooding, and a delight to drink even now. At the time of writing (2013) we have two bottles left, both given back to us by people who purchased them in 1983; they are waiting to be shared with them. But we know that the wine is good, very good. However, I was advised not to show it—my adviser said it would be considered too ripe. I wish I'd shown it anyway for it was, I think, the best wine I made that decade.

The benchmark for full-bodied red wines was of course Bordeaux, and the '82 wines were made to achieve a more

Bordeaux-like 12.5 per cent alcohol, although still matured in American oak. (Even if we had shown a preference for French oak, we could not have afforded it.)

And so in 1982 we began selling the 1980 vintage. It sold slowly but steadily, at a fair price, for at that stage the government had not realised that small 'boutique' wineries could be a cash cow almost ready for milking. Things were different then—there were so few boutique wineries, so few labels on shelves, and potential customers greeted any little write-up with interest. For instance, a short complimentary paragraph in the *Nation Review* would provoke enquiries about the wine and the shops would ring the appropriate winery.

In 1982 we bought an old ex-Telecom orange Toyota utility that, because of its long tray, had a great carrying capacity. So if we got a write-up on Saturday, I'd load twenty-six dozen on the Tuesday if the weather was fine, drive to Melbourne and call at the shops—Saleeba's Victorian Wine Centre in North Melbourne, King and Godfree and Carlton Cellars in Carlton, Richmond Hill Cellars, and so on, until it was gone. When the orange ute was spotted outside the shop, usually somebody would come out with a trolley, grinning: 'Saw the write-up, thought you'd be along soon, we'll have two dozen (or three, or four).'

I'd write out the invoice, have a coffee or a taste of something they'd recently opened, then off to the next one and so on, until the ute was empty and I made the two-and-a-half-hour drive back to Kingower. No typed invoices, no computer involvement, just a hand-written invoice in an invoice book with a carbon copy back-up. Good wines and goodwill! The sense of achievement was intoxicating; there was our wine on the shelves beside some of the best!

As I've mentioned, regarding Victorian wineries—and indeed Australian wineries in general—there were not many small vineyards operating then. We were at the genesis of the 'boutique bubble' when enthusiastic amateurs like me (but usually better equipped) were trying their hands and risking their resources to pursue the dream to make great wine. Many of the earlier established vineyards at Geelong, Bendigo and the Yarra Valley had been eliminated by economic considerations, or by the scourge of phylloxera, the vine-root sucking louse, around the turn of the century. Some Yarra Valley boutique wineries were making impressive products, and Stuart Anderson was forging the renaissance of Bendigo wine at Balgownie, as was Phil Leamon at Chateau Leamon, although if one sought the 'Chateau' one sought in vain. The mainstays of the small (and indeed the large) vineyards and wineries were at Rutherglen and the Goulburn Valley, where the phylloxera had failed to invade. The Barossa and Southern Vales in South Australia and the Hunter Valley in New South Wales provided most of our wine from interstate.

Thus, at that time, there was a small and exclusive club of boutique winemakers and we were aspiring to join it. We needed wine of exemplary quality, the recognition of the wine judges and the wine writers to achieve that goal. It was always going to be a challenge for a retired sparky and a journalist, but we seemed to be getting there!

At about that time, in 1982, Stuart Anderson brought Kit Stevens MW (Master of Wine) on a surprise visit to the winery on a 41-degree day. I'd hurt my back doing something stupid with the Furphy tank and was lying down when Sue said there were two men at the tasting room, so I limped over to greet Stuart and be introduced to Kit. There was no air-conditioning in the tasting room back then, and the glasses were warm to the touch, but they tasted and approved.

They tasted the pinot first, moving Kit to say, 'This is not pinot noir!'

'It's 100 per cent pinot noir,' I responded.

To which he replied, 'That's not what I meant.'

But of course I knew what he meant, for the pinot noir grape and a climate that produces summer days of 41 degrees Celsius are not natural bedfellows. However, he was very impressed with the shiraz cabernet and asked if he could take a bottle, for he was doing an 'options' game tasting with James Halliday, Len Evans and others in Sydney the next day, and thought he could have some fun with a wine from a vineyard of which no one had ever heard.

A few days later, Rod Whiteway, a friend from Canberra, rang and said he'd attended a talk given by Kit Stevens, who said that he had recently had the best pinot noir he'd ever tasted from the Southern Hemisphere—and it was from a vineyard in Central Victoria called Passing Clouds!

The fate of the 1980 bottle of shiraz cabernet that Kit Stevens took to Sydney was later revealed, for I was given a report on that options game. I don't know who thought up this game, but it's a fun way of testing people's analytic skills quickly. Contestants taste wine before being asked questions about it. If they are wrong they drop out; if their answers are correct, they carry on to the next question until only one person, the winner, remains.

The preliminaries were gone through—Country of origin? Then which part of that country? and so on—and ended up with Bendigo. James Halliday appears to have been the last man standing and was asked, 'Balgownie, Chateau Leamon or Blanche Barkly?' He responded, 'A nice one from Blanche Barkly,' and it was revealed as Passing Clouds. He had picked the wine from a vineyard he had never heard of, half a mile from Blanche Barkly, from which he'd probably only tasted one or two wines. I guess that's why he's a leading authority and wine judge and we are merely winemakers.

With the tasting room operating, the '82 wine in barrel and the vineyard pretty well sorted, we weren't looking too bad.

There was a man named Dennis Carstairs who had a wine shop in Banana Alley, one of those subterranean vaults under the train line south of Flinders Street Station. The location of his business put him geographically close to the money end of town, and he exploited it magnificently, being recognised as the best telephone salesman for wine in Melbourne. It was as well, perhaps, that he was brilliant on the telephone for, in his enthusiasm to telephone-sell wine, he often dropped the odd bit of pie and sauce onto his tie and shirt, earning himself in some quarters the unfortunate epithet of 'Dirty Dennis'.

Dennis had a fantastic list of contacts so he must have known about the reference to the wine. He rang me to ask how much 1980 pinot noir I'd made. I replied that there would be about fifteen dozen to sell from the barrique. He said, 'Okay; I'll take the lot!' Later, when it was bottled and labelled, a sample was sent to *Nation Review* for review. A couple of Saturdays later, I was surprised to see a car at the tasting room at about half-past eight in the morning. Its driver turned out to be Dennis Carstairs.

After greetings were exchanged he said, 'I'm here to collect the wine; I'm buying it all, remember?'

I said, 'Yes, we agreed on that, but not on the price.'

'Well, what do you want?' he asked, and I gave him the outrageously high price of $120 a dozen.

'Okay,' he said, pulling a huge roll of notes from his pocket and peeling off the cash. We loaded his car, he had a coffee and off he went on his two-and-a-half-hour drive back to Melbourne.

People rang me later in the day about the 'rave' review the Passing Clouds Pinot Noir had been given in the *Nation Review*. Dennis's contacts were good indeed. We both had a win there; he charged a very healthy price for the wine and some of it was sold in Sydney for more than $20 per bottle, a hefty price then.

So, ironically, the grape that shouldn't have been grown here was the most sought after, no doubt mainly because of the novelty of its great weight, colour and general character. It wasn't long before people were growing pinot in more appropriate areas, and also started using better trellising techniques and limiting the crop, leaving us far behind. For instance, we have been making our Passing Clouds Pinot Noir from fruit that we've been purchasing from Robert and Vanessa McKernan at Coldstream, in the Yarra Valley, since 2000. The valley is a much cooler and more appropriate site for growing pinot noir than the roasting shiraz-friendly vineyard at Kingower.

There had been snow at Kingower at the end of the growing season of 1981–82, an unheard-of occurrence. It built up on the pine trees and roofs and Sebastian woke me one morning by throwing a snowball at me as I lay in bed. That was the end of the precipitation for a while.

And then came our first taste of real drought, the 1983–84 season. It heralded another era: hungry wallabies knocking over flowerpots on the verandahs and insufficient water to grow as many vegetables as we wanted, for the dams had shrunk rapidly. Our vines struggled to produce a crop; we only succeeded in making two barrels that year, so we turned our minds to building.

Sebastian had taken a year off school prior to his HSC and was working with me on the vineyard in 1983. He remembers watering some chardonnay vines outside the tasting room when the world went dark. He glanced up to see a giant dust cloud obscuring the sky. It looked as if half of the Mallee's topsoil was blowing towards Melbourne. It transpired that the dust cloud not only travelled to Melbourne but also across the Tasman Sea to New Zealand where red rain fell on motor cars and clotheslines.

The double garage near the house had morphed into a winery and had generally grown like Topsy. Things had to be rationalised, so Seb and I dismantled the structure, carried it all across the dry creek and re-erected it on an open patch of ground, about 150 metres from the house, adding an additional area for barrel storage, as the barrels were now maturing on the front verandah of the house, or in the tasting room. This not only provided the opportunity for future expansion—perhaps concrete, in our wildest dreams a forklift—but also freed up the area close to the house for the next project—the brick guest wing, bathroom and toilet!

Rats in the rafters

The house was still as primitive as ever so I had decided to build a couple of nice solid brick rooms onto it, still keeping to the lovely old roofline and including a bathroom and toilet. In the years until then we had cleaned ourselves by filling a camp shower with warm water and suspending it above the bath, for in those days we didn't have plumbing as it is known. There was no pressurised water—only one rainwater tank on an elevated stand outside the bathroom that supplied water to the kitchen and to a tap above the bath, which was fairly useless as there was no hot water to mix with it.

But the bath was good for soaking vine rootlings before planting, the idea being to steep them for a couple of days in water with some seaweed concentrate added, which produced a jolly dark tea-coloured brew smelling strongly of rotting kelp.

A visiting architect's wife once strayed into the cement sheet and corrugated iron lean-to which rejoiced in the name of bathroom, only because of the presence of the old white enamelled bath, and to her horror found the bundles of stick-like rootlings luxuriating in their pre-planting mode. To her credit she never mentioned it to us, but a few years later another visitor, a charming young woman, was most interested to see 'the bath' that her Aunt Phyllis had spoken of, for apparently she'd been entertaining people for years with the story.

Little did Aunt Phyllis know that she could have provided additional entertainment had she seen our other visitor that day. As we were all having a cup of tea at the kitchen table in the ironbark slab and mud-walled kitchen, under the roof of split shingles supported by timber poles selected from the bush by the Taigs, the original builders, a rat had decided to make its way across the room on a horizontal beam a metre above our guests' heads. As hosts, it was quite a tense moment. I caught the look in Sue's eyes as she spotted it, one not quite of horror, but certainly of concern. I glanced up quickly and saw the rat pursuing its journey along the beam. Why it had chosen to venture forth in such circumstances, with four noisy humans just below, I'll never know, but it did. I was telling a story at the time and made my voice louder, my gestures more expansive, to hold our visitors' attention until the rat completed its crossing and was gone. David and Phyllis never knew how close to nature they were—and how close nature was to them!

As well as a rat or two, we always had geese, and when they had goslings, if the kitchen was quiet, they'd bring the young ones in, for all the world as if they were saying, 'See, this is the big house, where the *people* live!' They would inspect everything and solemnly exit, leaving you to continue reading your newspaper or making out invoices.

While there was water in the dam the geese were safe enough from the predations of foxes. They apparently had one awake on watch at night and if Brer Fox was detected they would all jump into the water with a cacophony of honking, similar to that which saved Rome in ancient times. However, nesting time made them vulnerable, for the female would be sitting on the eggs. In the daytime she relied on her camouflage for protection, her grey blending her with the surrounding bush, while the male, poor sap, having done his job fertilising the eggs, paraded around in his white finery, a pushover for predators. At this point it was then necessary to put the females into the 'maternity ward', a good-sized fox-proof pen, organised so they could enter and exit during the day for feeding or a swim, and could be safe at night. The rest of the flock stayed on the dam bank as usual, protected by the now rapidly diminishing water.

The goose is an awkward bird, too much for one, but not enough for two (echoing the words of Trollope), which we discovered when we ate our first. From then on we made sure that we had three for two people. They were delicious, especially when cold, the day after cooking.

The foxes were not bothered by such niceties but simply bit them on the neck for a quick kill then dragged them off. But if the fox gets into the chook pen it's a different story—feathers and bodies everywhere, the legacy of indiscriminate slaughter. It is the fox's nature to return as often as it can during a night to remove more carcasses for burial elsewhere. We never lost a fowl to foxes over many years—our memories were good enough to ensure that the gate was closed at night and I kept the pens in good repair. But I know plenty of people who were confronted with a bloody mess of feathers on one or more unpleasant mornings.

Foxes were particularly active during cubbing time when the vixens would take greater risks than normal to feed their

young. Strychnine was used to poison foxes in those days and
a technique was used to target the vixen, the rationale being
that if she died the cubs would most likely die, too, and the
opportunity for further litters would therefore be reduced. The
practice was to secrete strychnine inside a ball of butter and
freeze it, then place it later that night on one of her tracks. If
she took the bait she would try to take it back to the cubs, but it
would melt in her mouth and she would be more or less obliged
to eat it, and die. I bought the strychnine from our friendly
old pharmacist, Mr Jones, and on one occasion gave him a
conspiratorial wink as I said, 'Don't tell Sue!'

In Western Australia the foxes have become so sophisticated that the only way they'll take a bait is if it is put into a
dead parrot, the parrot buried with a feather or two showing
above the ground in the manner that foxes bury them. In this
case the fox finds the buried parrot, assumes it's the hidden
booty of another fox and eats it. If anyone thinks this is cruel,
let them see a lamb that has been attacked by a fox and left alive
with its tongue eaten out.

While admiring their guile, cunning and perseverance, I
dislike foxes intensely. They do not belong in Australia, and a
pox on the memory of those who introduced them. One year,
a particular fox had been eating noticeable amounts of shiraz
grapes. Even if it didn't eat the whole bunch, it would ruin it
by tearing the berries and leaving saliva on the remainder. I
determined to shoot it, as I had shot several others before. I
could see the track it had worn over the creek bed and into the
shiraz, so one very early morning when the moon was bright
and the breeze put me downwind of the fox, I put my plan
into action and lay out on the ground on the other side of the
creek bed opposite the shiraz with my rifle at the ready. The
fox didn't come along so when it was quite light, far too late
for it to break cover, I returned to the house for breakfast then
went to the vineyard to do some work. Coming back I was
amazed to see the fox, bold as brass, walking down the middle
of the bitumen road on its way home—having out-waited and
outwitted me!

Kangaroos, too, became an increasing problem in drought times. Their numbers were growing as they had become protected and people weren't shooting them anymore to protect their crops, or to gain cheap dog food, and the vineyards were very green!

But droughts don't last forever, and that one had really only lasted over the growing season of 1982–83, breaking spectacularly with a 4-inch rain prior to the 1983–84 growing season. We lost some topsoil then for I was cultivating as recommended by the agriculture department, so that the whole vineyard looked almost like a carpet and I was proud of my housework. But that sort of horticultural practice leaves the vineyard vulnerable to the depredations of soil erosion, and I've kept grass roots in the soil since. Perhaps it doesn't look as good, and it does require some soil water to keep it going, but it retains the soil structure and the whole biological balance. In the old days in the Barossa Valley, and doubtless other places, they would 'sheep' the vineyard right up to budburst after which time it was too dry on the surface for much grass growth to occur—an effective, organic weed control. This is done increasingly now, but one always has to be aware of where the sheep come from because of the risk of spreading that nasty louse phylloxera.

Denouement of the dunny

I had managed to complete the building of not just one but two new rooms with bathrooms and toilets, and had pondered the destruction of the old 'thunderbox' toilet. I hated the thing. The job of emptying it was mine and mine alone—and I particularly hated it when the influx of visiting little girls and their mothers would fill it at an astonishing and unexpected rate. Often this was not revealed to me until it had reached or overreached capacity.

Of all of the jobs associated with country life, that was the most onerous and odious, and after the 'box' became redundant it was used occasionally as a tool shed. Still I resented it, lurking there as a reminder of my past miseries. But I never quite knew what to do with it.

One day Dorothy Reading returned from Singapore with some novel fireworks in her suitcase (those were the days!) and presented us with some rockets and catherine wheels. In that package we also discovered three little cardboard tanks. All that was necessary was to light the wick and these little critters would propel themselves forward, their cardboard guns shooting flames ahead.

The means of disposal of the dunny came in a sudden inspirational flash. As the glorious Kingower sunset of apricot and china blue faded, and night fell, we were sitting on chairs a safe distance from the doomed dunny, armed with glasses of bubbly. I had laid a nice wide plank from the ground outside to the dunny seat (over which I had laboured and gagged for years). I had liberally splashed the weatherboard walls of the despised edifice with diesel fuel and when all was ready threw a dog-food can full of petrol onto the seat. All that remained now was to light the touch paper on the little tanks and watch them do their work.

They did it magnificently. In the Kingower gloaming they laboured up the sloping plank propelled by the little catherine wheels on their sides, with their dear little guns banging and spouting flame before them as they entered the dark void of the interior, all guns blazing. The denouement was dramatic to say the least. The whole structure emitted a roar, a sheet of flame erupted from the doorway and within seconds a huge pillar of fire leapt 8 metres into the air, taking the roof with it. With a loud and satisfying crackling the inferno took hold and the dunny burned to the ground, its demise toasted by us with Great Western's finest. Unfortunately, I had failed to inform my neighbours, Dawn and John Sendy, some 300 metres away across the vineyard, of the impending incineration and John, inspecting his cabbages for grubs by torchlight, was surprised and perturbed to see a column of flame ascend skywards from our house. But when he raced over he was relieved, and joined in the celebration.

Triumph

In September 1984, the Royal Melbourne Show was anticipated with much excitement, for our entries had been made
and the bottles sent down weeks before. As always, the doors
at the J.V. Plummer Hall were opened at 8.30 a.m. and the
winemakers (for only winemakers could get tickets in those
days) rushed in and headed for the table where the bottles of
the winner of the Jimmy Watson Trophy, announced the night
before at the show dinner, were displayed. After tasting that,
the ranks then thinned out and spread to the other tables,
eagerly scanning the results book for medals, and beginning
the task of comparing one's own wine to others, particularly
the winners, in earnest.

I was not there at opening time; it would have meant
getting up at about 4.30 a.m. at Kingower and I didn't need to
do that for I was planning to drive back the same day. It was my
first time there. I received my results booklet upon presentation
of my ticket and searched for the appropriate table—Victorian
shiraz blends, 1982 and older—and, after some searching,
found it. Feelings of dread fought with bright optimism in my
soul as I took the book to the appropriate table.

There were dozens and dozens of bottles in a serried double
line along the trestle table and then, and only then, did I look at
the book, starting hopefully at the bronzes, but it wasn't there.
Did I dare look at the silvers, or should I go through the also-
rans, the ones that had failed to get bronze? To hell with it, I
looked at the top: Trophy, Maltby of Anakie. Next one down,
Passing Clouds of Kingower. Oh, God in Heaven! We had won
a gold medal with our first show entry!

I hurried away down the stairs to ring Sue and Ondine but
there was someone in the phone box—John Glaetzer, master
winemaker for Wolf Blass. The door was open to let out the
cigarette smoke as he reeled off a list of medals to Wolf in
Adelaide. David Fyffe from Yarra Burn and Domenic Portet
from Taltarni were outside, near the phone box, having a cigarette and a bit of a giggle.

I congratulated David on his trophy in 'Victorian wines of cabernet sauvignon 1982 and older', which I had noticed on the way down, and asked them what the joke was. 'That's what we're laughing about,' responded David. 'Before I sent the wine off to the show, I tasted a bottle and it was like capsicums. I thought I had better not send off a wine with such a peculiar flavour, but I'd paid my entry fee so I did send it, and it's won the bloody trophy!' The capsicum flavour was unusual then, for not many people were planting cabernet in cooler areas like the Yarra Valley.

Sue, of course, could hardly believe the news when I delivered it to her. I went back to the hall, tasted several wines, including the Maltby wine—it deserved the trophy. I finished up at the 'Champagne Style' class, filled a tasting glass and drank it. Then I called into a couple of shops to tell of our good news and show them the results book, and drove home to celebrate and share my euphoria.

But now we were in a situation of having established an excellent credential, with no wine to follow up—a marketing disaster in anybody's terms. The 1983–84 season had been good to everybody and I had an idea that if I could purchase some quality grapes from elsewhere to make more wine, an extra batch, I might be able to combine it with our 1983 crop to make a blend, and to that end I was soon looking at other vineyards. I met the Willersdorfs at Carisbrook and the Jacksons at Harcourt and arranged the purchase of grapes from them for the coming vintage. We had to take advantage of that gold medal and strike while the iron was hot, so we needed another $100,000 or so going through the books.

They were duly harvested and so began my peregrinations around the countryside towing trailers full of grapes, comforted by the thought that we could have a continuity of wine, and save ourselves from some financial embarrassment.

Things happened in 1984, not all of them good, but the Carisbrook and Harcourt wines were great, showing an elegance and a high natural acidity not characteristic of the Kingower fruit, and I used both of them for years afterwards to add to the complexity and acidity of the Passing Clouds wines. I stopped using the Jackson Harcourt fruit when it became easier for them to sell to Blackjack, which had set up next door, and a few bad years at Carisbrook saw that crop fall away dramatically. The Willesdorfs had sold the property and it was hard for the new owner to run it from a distance. When my brother Robin later bought the vineyard we used fruit from it again as well as made the wine for his label, Rainbow's End.

Another ending, another beginning

Meanwhile things had changed again domestically. Ondine had completed her HSC at her beloved Princes Hill High School. She was a spectacular girl. We were great mates and she had become the person I loved and admired most in the world. She was now working in Melbourne at a job Ann Polis had helped her get at APSTE, and one of the greatest joys of my life was to have lunch with her there.

I lived vicariously through Ondine then. She would tell me of films and plays that she had seen, and the books that she had read, and we would discuss these things until her lunch hour had flown. I could not be there on weekends because of the tyranny of the cellar door at Kingower.

In 1984 she helped me after work at the Victorian Winemakers Exhibition at the Victoria Hotel in Melbourne, and was delighted to be part of Passing Clouds. She always believed in us, and that is probably why she (almost) always uncomplainingly put up with life in a sub-standard house while she lived at Kingower. It was never considered a sub-standard *household*, though; and although Sue was partially crippled with her muscular disease, she showed her characteristic sense of humour, intelligence and style that won the respect and admiration of youngsters. The house was always host to many children, local and from Melbourne; some cried when the time came to go home.

Sue and I were as enthusiastic as ever about Passing Clouds and there was never any talk of giving up. But something was missing in our relationship and it was in 1984 that Sue returned to Melbourne to live at her house at 28 Carlton Street again, taking work with Sally Milner on *This Australia* magazine, while I kept myself busy courting Julien, an old friend from trout-fishing and La Mama days, and Ondine's then landlady at her house in Brunswick.

I used to visit Ondine there and have occasional meals, often cooked by me, with them both, and eventually a romance developed between Julien and me. We married in October 1984. She came to live at Kingower in the expectation that I would semi-retire and move to Daylesford, where I had always planned to retire.

Sue and I had built a lifestyle and a business that she loved and I was effectively taking it away from her. I had let her down, badly. Of course, she didn't know then that she was to return to Passing Clouds, in 1989, and nor did I. So I was exceptionally fortunate when she did come back as kindred spirit, true friend and business partner, and I could share again her generosity of spirit, her intellect, and her inimitable sense of humour, while she relieved me of many of the tedious tasks essential to the running of a small winery business.

But this was later. Right then, in 1984, things were tough and about to get a lot tougher. But of course I didn't know that then, either . . .

7

Ondine, my daughter

On Christmas Day 1984, Julien and I were busy with cooking, me with some winemaking, while Ondine, her brother Sebastian and their new-found cousin, Marilyn, set about decorating the tasting room—for Ondine had determined that it was to be transformed into a banquet hall, so of course it was. Marilyn, the daughter of my brother Greg, had been in adoptive care almost since birth. They made contact eighteen years later, and there was never any doubt that she was a Leith: her mannerisms and speech characteristics bore an uncanny similarity to our sister Carolyn's, although of course they'd never met; she was almost a clone of Carolyn. Within half an hour of meeting, Sebastian, Ondine and Marilyn were chatting excitedly like long lost friends, Sebastian and Marilyn reciting together the Monty Python scripts which for some reason they had independently memorised. It was an eerie experience, and a pleasant one.

We took the food and wine over there and had as good a Christmas dinner as it was possible to have—good food, good wine, much laughter and much love, ending the night with Ondine and I having one of our mock arguments in part-Italian, part-English and part-laughter; we both so much liked to act. When we'd cleared up the dishes and taken them over to the house, I returned and turned the lights off in the tasting room, not knowing that the light was soon to go from my life.

On Boxing Day we all spent time together. It was planned to be the last meeting of Sebastian and Ondine for some time, for Seb had gained his agricultural diploma and was heading off to New South Wales to commence work as a jackaroo, the next step on his career path.

Oni and I went through the script of a play she was rehearsing—she had been selected to attend a drama group in Adelaide—and she encouraged me to audition for some commercial voice-overs, she having gained some extra experience and money from doing such work after her day job over the preceding weeks. 'With your voice, Poon, you'll get plenty of work,' she said.

We had time, too, to make rough plans for her approaching twenty-first birthday party on 21 May, to be held in the Passing Clouds tasting room. There were to be tents hired for people to sleep in, music provided by musical friends, a performance put on by her acting friends, and a bonfire. And she was going to organise her mother, Vosje, to be there if I thought that I could handle it. It was a happy family day, with Ondine having already exchanged presents with Sue in Carlton.

Ondine's car had been sideswiped while it was parked outside Julien's house, and was immobilised. I was contemplating lending her our spare family car, for her imminent visit to Rod Parker's mother who lived at Guerilla Bay on the New South Wales coast south of Sydney. She planned to take presents to her sister, Abigail, and spend some happy days in the sun with Abi and the others.

In the meantime, Ondine's boyfriend of some years, David Jones, rang. His hand had been injured in an accident at work and was seriously stitched up. He was therefore off work for at least a week, but could drive Ondine to Geurilla Bay. It had been arranged that he would spend Christmas and Boxing Day with his family and friends in Melbourne, come to Kingower to collect Ondine, then proceed to Geurilla Bay in the afternoon of the 27th, choosing to drive through the night and have a sleep along the way.

I had not seen much of David in the preceding years, for I would contact Ondine by telephone or see her alone at one of our lunches and she would, naturally, spend most of her spare time with him and her other friends in Melbourne; weekends usually saw me at the tasting room at Kingower selling wine. However, one night I stayed in Melbourne after a Passing Clouds wine sales event and the next morning I went for a run, as I often did. Ondine was living at Clifton Hill then, about 3 kilometres away, so I decided to pay her a surprise visit. As I jogged around the corner I recognised David's car outside the house where she was lodging. Was he staying there and was he sleeping with my sixteen-year-old daughter? Confused and, I have to confess, angry, I went into the house and approached her room and opened the door. Before me, asleep, with a shaft of sunlight playing on their faces, were two beautiful young people, as I would have imagined Romeo and Juliet before it all went wrong. I gently closed the door and left the house, adjusting my morality as I jogged away.

As planned, David arrived in the mid-afternoon of 27 December and we sat around outside the tasting room, chatting, joking and taking photographs. I had a few glasses of wine and observed that David did not have any alcoholic drink. Before they left he proudly showed me the work he and his mates had done on his ute. It really was a great restoration job and I admired it. Just before they left it occurred to me that if they wanted a sleep along the way, they could pull up at some secluded spot below a tree and sleep in the back of the ute beneath the benevolent stars as I had so often done. So I threw a mattress into the back of the ute and they headed off under the beautiful china blue sky and apricot-tinged clouds that preceded a Kingower sunset.

The next afternoon, on 28 December, Rod Parker rang to inform me that Ondine and David had not arrived at Geurilla Bay, and should they be worried? Yes, they should be worried. We should all be worried. And fearful. For there was no way they would have failed to meet a deadline without contacting us. We decided to leave things for another night before contacting the police—after all, if the police knew anything they would have alerted us.

The only place I could sleep with a phone close to my ear was the tasting room, so Julien and I made up a bed there to spend the tortured night, hoping against hope that a call would come. But none came.

For years Ondine and I had been able to communicate telepathically in some way. I had always been able to *will* her to telephone me, and soon after she would ring: 'Okay, Poon, you got me, what's going on?' After she went missing I had delayed trying to make contact with her in my mind, fearing the worst. Then that night I tried, but there was no response. Poor Julien, lying beside me. I screamed and shrieked far worse than any wounded beast, for I knew Ondine was dead.

In the morning, after consultation with Rod, we called the police. They treated the matter seriously and were soon checking motels and caravan parks between Melbourne and Sydney, but to no avail. How can two people and a vehicle disappear from the face of the earth?

I had only one possible solution. We had discussed various routes to Geurilla Bay and I had mentioned the road through Corryong and over the Snowy Mountains through Kiandra and Cooma, then down the Brown Mountain to the coast. David had not seemed keen on the idea, but it was just possible that Ondine had persuaded him to adopt her father's suggestion, for she and Sebastian had been camping with me some years previously in that magnificent country. If this was so, it was possible they had run off the road and their vehicle was lying, like many others from times past, in some crevasse invisible from the road.

I had contacts up that way, Ian and Juliet, winemakers who had established a vineyard at Tumbarumba below those mountains, and I turned to them for help. I needed an aeroplane to search those mountain roads. Juliet organised a plane and a spotter, but they called back with a negative result. Larry Hewitt, a friend of a friend of Julien's, had a small elderly Cessna aeroplane that he kept at the airport at Khancoban. He was there on holiday and generously offered to fly me above those precipitous mountains in search of the wrecked vehicle.

Then our old friend and lodger at Julien's house, James Jenkinson, offered to accompany me to the mountains and we set off on the seven-hour trip in my car—the car I *could* have loaned Ondine to drive herself to Geurilla Bay.

At Albury we stopped for fuel, and after paying I returned to the car with a packet of cigarettes. 'You don't smoke,' said James.

'Yes, but I used to, and right now I think I need the consolations of Madam Nicotine again.'

We camped in the Recreation Hall at Khancoban, which the local policeman had considerately arranged for us. I remember the revelry of a New Year's Eve party being held in the hall, in bizarre contrast to the desolation in my soul. I knew that Ondine was dead, but there was a remote possibility that David was alive. In any case, their whereabouts had to be resolved.

The next morning James drove me to the airstrip to meet up with Larry and his Cessna. We took off and began our search. The little aeroplane was perfect for the job, being slow and manoeuvrable, and Larry and I spent many hours flying above those lonely roads where we spotted several old wrecked cars lying in inaccessible gullies, but not the restored green Holden ute.

After two loads of fuel we had exhausted our options and I returned to the Recreation Hall, to meet up with Rod Parker and his partner Cheryl. They had driven there, over Brown Mountain, searching from the road for signs of a vehicular misadventure. They, like me, had nothing else to do but clutch at straws. With the aid of the policeman, I began ringing police of higher and higher rank, seeking help. I was convinced that Ondine and David's bodies were somewhere out there in the mountains and that they could be found. I was obsessed and becoming deranged, maintaining that I would hire helicopters until my funds were exhausted.

Then, at five-thirty the next morning, the policeman arrived at our temporary lodgings and took me aside. 'I've got some terrible news for you, mate.'

'Yes,' I responded. 'They're dead. What happened?'

With sensitivity and compassion he told me that the bodies of Ondine and David had been found in David's ute, which had been dumped in Kings Cross in Sydney; their bodies were only discovered when somebody tried to steal the tonneau cover.

It was necessary for me to go to the morgue and identify Ondine's body. David's uncle had flown from Melbourne to identify him. James dropped me at the airstrip at Khancoban for the flight to Albury airport, once again provided by the generosity of Larry, and took the car back to Melbourne. Rod and Cheryl departed. The wheel had turned full circle.

I was met by police at Sydney airport and driven to the mortuary. There we met David's uncle, ashen faced and distraught. He had been unable to identify David's body, could I do it? I demurred but was told that if I couldn't do it then David's mother would have to be brought up from Melbourne. That was unthinkable, so I agreed, and a ghastly half-hour followed until at last I said: 'That is the body of David Jones.'

It was then that I had to identify Ondine's body. I protested—I just couldn't do it. It was explained to me that if I couldn't do it, my sister Carolyn, who lived in Sydney, would be asked. That, too, was unthinkable. Mercifully, I was able to identify them, in black and white, through the lens of a television camera transmitted to a screen. There was a scar on her leg, the legacy of a fall at the Inglewood swimming pool some years earlier, and through that I was legitimately able to say, 'This is the body of my daughter, Ondine Leith.' And so I was saved from having to view my beautiful Ondine's face, apparently unrecognisable due to the activity of the blowfly maggots; their bodies had been in the back of that ute for four days in the summer heat.

I was then taken to the Darlinghurst Police Station to be interviewed. Three detectives questioned me at length about Ondine and David. They came and went from the room, their questions repetitive and circular. Eventually one of them asked, 'Would you like a drink?'

The day was wearing on, the sun was weakening outside. 'Yes, I'd like a drink.'

'What would you like?'

'Scotch, if it's possible.'

A half-bottle of Scotch and a glass duly appeared on the desk, some stubbies of beer, too, for the police. More detectives appeared and at one stage there were about twelve of them in the room when the penny dropped and I realised that I was a suspect! Not only that, but the bodies had been found near Kings Cross, Australia's centre of sleaze and drugs. Of course! The murders were going to be seen by some as drug related, and my beautiful girl, who hated drugs, who wouldn't even smoke a joint, so much did she respect her mind and body, was going to be regarded with suspicion by people who never knew her.

At last the questioning ceased. The whisky was gone with the day and I was apparently considered innocent of any involvement in the murder of my daughter.

The police took me to the airport and I flew to Melbourne. The alcohol had had little effect on me—the adrenalin had quickly chewed that up. I was hoping to remain anonymous but I was paged, and when I went to the desk the cameras were onto me. A friend, Greg Kelly, put me in a taxi to escape the reporters and photographers. I went to see Sue at Carlton Street where the ghastly task of contacting Oma in Holland had to be addressed. Knowing my Dutch language skills would not be up to the task, I contacted a Dutch friend who came to Sue's and we made the dreaded call together. I rang Vosje, who knew all about the deaths by then of course—I think Rod Parker had been speaking to her. She seemed to be handling the situation better than me; it was as if she thought that they'd just gone away somewhere. I assumed somebody was looking after her with antidepressants.

Somebody drove me to Kingower. I don't remember who it was but I bless them for it. My friend Robert Roles was there. He had come to stay and give Julien moral support, and had sent away reporters and a journalist who had helicoptered in. Julien and Robert were wonderfully considerate and supportive. I was ranting and raving, swallowing sleeping tablets and drinking wine, needing sleep but wound up like a clock spring.

In the morning I awoke before them, put the jug on for tea and a slice of bread into the toaster, which didn't work properly—a mouse had died in there and two maggots crawled out. My devastation was complete.

Within days the police had a pair of suspects—Robert Pickford and Michelle Archer, his de facto wife, both heroin addicts. They were members of the Australian Defence Force and were based at the army barracks at Ingleburn, a south-western suburb of Sydney. The man had bought heroin from the occupants of a flat in Melbourne, and the couple had shot up a capsule each. While the woman took their twenty-month-old toddler back to the car, the man held up the dealers and, with the aid of a silencer-equipped rifle, robbed them of $170.

One of the pair had driven David's ute back to their house at Ingleburn with the bodies of Ondine and David in the back, parked it in their carport with their own car, and ransacked it. It later transpired that both vehicles had been apprehended at Tarcutta, because they were being driven erratically, but the police officer let them continue on their way, for neither vehicle was stolen. Later, outside the court in Melbourne, the policeman involved told me he sensed something profoundly evil at the time and was glad to see them continue their journey north on the Hume.

There was television footage of the ute in Kings Cross where they had dumped it. It was a distinctive vehicle, and one of their neighbours easily recognised it as being the vehicle that had been parked in the carport of the Pickford–Archer residence; they contacted the police. The two were arrested at Avalon, north of Sydney, where they were spending a day at the beach with their toddler.

It was necessary for me and members of David's family to fly to Sydney to examine the pair's house with the police. David's mother Val, her husband Bob (David's stepfather), a mate of David's and I duly took the flight, and at Sydney's Mascot airport we were met by police who drove us to the army settlement at Ingleburn. We were to look for anything belonging to Ondine and David.

The house was a chaotic mess of strewn clothes, dirty nappies and cheap books about violence and killing. Only Pickford's army uniform was folded, clean and neat. There were also plenty of new packs of disposable nappies; they must have been spending up big with Ondine and David's holiday money, I thought. Under a cushion on a settee there was a large dagger, no doubt in case of unexpected 'guests', and there were some letters from army members from various countries in which they were serving, with references to 'good gear'. It seemed that there was quite a little nest of heroin users in our armed forces. And then there, incongruously among the cheap rubbishy products on the bathroom shelf, was the bottle of 'Opium' perfume that I had given Ondine for Christmas little more than a week before, and also the perfume that Ondine was taking to Geurilla Bay to give to her sister Abigail. There were other things, too—some of Ondine's clothes, David's running shoes and a pair of David's jeans that Val involuntarily hugged to herself when she found them.

Back home there was now much to be done, and we liaised with Val and Bob. Our children's bodies had to be flown from Sydney, funeral arrangements had to be made, and I had a eulogy to write; friends were sending cards and letters of sympathy and some of their sentiments could be included in it.

Another problem had to be solved; the always emotional and dramatic Vosje would, if discovered by the press, provide all too colourful interviews, particularly if she'd had a few drinks, so she was spirited away to the Daylesford house where Robert Roles, Jane Buck, Mary Rogers and Kate Millard looked after her on a roster system and helped her through her grief.

The cremation was conducted, the funeral held, the eulogy read by John O'May, an actor friend of Rod Parker's family, a man who knew Ondine. The next day Ondine and David's ashes were buried at the Kingower cemetery. In the oppressive Central Victorian heat my neighbour, John Sendy, gave a short and poignant speech. And then the earth was cast in to cover their ashes.

♣

Some days later a committal hearing was held at a small court-room in Russell Street in Melbourne and only when a question was directed to 'Robert Pickford' did I realise that I was sitting two metres away from my daughter's killer. Julien realised it, too, and quickly positioned herself between me and Pickford. I was strong and fit but no match for a trained killer, a physical fitness instructor in the army. I looked around for a weapon, but there was nothing except a fire extinguisher on the wall, with policemen between it and me. Had I known that I was going to be in the presence of that man I would have secreted a short length of heavy chain on my person and smashed his head to a pulp.

Many, many stressful months later, the trial was held. Pickford had contracted hepatitis and someone had bungled blood samples and other things to do with the evidence in a similar manner to the Lindy Chamberlain case. When the trial was eventually held I was, of course, called as one of the witnesses. The defence barrister questioned me: 'Did I know that David had a toolbox below a panel on the floor of his ute?' 'No, I didn't.' And so on . . . I only attended on the one day I was needed. I could not bear to endure the agony of the complete trial, and what was the point? Very little mattered anymore. Ondine and David were dead.

A friend of mine, Robin Hardiman, attended every day of the trial but I never spoke to him about it. He's now dead so I don't know the particulars of the proceedings, but it was apparently established that Pickford had probably shot them both while they were sleeping in the back of the ute, the motive apparently robbery. Pickford and Archer had earlier driven to Melbourne where they had taken part in that abortive drug-related robbery during which he apparently fired shots. Thus it seemed that there was an angry, frustrated drug addict driving north up the Hume Highway, possibly out of money and needing another fix, when he encountered Ondine and David in a lay-by. Pickford was given two life sentences, so is, of course, now released. Archer was not charged with murder.

I used to think that if Ondine went to New York (as she hoped one day to do), and was ever confronted by a mugger, that she would simply give him her money. But I never dreamed that it could happen in a lay-by on the Hume Highway, in Australia, and it's probable that there was no time for negotiation with a drug-crazed madman in a killing frenzy. I suppose they awoke and confronted him, and so met their deaths. Thus two innocent people with so much to live for had their lives brutally taken by a loser, a poor example of humanity. Charles Darwin, where are we now? The rules have changed!

Ondine would have come into her fiftieth year in 2013. How many hopes and dreams would have been fulfilled? Some years after her death, I was moved by such thoughts to write:

> The chair is empty where she sits, or sat,
> From where she charmed us with her wit, oh that
> She were here again!
> How is it now that good by evil is outdone?
> The murderer breathes his air, my daughter none.

8

Life goes on

The climb back from Hell

As I write this, the 21st of May approaches—my daughter's birthday. As the days creep closer towards it, I am increasingly overcome with sadness and despair, with misery and anger, although less anger as the years pass—and twenty-eight years have passed since my daughter's death.

I would have given my life so that my child could have lived even another hour on earth. She was the person I loved, admired and respected most in the world. Many fathers love their daughters as much as I loved mine, but none could have loved more.

In the immediate months surrounding the deaths, the funerals, the court case and conviction, I wondered how I could bear to live with such grief. They were the hardest of times then, as mind and body adjusted to the anguish. Three hours' sleep, often induced with sleeping pills or alcohol, became standard fare before the gunshots in my head woke me in the night and early morning, the desperate hours until dawn.

In my hours of despair I wondered if, as I grew older and the strength of comparative youth ebbed, I might not be able to endure such pain. Now I am seventy-three years of age and I still don't know the answer to that one. Even now I sometimes draw a great involuntary gasp, when the horror and the loss suddenly overwhelm me.

Over the years there have been good, productive and happy times. I have had a close bond with my oldest son Sebastian, and later, with my two younger sons, Cameron and Jesse. I've been lucky enough to have known other loves and many friends.

But back then, in 1985, daily life and work ground on in a haze of grief and exhaustion. Winemaking had become difficult, as I had lost my sense of taste and smell. There were other manifestations of my condition. When I thought of the murders my body would instantly exude an unpleasant and alien odour. And for years the electricity in my body would cause a spark to jump to metal objects, so painfully that before I opened my car door I would first test it with my elbow as a matter of course, the elbow being less sensitive than the fingertips.

I have been reading Ondine's diaries lately, seeing life through the eyes of a girl between the ages of fourteen and twenty years; reading of the pain and the joys of growing up. A girl of intelligence and charm, ambition and industry—a girl who tells her diary: 'I will succeed. I can do it!'

Ondine had to mother her mother, Vosje, who fell victim to alcoholism and physical violence. Some time ago I read one of Ondine's HSC papers, an essay on Bob Dylan: the teacher praised the work, but commented that it was three days late. The diary shows that during those days Ondine was helping her mother recover from a bashing administered by her then boyfriend. She was physically relocating her mother, dealing with the medical, legal, financial and psychological issues associated with her mother's predicament, doing her school assignments and sparing me, the divorced husband, some grief that I would have voluntarily taken from her shoulders, as I did later when I realised the magnitude of the problem.

But the diary takes me back to good times, too, to the teenage intrigues of her life, to the memories of those lovely girls, her friends, whose faces still appear in my mind's eye—Laura, Hanna, Karina and all; they know who they are, and I hope that we can meet up again one day. It would be great if we could get together with our families and remember Ondine and those good times and see what changes a quarter of a century has wrought.

One of the greatest changes for me came only days after Ondine's cremation and burial, when Julien told me she was pregnant. 'Thank you, God. My life's love, my life's work, gone, and now you're giving me another baby!'

Good friends and loyal helpers

The year 1985 was difficult, exacerbated by Julien developing a problem with her wrists that appeared to be carpel tunnel syndrome but was later found to be a calcium deficiency and easily remedied when diagnosed. At times she could not lift our new baby, Cameron, and eventually she went to live for a while with her sister Eryl, in East Gippsland.

Because I was managing to sleep only a few hours a night for the year following Ondine's death, I lost my concentration. And with my sense of taste and smell gone, I don't remember much about the 1985 vintage.

The 1984 vintage had produced fine wine: it had been a year of average rainfall, the vines were in good balance and, with the addition of the Carisbrook and Harcourt fruit, it was more elegant than the straight Kingower wine. The wine critic Mark Shields wrote of it as 'Vivaldi in a bottle'.

The 1983–84 vintage had turned out successfully, too. James Halliday, Philip White and others wrote well of it and, although a few people who did not approve of mixed vintages didn't buy it, it sold well enough for us. I had put a pink label on it, a sort of 'sporting globe' pink, to differentiate it from our regular vintage wines, and that was a novelty. It even had a pink-printed lead capsule over the cork and it became a cult wine in some circles. It was quite an amazing wine and lasted in the bottle, never seeming to tire, doubtless due to its lively and lovely natural acid. Last week I dug out my remaining three bottles and gave one to Cameron and one to Jesse; the third I've kept to share with Sebastian.

Anyway, the '85 vintage was going to be difficult. But I did it, supported by good friends and loyal helpers. The old team was there for me—including Vanessa Buck and China Gleeson—and some new friends that year, particularly Regina, and between us all we got through it somehow. We were still picking at a ripeness of 12.5 degrees baumé or so. (Later on I decided that shiraz was better a bit riper and moved the picking time to coincide with about 13.2 degrees baumé and cabernet at about 12.8 degrees; I think that this gives a good balance of mouthfeel and varietal flavour. Of course, these days the big shiraz are picked at 14-plus baumé.)

Due to my loss of smell and taste the H_2S escaped me, and that took a bit of correcting later with the addition of tiny amounts of copper. But the wine seemed fine. We had a bottle

Resting in Perugia, 1961.

Left: Vosje.

Below: My mother, Mavis Jessie Leith, with Sebastian, c. 1965.

Ondine and Sebastian, MacKenzie Falls,
Grampians, Victoria.

Top: Ondine and Sebastian, 1970.

Above: Ondine and I planting vegetables at Kingower, 1975.

Sebastian and I with organically grown vegetables, 1978.

Top: Sue with Protos and Amy.

Above: Ondine, Protos and friends.

Top: The original Kingower winery in 1982.

Above: The exterior rear wall of the kitchen, Kingower, 1980s.

Top: The original laboratory, Kingower, 1984.

Above: Ondine at Nancy Sawyer's house. Nancy was Rod Parker's mother.

Top: Sue and Ondine in the Kingower kitchen, 1983.

Above: Winery assistant, Stefano de Pieri, now a celebrity chef, in 1984.

Top: Ondine and Sebastian at the Kingower tasting room on Boxing Day, 1984—the day before Ondine was killed.

Above: Winemaking in Burgundy, 1985.

Top: Catching up on paperwork, with Bridgewater, 1987.

Above: Sue with François and Anne Marie, France, 1985.

Top: Sue and friends on her electric tricycle, 1990s.

Above: Picking the grapes at Kingower, 1990.

Top: The nearly 'All-girl Foot-stomping Team' with Mark Gilmore, the
proud father of two of the girls, 2004.

Above: Jill McFarlane, Sue's sister, and Virginia Trioli (right)
cooling down.

Top: Susie McDonald and I finishing netting the vineyard at Musk with Bob the kelpie and Bruno.

Above: Miwako Mizukami at Kingower.

Top: The Passing Clouds tasting room.

Above: My eldest son, Sebastian, with his daughter Ella. The clay bust on the right is one I sculpted in 1961 and gave to Vosje's mother, who then gave it to her grandson before she died in 2010.

With my two younger sons, Cameron (left) and Jesse.
ANTHONY WEBSTER, IMAGINE PICTURES

of it for Cameron's twenty-second birthday some years ago, because 1985 was the year of his birth, and it was fine—very fine, in fact!

Le viticulteur Australien

After vintage, towards the middle of that challenging 1985, Fernand and Catherine Chevrot arrived from France and invited me to Burgundy to work some of their vintage with them.

Some years earlier, fellow winemaker Stuart Anderson, who had worked and stayed with the Chevrots in Burgundy, had introduced them to us. The Chevrots were a young couple in their thirties who ran their vineyard and winery at Cheilly-lès-Maranges near Chagny, some distance from Beaune. They were progressive, and had travelled widely in Europe (perhaps unusually for Burgundians). They were well aware of tradition but not blinded by it.

Fernand was a red-headed Gaul if ever I saw one, looking as if he'd stepped from the pages of an *Asterix* comic book, and was possessed, unsurprisingly, of a Gallic sense of humour. Once, on his initial solo visit to Passing Clouds, I asked him if he missed his wife. He replied, 'When I get back 'ome you will 'ear zee bang from 'ere.' Catherine was part Spanish so she was not blinkered by Burgundian tradition. She was by no means a strident feminist but she was going to play a positive role in their mutual winemaking endeavours. This may have had something to do with their willingness to learn new ways from the New World, for they recognised that something good was happening here, in the United States and New Zealand with pinot noir, perhaps more so than with chardonnay. They were humble enough to think that they could learn something from us.

At that time in late 1985 I knew that I desperately needed a break so I gratefully agreed to visit for their vintage in October. Julien was recovered and back at Kingower so I left her holding the twin babies—our infant son Cameron and the vineyard. And I went to France for an unforgettable four weeks.

I caught an aeroplane to France at about the speed of sound, then the TGV Fast Train (*Train à Grande Vitesse*) across country to Lyon at the incredible speed of 250 kilometres per hour, then a slower train to Dijon, and finally a very slow antique bus to Chagny, where Fernand collected me and took me to Cheilly-lès-Maranges—and an earlier era. Apart from electric wires, vehicles and the occasional glimpse of a sparkling new wine press in an ancient shed behind an ancient wall, we could have been in the eighteenth century. For the picking, done by hand, we sped in the van from small block to smaller block owned by Fernand and Cathy, scattered as they were by Napoleonic decree, which meant that parcels of land continued to be divided among beneficiaries with the death of the father.

I was given a few days' picking and then put into the winery where they had to add tartaric acid for the first time and, being familiar with the procedure, I was asked to demonstrate. In fact, I was nicknamed *le viticulteur Australien*. There were winemaking consultants, newly appointed by the government, who would come over to the winery to take samples and make firm recommendations on what should be done, all in the interests of improving the quality of Burgundy, which had fallen to a low standard in some instances.

Apart from winemaking duties I did other jobs such as ferrying the old ladies (Fernand's mother and aunt) to the cemetery for the *fête des morts*, Day of the Dead, and taking pots of chrysanthemums to the various graves, or driving into town to collect parcels of food or winemaking equipment.

The first job of my day always involved the use of the little Renault 4, and invariably I would open the door and get in the right-hand side, close the door and find myself looking at the glove box.

'See *le viticulteur Australien*, he gets in the passenger door, sits down and closes the door; he then opens the door and gets out. He walks around to the driver's side, he gets in, he closes the door and he drives off. Why do you think he does this, Jean Paul, is it Australian tradition?'

'I don't know, Claude, it seems very strange to me, also!'

Because I lived in the house with the Chevrots, I would leave them to themselves for a while between work and dinner and go to the local bar for a pastis or a beer. A group of locals, clearly suspicious, used to look at me and mutter until they finally elected a spokesman to approach me. They wanted to know, if I was a *viticulteur*, how I could be in France when vintage was on? Who was looking after my vineyard then, eh?

They thought they had me. I explained as best I could in my schoolboy French about the Southern Hemisphere having the opposite season but they clearly didn't believe me. However, they must have checked later with somebody because they never baited me again on that score.

But they weren't yet finished with me, and a few nights later the spokesman approached and asked if it was true that we harvested at night in Australia. I said, yes, sometimes we did. He reported back to his group and they sent him back to ask why. I said it was to preserve the fruit flavour. After animated discussion with his panel he returned triumphant: 'If you want fruit flavour, why don't you drink 7-Up?' He had me there. France 1, Australia 1.

I loved my time in Cheilly-lès-Maranges; it was exciting, energising and educational, and it occasionally dulled the pain of the loss of Ondine. I met characters who will never occur in the next generation. Cathy and Fernand's sons Pablo and Vincent have a great deal to do with the winery and vineyard now, but I haven't seen them since they were children. Sebastian and Cameron have both been there, and Cathy and Fernand visited us in Australia a second time, but I've yet to return to Burgundy and would love to go again.

Sue joined us all for the last two weeks of my stay. Then she and I drove to Holland where I wanted to meet up with my ex-mother-in-law, Vosje's mother, Oma, whom I hadn't seen since she'd stayed with us at Sue's house about ten years earlier. Oma had found us a nice little place to stay for the night and we were made most welcome at her flat, where a meal, prepared by a girl she had hired for the occasion, awaited us. We reminisced about her time in Melbourne and at Kingower, where she used to sit on a chair in the sun; after a few days she'd be as brown as a berry, a legacy of her father's Italian blood. It was of course late autumn or early winter in Holland then, the leaves had mostly fallen from the trees and she proudly pointed out that she could see the windows of the palace from her flat and urged us to look, in the hope that we'd see the Queen walking around inside her 'house'.

Everybody, it seemed to me, ate very well in Burgundy, although often simply. I remember one day Fernand was away and there was just Cathy and me for lunch. The really frantic part of vintage was over—I'd been amazed at the short window of opportunity they have to pick there, between declaring the grapes ripe and the first cold winds blowing in from Switzerland, bringing with them the problems of mildew. We had a leisurely lunch and I was thinking how elegant and complete it was when I realised how simply we had actually eaten. The presentation, the plates, the glassware, had made it seem like a mini banquet. But it was a soup, two cheeses, bread and a small green salad, a taste of chardonnay, a taste of pinot and a coffee—but elegance indeed.

Cathy, taking advantage of Fernand's absence and wanting to know if there was anything she could learn from me, anything that could improve their winemaking skills, interrogated me as to what I thought they could improve. Hesitantly, I suggested that the gaps between the large concrete fermenters were breeding places for the drosophile, the wine fly, and that they could be sealed with mortar or silicone. Also, I ventured, they could strain the newly fermented wine from the concrete fermenters through a stainless-steel mesh screen instead of a bunch of troublesome vine prunings, *les fagots*, the traditional method. After further prompting from Cathy, I suggested also that if you were pumping wine and lunchtime snuck up on you, then you didn't just turn the pump off and go to lunch, but rather finished the job, then cleaned the hose with water.

These things were relevant to me, having come from a warm climate, but probably not so important in Burgundy where it's quite cold at vintage. However, I gained the impression that Fernand would have embraced Cathy's suggestions if he wanted to continue to enjoy Cathy's embraces!

I had brought a bottle of my '81 pinot with me and Fernand had a Brown Brothers and a Balgownie pinot, so a degustation was arranged, to be attended by some local vignerons and a couple of wine merchants, one of whom had brought along a South African wine to add to the mix. All wines were tasted blind and were scored according to tradition, the only difference being we were to put an F or A in front of the wine to indicate our opinion of its nationality. I told Fernand I wouldn't repeat this story, but twenty years have passed, so . . . All the French tasters considered the Australian wines to be French and vice versa. Also, they rated the Australian wines higher than the French, with the South African one leading the pack! After the wines were unmasked it was a very subdued little group of Burgundians who left the degustation to ponder the wonders and injustices of the world.

Towards the end of vintage, before Cathy and Fernand left for their holiday in Aix-en-Provence, leaving me to deal with the intricacies of cellar door sales, we ate at two restaurants some way from Cheilly, one specialising in steak tartare, of which I was a fan, and another in pork, particularly the offal. I noticed Cathy and Fernand looking expectantly at me as I ate the last sausage. When I'd finished they leaned back, relieved and gleeful. 'Now,' said Fernand, his eyes sparkling, 'now you can say you have eaten every single part of the pig!' No, I didn't ask!

As a short aside, I think I got my own back. Some years later, when Cathy and Fernand came to stay with us at Kingower, I played a trick on them, for I felt I owed them for the 'pig sausage'. It was their first night and I explained that I had some nets set for the yabbies we were to eat for dinner. I then drove them to a lonely dam in the bush and from the clay-coloured water I retrieved the yabby 'opera house' traps, which I had set earlier, and placed their clawing contents in the hessian sugar bag I'd brought along. 'Would you like a drink?' I asked my guests and, bemused, they answered yes. I then led them to a little clearing in the scrubby bush and there was a fully set table with a candelabra and a small brass bell upon it, surrounded by four chairs. I rang the bell and some seconds later a man (my employee, John Hopwood) appeared through the scrub dressed in formal waiter's livery, bearing a silver tray with a printed menu and a notebook. He presented the menu and lit the candles with a flourish while I scanned the menu. 'I think the Veuve Cliquot.' He wrote the order down on his pad, bowed and disappeared. Straight-faced, I then expounded on the differences between marron and the Australian yabby until our waiter returned with glasses and the Champagne (for which I had saved) in a silver ice bucket.

I can't remember exactly when they got the joke but when they did we all had a good laugh and the story has apparently been told many times at Cheilly-lès-Maranges in Burgundy.

After some hard work with the cement mixer—for we poured a new concrete slab with the enthusiastic help of the Chevrots—we holidayed in Tasmania for a few days where the couple learned something about trout-fishing—which they found a little more challenging than yabby catching in the Kingower dam!

But back to my time in Burgundy. The meals the Chevrots' pickers ate were obviously to a traditional formula. When I first arrived at Cheilly-lès-Maranges there were cages just about bursting with live rabbits, but when Sue and I left only a few breeding pairs remained; the rest had become *civet de lapin*. We ate all the other traditional Burgundian dishes too—*coq au vin*, *boeuf Bourguignon* and salt fish. It was obviously a matter of pride and tradition to ensure that the pickers were provided with the very best. The older women got going with the cooking very early in the morning, and as we assembled in the gloom for work, the aromas of lunch would already be wafting across the courtyard. By about 10.30 a.m. they had big pots simmering, and the women could take a break to have a coffee and chat, or a lie-down.

One day we visited an old friend of the Chevrots, Riton, a giant of a man who every second day would have a two-hour lunch at one of Beaune's best restaurants, usually with his son—eating his inheritance, as Fernand put it. The day we visited was not a lunch day so Riton showed us around his cellars. Before the German invasion of World War II they had bricked up part of the cellar to hide their treasured old bottles, and when peace was declared in 1945 they had knocked rough doorways into the walls. The bricks were still lying there on the floor; in the event of another occupation they would save considerable time and effort.

On the way around the cellars, tasting and spitting some of his excellent wines, Riton asked me how old I was and other questions about viticulture in Australia. When we returned to his little office he took a large sausage down from a hook, took out some bread from his desk drawer and opened a bottle of wine. We had to play the Burgundian game of guessing the age of the wine and I plumped for 1975.

His face wore a satisfied grin. 'No, no! This is the year of your birth. This is 1940!' What a gesture! I felt humbled and privileged in equal parts. The wine was still in excellent condition after all those years—those old Burgundies hang on for a long time, due largely to their high natural acid content.

The Chevrots had another friend, François, who used to help Fernand with various jobs around the winery. He had a little hut in the forest, and a few days later we went there to collect mushrooms. We came back to the hut with our baskets full, and he sorted them in terms of taste, rejecting those that were toxic, then cooked them together slowly in a big cast-iron pot while we sat outside on the grass in the late autumn sun, smelling the magnificent odours, sipping the ubiquitous Aligote, a high-yielding grape that makes a straightforward wine, and eating cheese and bread until they were ready. We had nothing with the meal but bread and a magnum of twenty-year-old red Burgundy—a simple meal to remember forever; that velvety richness and complexity of flavour is indelible in my mind.

Vintages and farewells

In November of 1985 it was back to Kingower to spray the vines, bottle the 1985 whites and prepare for the 1986 vintage—I don't remember much, but I must have done for I have the bottles to prove it. I know that it was very popular and sold strongly, even though my vines had suffered their first case of downy mildew. This infection occurred because I'd taken the family fishing and stayed away too long, returning to relentless rain and humidity. I spent several days in impotent frustration as the warm rain poured down and the humidity rose—perfect conditions for downy mildew.

Vosje seemed to have settled down a bit; she was still enjoying a drink and would occasionally ring me at the vine-yard with some outrageous request: 'I've got a place with an open fire now, do you think you could bring me down a ton of wood from the country?' or 'Can you take me out to lunch at that place where you used to take Ondine?' Sue particularly liked the one that went: 'I've accidentally got some rice stuck in the washing machine. Do you think Graeme could clear it out for me next time he's in Melbourne?' From then on, Sue and I referred to spurious and deceptive requests as 'rice in the washing machines'.

One day I got a call from her phone, but it wasn't from Vosje, it was from her current boyfriend. Vosje used to like defying traffic and would often cross a street and expect the cars to stop for her, which they always seemed to do. But this day, crossing Fitzroy Street in St Kilda, a driver hadn't seen her and she was dead. I was very sad she'd died that way, but I was also angry with her for having caused the driver, an innocent man, to suffer for the accident which, for all I know, haunts him still.

For Vosje it was a tragic end to what had become a tragic life. But had the cards been played a little differently by her or by me, it could so easily have been a wonderful life. She tried several times over the years to reignite our love but even if that had been possible, it was never the right time. I was always in love with someone else. More sleep-starved nights lay ahead.

So another phone call had to be made to Holland. In my halting Dutch I had to explain to Oma that her daughter was also dead; probably only someone who has experienced that will know how hard it is. Another funeral had to be organised, another burial, another eulogy written. There'd be no more sparks from Vosje . . .

❧

The year 1987 was a wet year and the wine reflected that—like most wet years, a big crop with poor concentration of fruit and colour. Ironically it is sometimes a fact that you make money from wine from a wet year: people remember the quality of the year before, which was often drier and better, so they buy the new one. They may then find it less than inspiring and don't buy the next year, which might be terrific if it's another drier year. This is where wine writers are invaluable, or should be, for they get to do your tasting for you.

In 1987 we made cabernet and shiraz-cabernet blend. There was more cab than I needed for the 60/40 shiraz-cab so it was either change the proportions of the blend or make a straight cabernet sauvignon, and I chose the latter path.

From a marketing point of view it would have been better to change the proportions, but of course I wanted to know what a straight cabernet would be like. As it happened the shiraz had put on more bulk, or less concentration and more water, and the cab sauv was more concentrated so a much better wine; I suspect that I also had left a little H_2S in the shiraz.

At that stage I was beginning to get my sense of smell and taste back, and sometimes in the vineyard I realised that I could smell something, so I'd immediately rush to the winery and taste as many barrels as I could before I ran out of smelling capacity. For a few years, after my first encounter with H_2S in 1985, Steve Goodwin and Dave Brown kindly came to the winery before bottling time and tasted all the barrels for H_2S. I have been lucky with my friends.

The 'green label' year was 1987, so 1988 became the red label. It was bigger, more solid, but lacking somehow. I thought later that summer pruning could have been the culprit. I know some of the bottled wine was heat affected; I had run out of storage space and had to take some to Bridgewater, where a friend kindly allowed me to store it in his shed. His son, however, didn't understand about sunlight into wine, and one day I went to collect some wine and found the sun's rays shining directly onto several pallets and very little air space left in the bottle.

During 1988 another distressing phone call came. It was from Vosje's daughter, Abigail. Her father, Rod, had been diagnosed with a brain tumour and was not expected to live. Poor Rod! The best person in his life of course was Abi, and he would have to leave her. Poor Abi! Her sister, Ondine, and her mother, Vosje, gone in awful circumstances, and now her father doomed. Why should this lovely innocent girl's life become a Gothic tragedy? If there is a God, he has very strange priorities.

I'd set aside some shiraz grapes to make a sparkling red, and had ripened up another patch to the maximum in order to try my hand at vintage port. This is tricky to make, requiring very ripe fruit and the addition of brandy spirit at a certain stage of the fermentation so that enough residual sugar is retained to give the wine its characteristic sweetness. My idea was to make the wine and call it Ondine in memory of her, the base wine being sweetened slightly by the addition of vintage port made by me, her father. The project worked well. When entered in the Victorian Wines Show the next year, the vintage port component achieved the same point score as the Brown Brothers and Stanton and Killeen, and they'd been making vintage port for generations. I was very pleased with myself! When judiciously added to the base wine, the result was indeed pleasing. Sue and I organised some people to help us with attractive packaging and the operation was deemed a success. (Twenty-five years later we have two bottles remaining. The wine will be all right but the corks may not.)

The year 1989 was again cool and wet, and I realised I was doing myself a disservice by maintaining a basic trellising system. I had already turned the front paddock shiraz over to a 'T' trellis system and this had proved successful, with better ripening of the fruit, so now it was the turn of the cabernet. I chose not to use the 'T' trellis but instead started using a technique known as VSP, or vertical shoot positioning: the vines are trained to two vertical wires, and extensions are added to the posts so that a pair of foliage wires can be installed above the fruiting wires. These green shoots grow into new canes that carry this year's crop. They can then be lifted to expose the fruit to sun and air without reducing the actual number of leaves in the canopy. It was really held up in the manner of, say, a bunch of celery, if you imagine the fruit being positioned low on the stalks.

The year before, in 1988, I had cut off leaves in the fruiting zone and had used a hired reciprocating hedge trimmer mounted on a chainsaw for the event. I was able to mount the trimmer-chainsaw on a piece of timber tied to the windscreen of the Suzuki jeep by using an octopus strap to hold the handle and cushion any kickback. All I had to do was start the chainsaw motor, slowly drive up close to the vines and let the hedge trimmer do its work. With this appropriated equipment I was able to summer-prune the whole vineyard in little more than a day. The disadvantage was that it would sometimes cut quite close to the bunch, leaving perhaps only two or three leaves on that cane to ripen a bunch or two. This was insufficient for fruit-flavour ripeness although enough for sugar ripeness, and is probably what caused the '88 to be a bit boring.

Angel Blend

Thus the 1989 cabernet vines adapted to their new training, and the results in the 1990 wines were gratifying—so much so that I decided to make a straight cabernet, to be called the Angel Blend in memory of Ondine.

The 1988 'sparkling Ondine' was almost ready for release, resplendent in its smart new packaging, and I had not anticipated making another—the straightforward flavour profile of the '88 crop seemed to lend itself to tweaking with the vintage port; it had been a success and I had no reason to experiment further.

However, in the years following Ondine's death we kept observing extraordinary coincidences in the winery. Often a tank containing a certain amount of wine would exactly fill the barrels allocated to it—not just fill them, fill them *exactly*, with not a drop too much or too little. It reached the stage where we would often wait expectantly as the last barrel was being filled, and when it filled to perfection we'd say: 'The Angel has done it again.'

There were other strange things going on, too. The light over the kitchen table would stop working whenever I went fishing in Tasmania—not to Daylesford to be with family, or to Melbourne for a sales trip—just fishing trips to Tasmania. It was as if the Angel didn't like me going away fishing, for the light would mysteriously begin working normally again on my return. And once, eerily, when we were sitting around the kitchen table, Ondine's name was mentioned and the light went out for about three seconds . . . and then came on again.

We accepted that there was something more than coincidence going on, something wonderful and special. We accepted that we had a guardian angel—and that's why I decided to create a wine and a label in recognition of her.

The 2000 cabernet for the Angel Blend was put into French oak barrels made by Schahinger's. They were mostly puncheons, the big ones of 480 litres or so, which meant the wine would mature slowly (as a rule of thumb, the smaller the barrel, the quicker the maturation). Years later I decided it was all a bit too slow, and that's when I started adding merlot and cabernet franc to soften the wine a little, and give it a touch of perfume. An alternative would have been to use hogsheads of 300 litres or barriques of 220 litres, more expensive options costing more per litre for the oak component. In any case the winery was designed around larger barrels. It was galling at times to realise that winemakers in more fortunate circumstances could simply order whatever barrels they wanted, particularly if the vineyard owners were wealthy and ambitious to win medals and reputations. Of course, it is not unknown for red wines to be 'double dipped'—that is, exposed to two brand new barrels in the course of their maturation; it can be advantageous for a particular class of a particular wine show. The class from which the Jimmy Watson Trophy winner is selected, for instance, is judged within the chilly confines of a concrete building in Melbourne in September, and the wine has to be very heavily oaked to show up in these circumstances. The same wine might taste drastically over-oaked at a higher temperature.

I fancied doing something quite different for the Angel label, and the idea of emulating those gaudy Italian religious paintings appealed to me. My theory was that, as it wasn't going to sell on its label but its quality, I could do what I liked with the label and it would be a joke between the Angel and me. I put down a little watercolour of what I wanted and Alan Wolf Tasker from Lake House agreed to 'professionalise' it for me; he did a terrific job.

The label itself continues to divide opinion. For instance, some people at the tasting room say that they like the wine but could not buy anything with such a ghastly label. Others, usually women, have been known to say they don't drink red wine but must have a bottle for the label! There was once a plane-load of English wine sellers who were brought out here, I think by the indefatigable Hazel Murphy, and at a tasting one of them took me aside and asked me if we were going to change the Angel label. 'More flak coming,' I thought. I told him we were not.

He looked relieved. 'That's good,' he said. 'I come into the shop in the mornings in winter and it's freezing. I turn the lights and heating on and as I go back, rubbing my hands, I often stop and look at the Angel Blend label. It makes me feel warm.'

The Angel always won medals, usually high bronze, once a silver, but it was not until I had refined the proportions of merlot and cab franc to 5 per cent each, and invested in a couple of French oak hogsheads, that we won a gold medal at Melbourne, again frustratingly beaten by a half-point for the trophy, again by a wine which I considered was superior to ours. It was Yarra Ridge Reserve Cabernet, I think, and I was told later that it had been put through an osmotic filter to gain extra concentration, but don't know whether that is so or not. Our wine, the 1994, was very elegant and well structured and what remains in our museum stock is ageing beautifully. Meanwhile, the 1991 shiraz cabernets were powering along, good wines both, and the 1992s a worthy follow-up.

Daylesford and domestic changes

In 1989 it was time for Cameron to go to primary school, so although I'd been building rooms onto the Kingower house, including a good kitchen, another bathroom and toilet, and a large sitting-room—probably subconsciously trying to delay the inevitable—we moved to Daylesford, 100 kilometres south, in another climate, almost another world, for it had long been my plan to retire there and it was what I had previously promised Julien before Ondine's death.

In 1984 Julien and I had bought a double block of land there with much difficulty at a price that even then was a bargain. The house was in a state of severe disrepair but of such charm that it had to be renovated and extended, too, to accommodate a growing family, for we now had another son, Jesse Norman, born in October 1989—another important part of my life and another great mate. The house extensions were made that year on a grander and grander scale.

Builders, bricklayers, stonemasons, electricians, plumbers and painters were employed while bank interest rates rose to an astronomic all-time high. Some years previously the government had put a 10 per cent tax on wine that had taken some swallowing, for we were reckoning on a wage of 10 per cent of our gross. Raising the price of the wine was not simple: it put it into a higher price bracket, and the multiplying effect as it passed through the hands of wholesaler and retailer led to a significant increase. So we were not rolling in money and eventually, when the money ran out, the Daylesford house works had to be halted. It was habitable but there was still much work to be done, so I was assured of projects over the ensuing twenty years in my 'spare time'.

But there were also other things to attend to. As I was going to Daylesford and Sue Mackinnon was coming back to live at Kingower to resume her role as working partner, a house was designed for her by an architect friend, Hugh Flockart. Being the owner-builder meant I was in charge of employing and coordinating the contractors, ordering materials and so on. It rained incessantly and the whole building site became a sea of jelly-like mud, much like the vineyard when we planted in 1974, and we couldn't get concrete trucks in to pour the slab.

The plan had evolved, as a compromise, that I would bring the original Kingower house up to an acceptable standard for it to be run as a bed-and-breakfast (B&B), catering for two couples. Cliff and Marg Stubbs were coming up from Melbourne to live there and run the accommodation facilities I had built into the place—two new rooms for guests and another ensuite incorporated. Cliff had always wanted to be involved in winemaking and Marg was keen to do the B&B, so they were an ideal couple to work with us and also to live at the house. If they could run the cellar door and Cliff could perform some winemaking duties, then I would have some time with my young family and also do some recently neglected sales trips to Melbourne and interstate. Importantly, I also needed to be able to spend some time with Sebastian, still jackarooing, and shamefully neglected by me, as I had hardly been able to see him since Ondine's death.

Eventually the rain stopped long enough for us to pour the slab at Sue's Kingower house, having first put down 30 cubic metres of gravel to give the concrete trucks access. I remember saying to myself at the time, 'I don't know what a nervous breakdown is, but I think I'm having one.' By 1991 Sue's house was finally finished. My and Julien's house at 2 Ruthven Street in Daylesford was as finished as it was going to be for quite some time, and Cliff and Marg moved in at Kingower. It had been a busy two years.

So the children grew—Cameron at school virtually over the road from our house, Jesse at a nearby crèche. Julien was working in Daylesford with her network of social worker mates, Sue had settled in at Kingower managing the administration and sales, and Cliff and Marg were handling their side of things.

Somehow it worked, although for me it meant the drive to Kingower and back every day, 100 kilometres each way, or on the days I was going to Melbourne, 100 kilometres each way the other way. We bought a little Alfasud second-hand from our friend Bill Purton, who still clearly remembers the test drive around Melbourne's Yarra Boulevard at night. That little red machine became a familiar sight to many people along the route. After Maldon the roads were wide and deserted and while it might be economical to drive at 100–110 kilometres per hour, if called upon it could easily top 170 and often had to do so to meet a deadline—usually to be back at Daylesford before 6 p.m. when Cameron was put to bed. It often carried sixteen cases of wine, too, as I'd use it for deliveries on the way down to Melbourne and at towns on the way home to Daylesford.

9

Musk and more

A sprig of cherry blossom

But for her persistence, Miwako would never have worked with us at all. In 2002 she came to us via a circuitous route. She first made a phone enquiry, and Sue told me that a Japanese girl wanted to work in the winery for vintage; the concept of a non-English-speaking Japanese girl working in the winery sounded bizarre to me, and rudely I let it go. But after Sue reminded me another two or three times over the next few weeks—'Your Japanese girlfriend rang again'—I decided at least to contact her. With limited English she convinced me of her enthusiasm; but it was her competence I was concerned about.

It transpired that she was learning English from Cecilia, a friend of Richard Thomas, an old mate and maker of some exquisite commercial and some feral experimental cheeses, so I had to do my best for her. It's a long way to come for a job interview so I suggested she pack some clothes and come up prepared to stay a week, and if things worked out well she could complete the vintage.

I've always appreciated having a female working in the winery. For more than a decade, Vanessa Buck has worked every vintage for a weekend or two, and other women have come and gone for short spells, though unfortunately none of them have been there long enough to learn what happens on a daily basis and be ahead of the job. I have found women to be generally neater, tidier, better organised, and often with more staying power, than men.

Lacking a woman's natural caution in the face of large inanimate and barely understood objects, men can get themselves into all sorts of trouble in the winery. They want to take over, they want to push that button, or roll that barrel out of the way, or take on any masculine challenge, but they do not always want to coil that hose neatly when they've finished. Men, sometimes desperately, want to do what the winemaker is doing and as soon as the winemaker goes to answer the phone they jump to it without realising that a little knowledge is a dangerous thing.

Of course, there are exceptions to this perception of men. If you watch a group of Balinese men harvesting coconuts, you see them all working as a harmonious unit. One man goes up a tree and cuts the branches that have to be removed, then begins to drop the fruit in earnest. The men on the ground keep clear and work a few trees behind him, cutting the slots in the coconut so that they can be strapped into bundles, carrying the bundles, and generally doing less dramatic jobs. When the climber stops to have a drink of coconut milk, or to eat some of the flesh, none of the others try to scamper up the tree and take his job. In Australia, they couldn't wait to get up there and make fools of themselves and possibly break something—their necks, for instance. Women tend to work in the same way as those Balinese coconut harvesters, so there is often less tension when they are working in the winery.

I won't forget the day, in 1982 in the early years of the winery, when we finished picking grenache grapes, of which we had only a tiny patch of 250 vines. I was wishing aloud that there had been a bit more fruit, worrying there wouldn't be enough to make up the amount for a full barrel. Ondine had been picking with the others and it had been hot work in the sun—in fact, I was leaving the grapes to cool for a bit before crushing them. I noticed that she was not there with the others and felt a twinge of annoyance that she hadn't told me she was going (for a wash or swim or whatever). The others were having after-work drinks and chats when Ondine reappeared, saying, 'I've got some more grapes for you, Poon.' We took the ute to collect them. By going over the last rows and gleaning bunches the pickers had missed, she had filled three more 10-litre buckets. Staying power!

Anyway, Miwako, aged about twenty-six, joined us in 2002. But we immediately hit a hurdle. After collecting her from the bus at Inglewood we had returned to Kingower—and to Bruno doing his golden retriever welcome. He was little more than a pup then and frolicked up to us, wagging his tail. Miwako shrieked and jumped back into the ute. This, I thought, is all I need, a woman who is terrified of dogs. At Passing Clouds—dog heaven—sometimes as many as seven canines appear on the weekend. It transpired that she had been bitten by a dog as a child and had been scared of them ever since. She had to be mollified and I had to show her how harmless Bruno was, until finally she timorously touched him. Twenty hours later he was sleeping in her bedroom, and later when she would practise driving after work in the old Telecom utility, she would take him with her in the passenger seat where he would sit up, tongue lolling happily, for all the world as if he was being taken for a joyride by his girl-friend. They had become the best mates imaginable.

We gave Miwako the 'Sebastian Suite', a bedroom with ensuite originally built as Sebastian's room, and she quickly settled into the lifestyle. This was basically have breakfast and start work at 7.30 or 8 a.m., then until about coffee time plunge vats (as they are twice daily to force the hard cap of pips and skins down, to mix with the liquid wine beneath), take readings for temperature, baumé and pH, and adjust the cooling as required. This is ideally a two-person job, for the cooling coil and its associated hoses are heavy with liquid.

Miwako proved quite capable of all that. She was meticulous at taking readings and recording them on the whiteboard, which was soon set up with absolute symmetry; for instance, where I had ruled lines she now had carefully cut tapes to divide the various columns. She was quite a solid girl, not the sylph-like creature that Sue had possibly imagined, but she was agile enough to get up on top of the vats, so I was able to leave the plunging to her and ready ourselves for pressing, or whatever else was on the agenda for the day. She became an extremely dependable assistant.

She and Sue got on increasingly well, too, and I had to be careful about sending her to Sue's house for anything as Sue would keep her talking for as long as possible. By this time Sue's sister Jill had moved from Coff's Harbour into an extension she'd had built onto Sue's house. It suited Jill well, for she could not only help her sister but also be geographically closer to her daughter in Melbourne and her friends in South Australia and Victoria.

Miwako was loyal and cooperative, but she slowly and insidiously began to change my living pattern. It started with breakfast. Sue and Jill, or 'the sisters', as they were known, always kept hens so we had sufficient fresh eggs for breakfast daily. I would get up around 7.20 a.m. (at that time we were starting work at eight), and make breakfast for us both. Miwako began coming to the kitchen earlier and earlier until one morning I came out and she had already cooked breakfast. The eggs were poached to perfection, but the plate had the addition of very finely chopped straws of carrot and radish, a touch of green wasabi and a dab of chilli sauce, so the plate was beautifully presented, like a painting. Every day from then on there were slight variations, each worthy of a photograph.

My lunches were almost invariably bread rolls thawed from the freezer, with salad, cheese or Italian smallgoods that I buy from our friends at 'Istra' at Musk. Before long Miwako was leaving the winery before me at lunchtimes and the cuisine smartened up considerably. She was going shopping with me by then, so that when we went to Daylesford to stay with my family we stopped at Newstead where there is a little supermarket and also Central Victoria's leading butcher, Ross Barker—or so he seemed to me. Whenever I cooked steak for visitors, especially overseas ones, they always commented on the superb quality of the meat, which was invariably Ross's porterhouses, but when I asked him why they were so good he professed not to know. Ageing, I suppose.

Slowly Miwako took over the evening meal as well, and I was left with no cooking to do except that of the steak, at which I fancy myself a dab hand. One night I went into the other room to speak on the telephone and overcooked it. Miwako knew the meat was overcooking of course, because she was in the kitchen at the time, but she was letting me cook my own goose, as it were—she wanted that job! When we sat down to eat she cut into her steak, looked at it ominously, then said seriously: 'I think now, I cook the steak.' And from then on she did. To perfection.

Miwako liked her food, and her wine, but I don't think I ever saw her noticeably affected by alcohol—she could easily enjoy a bottle of full-bodied red wine with dinner.

When vintage was almost finished and we were able to take a day or two off at Daylesford, I took her fly-fishing at my neighbour's dam at Musk, which I had stocked with trout a few years previously. Normally I scarcely had time to fish it but was often rewarded when I did. Miwako showed great interest when I told her about fly-fishing and how it was done. Like most Japanese she was very respectful of fresh fish, although she had never caught one, nor seen one caught. Her father was a chef and she speculated on the pleasure she would gain from telling him about fishing in Australia.

So an unlikely alliance was formed, with me as the angler and Miwako as the spotter. One of the banks of the dam is very high, and if you stand quite still on the bank, it is usually not long, particularly with the aid of polaroid glasses, before you see a trout cruise by, say, 10 to 15 metres out from the waterline below. The problem is that you can't cast a fly to it from the high bank because one movement makes it disappear like, well, like a startled trout. The solution is to have the spotter high up on the bank who, when the trout appears, gives instructions to the angler below who can cast to, but not see, the fish; the fish can't see him for he is low to the water and the trout's field of vision is cone-shaped. Provided the spotter does not move, he or she can transmit verbal instructions, for the trout, like the kangaroo, does not notice a new object within its field of vision provided the object doesn't move. In these circumstances the fish will take most floating artificial flies, provided it sees them land on the water.

So we set our first trap, and as the trout approached, Miwako, unmoving as per instructions, said: 'Trout coming, free o'crock', then 'two o'crock', at which stage I would cast the fly to twelve o'clock. If we were in the right place relative to the sun and no shadow of the fly-line fell across the surface of the water, then the trout might take it. Our first one did, and was duly landed after a lengthy struggle, Miwako as excited as a Japanese gets, I suspect (although Kumi, a Japanese lady with whom I now play table tennis, gets pretty excited, too, over a good shot at a critical point in the game). I tapped our fish on the head with the 'priest' to kill it while Miwako discreetly averted her eyes, then I picked up the fishing gear and packed it in the car. (For non-fisher-folk, a priest is a small baton-like tool used for humanely delivering 'last rites' to a fish, usually a trout—for trout anglers are generally of a more sensitive and gentlemanly inclination than those who fish for coarser species, and would not leave a fish to gasp to death. They either kill them quickly or release them back into the water!)

On the drive home Miwako sat in the passenger seat of the car and held the trout as reverently as if she were holding the crown jewels. I cleaned the fish, which had beautifully coloured flesh; in that dam their diet is largely mayfly nymphs, water snails and yabbies, and the water that feeds it is from a pristine spring-fed creek. When Julien and the boys came home later in the afternoon, they were treated to the sight of sushimi and nori roles in the middle of preparation. Boy, it was good, we all loved it, and it was the first of several three-pounders from the dam.

The morning after the Japanese banquet Miwako and I were up early to pick wild pine mushrooms from the forest at Daylesford to take to Mildura, on the Murray River in northwestern Victoria. It was towards the end of Miwako's time here in 2003, after vintage, and we had organised a Passing Clouds dinner for the faithful at the Grand Hotel in Mildura. Old friend and previous Passing Clouds voluntary winery worker and cook, now (reluctant) celebrity chef extraordinaire, Stefano de Pieri, was going to add the mushrooms to a dish based on Murray River carp he was preparing.

We were having breakfast on the deck of the family house overlooking Lake Daylesford when Miwako spotted giant white flowers on the cypress trees on the opposite bank above Kerry and Ann Bolton's Book Barn, which had not been there the night before. She pointed excitedly, 'Rook, beautiful frowers on trees!' I stood up and clapped loudly and the flowers all flew away screeching, for they were, of course, white cockatoos.

Speaking of Kerry, he and I would sometimes hurl good-natured abuse at each other across the lake if I saw them having a barbecue in his back garden near the water's edge. Once, after Julien had bought me a three-burner barbecue on behalf of the family, Kerry bought himself a four-burner one, and terminated an exchange by yelling across the water, 'You're a three-burner person, Leith, and you always will be!'

So with a couple of boxes of mixed fungi in the car, Miwako and I went back to Passing Clouds to do a couple of winery jobs before heading off for the four-and-a-half-hour trip to Mildura. We arrived there, got our rooms organised and went downstairs to open up the wines: they were under natural cork so we had to check for cork taint. Then we relaxed and had a beer before dinner.

Dinner followed the usual winemakers' dinner format: introduction of the wines to go with the food; winemaker speaking between courses; then eat that course and so on. We had four wines with the meal then the sparkling Ondine 1988 Shiraz Cabernet with the cheese. It was a triumph—the food was superb and the wine by no means disgraced it. But it had been a big day, and we were ready for bed.

But Stefano wasn't. He'd been cooking all day and was looking forward to a drink or two and a bit of a chat. So down we went to the cantina to taste the wine he had been saving to drink with me, a 1985 Domaine Romanee Conti La Tache. I will never ever forget that wine! It was glorious and everything that a pinot noir should be, but I've forgotten quite a bit of what happened afterwards. We drank a bottle of Rhone shiraz that Stefano wanted to try. I know that. And I know that I tripped on the stairs from the cellar. On Japanese television there had been a mini-series about two lovers who eventually committed suicide after sharing a bottle of '85 La Tache, a circumstance that drove the price of any La Tache to stratospheric heights in Japan for a time. I remember Miwako had the empty bottle, almost the casket that would have held the holy grail—I hope she's got it set up now as a bed lamp at home in Japan.

We had breakfast with Stefano, said goodbye to Donata, his wife, and drove back to Kingower. Sue couldn't wait to interrogate Miwako about the night and when told that we had continued into the cellar, Sue asked how we'd handled all that wine so late at night. Miwako replied, 'First time I have seen Graeme a little bit dwunk!' Which was nice of her.

Sue and I had great memories of Miwako's requests for interpretations of some of my Australian utterances. Once she went over to Sue's house and asked her what 'Bearmybumenburkestreet' meant. Sue asked her in what context that statement had been made and was told that, after tasting a pinot noir, I had said that if it did not win a gold medal I would do just that. So Sue was able to enlighten her. And on the return journey from Mildura, Miwako had asked me why we drove to Mildura at 100 kilometres per hour on Friday but were returning on Saturday at 125 kilometres per hour. My response had been 'Orlacopsareaddafoody' which was probably a little harder to explain, embracing as it did some analysis of Australia's legal, cultural and sporting traditions.

It was a sad parting at Tullamarine Airport one cold late autumnal morning. If love is based on respect and admiration, then I loved that tough, inscrutable and incredibly loyal Japanese girl just then. We embraced for the first time, and both unexpectedly shed large tears, with the roaring of the jets in the background.

Postscript: A couple of years after Miwako's departure I caught a magnificent six-and-a-quarter-pound rainbow trout in that dam at Musk where Team Graeme and Miwako had taken that lovely trout. This time I cooked it the way suggested by Stefano de Pieri—making up a meringue of egg whites and salt, smothering the trout all over with it, and cooking it in the oven until the meringue just starts to brown. Then it's cooked and you take it from the oven and let it stand for fifteen minutes. This is a superb way to cook trout or Atlantic salmon and is a stunning presentation, for the meringue is cracked and folded away, taking the skin with it, revealing the steaming orange or pink flesh beneath.

Good times, hard times

In 1992 my mate Ben Vaughan from Tasmania, who wasn't doing much at the time due to legal complications associated with employment, used to come over and help me sometimes. We would taste all the shiraz and cabernets to rank them in order in terms of quality and suitability for the Graeme's Blend or Angel Blend. I had previously done this job by myself, so doing it with Ben was a good experience, though challenging and time-consuming, with decisions having to be made and compromises effected. I welcomed company and a second opinion, particularly as Ben had a fine and well-trained palate.

While rating the '92s with Ben from the barrel, we came across two beauties, cabernet and shiraz, that Ben said he'd love to see combined. Always keen to experiment, I performed the 'marriage ceremony' and told Sue that she had to get yet another label organised which, of course, she efficiently and uncomplainingly did. It was to be called Ben's Blend, and Ben was not to know about it. There would not be enough quantity to take it to the Victorian Wines Show, but I could enter it in the *Wine Wise* magazine small-winemaker competition, where lesser quantities were acceptable. I did this, and it gained a much coveted 'highly recommended' rating. It was, and still is, a great wine.

I didn't make a '93 Ben's Blend, the '94 was excellent, but I ruined the '95 by adding a small barrel of wine that I'd made from grapes from a local vineyard. They had obviously been grown under the drip zone of eucalyptus trees, and the eucalypt mint was strong enough to effectively ruin the good wine with which it was blended. I decided that was the end of that blend.

By that time the 1995–96 season was approaching and I had secured fruit from several good local sources—the Burdetts from Bridgewater, for whom I had been making some wine; Beau and Joy Foster from Wedderburn; and the Humphreys from Kingower, who also asked me to make some wine from their grapes for them, to be labelled 'Hallmark' in recognition of their modest dealings in antiques, particularly silver objects and claret jugs. The Burdetts had merlot and cab franc, as did the Humphreys. With pinot and cab franc from the Grahams up the road, and some cabernet and shiraz from the Fosters at Wedderburn, we looked like having a bumper crop of every-thing we'd need.

We had planned on employing a young couple, Greg and Paige Bennett. Greg had worked in the winery at Charles Sturt University (after it changed its name from Riverina College), and for Portavin bottling services, so he was pretty savvy with wine handling. But how he wanted to get his hands on some winemaking tools! Paige had worked on the Mornington Peninsula vineyard as a wine sales rep, so she was very familiar with the wine trade. My idea was to increase volume so the winery could produce enough money to pay us all a wage and maybe take the pressure off me.

We were committed to a particular price bracket and there didn't seem to be much chance of changing that, it being in line with our contemporaries after all, so an increase in volume seemed to be the only answer. We invested fairly heavily in new oak, Greg was set to start pre-vintage so that we could do the winemaking in shifts, and all looked ready to go. Then Greg dropped his motorbike at high speed and wrapped himself around a tree backwards and quite hard, doing himself serious injury and sidelining him for the vintage.

So once more into the breach! Once more to look at what had to be done that day, every day, and think, 'What I'm about to attempt is impossible, but it's impossible to do anything else, so here goes!' As a sign in one of our old workshops said: 'Difficult jobs done immediately—the impossible takes a little longer.'

My family would often come up from Daylesford during vintage. Some of Julien's friends, who had become mutual friends, were now part of our eclectic group and the tradition continued of great meals, good wine and fun after work. The wine press usually had to be tended during our feasting. But being just across the creek, that was easily done. And if it had to be unloaded and refilled that could be done, too, but in that case it might need tending until the early hours of morning.

My second son Cameron was about ten by then and increasingly keen on working in the winery. He'd been working with me since he was very young, and once, a couple of years previously, had said tearfully to his mother when she came to get him from the winery for dinner, 'But, Mum, we haven't finished yet!' He and our younger son Jesse loved pushing the huge, heavy and unwieldy dry cake of skins off the press and helping to get it onto the trailer. Later when they visited, Cam would go to the winery to see what was happening, and Jesse would go to the tasting room and print out the takings from the previous week. Horses for courses!

Somehow, in 1996, we processed 100 tons, as much as a large winery might swallow in a single hour. But for us it was hard work over a period of six weeks. From pinot noir to cabernet, thirty or so batches of wine, all kept separate from ferment to settling-in tanks and then into barrel, the barrels stacked higher than I'd ever had them before, within inches of the roof. We were going to need a new winery if we kept going like this! Greg, healed after his accident and raring to go, arrived after vintage, and he and Paige were installed in the house so we could think about the new winery.

The idea developed that I'd build the winery with Bill Ricardo, using Greg's help when we needed three people, and Greg would perform vineyard duties and share winemaking with me, or solo if the job didn't require two. Bill had recently come to work with us, having first met Sue when he knocked on her door to try to sell her some ducks that he used to raise before the drought. He came not as assistant winemaker but as a general handyman and assistant, who soon became fairly autonomous and indispensable. Or as indispensable as anybody ever becomes, for as my friend Jim Sloan used to say, 'The graveyards of the world are filled with people who thought they were indispensable.' Greg and Paige later bought some ducks from Bill for fattening, but after two months they all flew away. I mischievously encouraged somebody else to inform Greg that

Bill had trained his ducks to fly home after two months, when someone else had fattened them!

However, Bill did distinguish himself as a wine blender in the following manner. We were pumping shiraz from the barrels into the big tank, T1. There was a line of barrels, mostly shiraz but with a few of cabernet franc among them, with their contents written on the top of the barrel. The phone rang and I took it outside to answer it. It turned out to be a long call and when I returned I saw to my horror that Bill was working his way down the line and was pumping his second barrel of cab franc. I hadn't realised until then that he was functionally illiterate. I shrieked and frightened the hell out of Susie McDonald, Julien's niece (and therefore mine by marriage), and Bill but then contained myself and rationalised: 'Well, the Laughtons at Jasper Hill make a shiraz cab franc and it sells for a lot more than our wines do, so we'll see what happens.' It was labelled Bill's Blend and got a medal and a better score at the Melbourne Show than the Graeme's Blend of the same vintage, but we never did try to charge more money for it.

The winery project began. The building had to be quite high to accommodate our new variable capacity tanks, and a new catwalk would have to be built to work them from the top, higher than the forklift could reach. So it was necessary to mount a couple of wooden half-ton fruit boxes onto the forklift so that the trusses could be raised into place, quite hair-raising and definitely illegal, in contravention of workplace health and safety regulations. However, I figured that as I wasn't employed, then the rules would not apply to me anyway, so I got the 'top job'. It was finally finished and at last we had enough space to work in, although we still needed more tanks. It was a nightmare trying to shuffle different batches around with insufficient containers, so sometimes we used the milk vats under cover of CO_2 gas (as we did in 1980) or 1000-litre plastic food-grade containers.

Impatient to start work after his convalescence, Greg was sharing the winemaking with me, and we proceeded through 1996 to 1997, which was to be the last pinot noir made from

Kingower fruit. Greg was very keen to make pinot so I more or less let him have his head with the '97 pinot and he did a great job of it, winning a high bronze medal—not bad for a pinot grown north of Bendigo! From then I was planning to make pinot from superior Coldstream fruit, and rosé from Kingower fruit.

At the time the future of the wine industry for people like us was uncertain at best. We had hoped at one stage to be exempted from the GST, as promised, but then we found that it was to be replaced with the dreaded WET (Wine Equalisation Tax). For producers under a certain size this was modified, in that you'd pay the tax to the state government and the federal government would give it back. This could, and can, change at any time, but meanwhile it doubtless employs a lot of clerical staff and saves them the embarrassment of seeking more challenging work. The 2009 federal budget threatened to include an added wine tax but that didn't eventuate, due largely to the work of our industry body.

With all the confusion and uncertainty it began to look as if we would be doing well to get out of everything square if we paid off our bank loans. The future was maybe rosy enough if cellar door sales were very strong. But ours, like most others, was not increasing as more wineries proliferated in the Bendigo area. Various bodies were promoting tourism in the area, which meant one and two bottle sales more often, but the days of the old Renaults or Peugeots, or the new BMWs and Mercedes, backing up to the cellar door for their dozens, had almost gone. This, perhaps, is not surprising when you can buy a new television for the cost of a case of Angel Blend, and by industry standards Passing Clouds 'over-delivers'—that is, gives exceptional value for money.

Wine sold through a distributor doesn't return much, for the distributor takes 35 per cent of the price for their costs off wholesale, then sells to a shop, which then resells it at, say, 30 per cent or so mark-up—or more in the case of a restaurant. So a $100 per case wine wholesale gains the winemaker, say, $66 from the distributor and costs the consumer, say, $125. We rely on our distributor but small producers like us need a cellar door facility, too.

After ten years of drought the cycle of dry year, wet year, and the perpetual waiting for next year to be better was not looking promising. We had sales in the United States for our Reserve Shiraz that mercifully got 92 or 93 ratings by Robert Parker and the *Wine Spectator* (even a 96-plus for a wine I made but didn't particularly care for). But we were buying increasingly large parcels of fruit for that, and the supply from our near neighbours was literally drying up.

New vineyard at Musk

The answer, as I saw it, was to buy a property near Daylesford and plant vines there. It was close enough to be accessible to my family house at Ruthven Street, and would allow us to tap into the tourist market. Establishing a vineyard and cellar door presence there would gain us a greater percentage of the much more lucrative cellar door trade, for which we could and must charge retail price, particularly if we were to provide to a retailer of any sort.

I believed then, and still do firmly believe, in the enthusiasm for and consequent increased market share of organically grown local produce, and I had plans for an organically grown vegetable garden and orchard, a herd of cows and a cheesery. I calculated that to produce something interesting and in demand in the food line would require a property of, say, 30 to 40 acres, with good water available.

So in 1997 Passing Clouds bought such a property, or rather the bank did, and with extra borrowings for the purpose I started to establish another vineyard, at Musk, 6 kilometres from Daylesford, on magnificent chocolate scoria soil, with water right from the creek and the knowledge that any bore should encounter an aquifer of high-quality water. The place was at a higher altitude than I had planned on, but it faced due north and was on the northern slope of the Great Dividing

Range, reaching a height of 770 metres at Wheelers Hill, to the south-west, which helped protect the site from the southerlies.

Although I was motivated to a certain extent by sentimentality to purchase a property at Musk, having always loved that little corner of the world, the decision to set up a satellite vineyard for Passing Clouds, as opposed to anticipating and planning for retirement, was a conscious one made after much soul-searching. On the one hand I could wind down more, go fly-fishing and hiking in Tasmania (if my arthritic knees would hold out), and play golf at nearby Hepburn Springs. On the other hand, I could set up a business in which the family could share, especially if Kingower had to be sold due to continuing drought or increased financial pressure in the wine industry.

The tantalising prospect of discovering a new, special pinot noir and chardonnay site was always there, of course. But there were many questions.

I was hoping for an area that, like Burgundy, had a small window between adequate ripeness and the weather closing in. Tasmania was producing some of the best pinots, and Lindsay McCall on the Mornington Peninsula arguably the best in Victoria; certainly he was the winner of most trophies. But were some of the other very cool areas living up to expectations?

I hadn't tasted Norm Latta's Eastern Peak for a while; his winery was 40 kilometres away from Musk and produced a cool-climate wine if ever there was one. I remembered it as having fantastic natural acidity and delicate flavours but I didn't even know what clone the vines were. Not far down the road towards Woodend on Beacon Hill was another winery I had visited. It was a labour of love, of similar altitude to Musk, whose wines were made by Lou Knight, but where was the wine to taste?

If the Musk fruit failed to ripen, it could be made into sparkling the following year, of course, but that costs money and to sell at what price? And how much sparkling wine at $40 per bottle can the market bear? Hanging Rock is asking a good price for its Macedon, but how much are they selling? How much is it costing to wait all those years of maturation to achieve the desired result?

Then there were questions I asked of myself. Are my skills sufficient? Will we get enough money from the development and sale of the extra block of land in Daylesford to cover the cost of further development after the venue is established? Do I have enough determination, enough youthful enthusiasm, to establish another vineyard in a climate that is inhospitable for at least several months of the year? Will I have the support of my family?

Many of these questions were hypothetical, and many subsequently became irrelevant, as Julien, my wife, had apparently already decided to walk out on our marriage—or, more accurately, make *me* walk. She was legally able to do this, as we had a son at home, Jesse, who was fourteen and a half years old and for whom she could claim carer status, because I had another place to live—the house at Kingower. So it looked as if I was headed the same way as the old man kangaroo, forced away when he was no longer required for protection or propagation. I didn't think I was a bad husband, but I guess I must have been, in her eyes at least, and that is what mattered. I can't have been a bad father, though, as I still seem to have the respect of my sons and, when I come to think of it, to my mind there is no reason why I shouldn't have the respect of my now ex-wife as well.

For Kingower the timing was good as Greg and Paige had recently departed, me having decided that as I'd completed the planting and trellising at Musk I must now let them go and return to winemaking at Kingower. The realisation that I would not be living in 'my' house at Daylesford again unless I had a personality transplant was devastating. It was, of course, not as obscene as losing Ondine, but there were similar elements; they had both been twenty-year projects, working with and for a thing I loved, now taken away.

Thus there were plenty of questions and precious few answers at the time.

In discussing the Musk project with Sue in 1996 she asked if I wasn't perhaps spreading myself a bit thin. 'Of course not,' I said. 'Greg and Paige can continue handling things at Kingower with you for most of the time, and I'll continue covering the cellar door during their holidays. Greg and I will share the eight weeks or so of vintage, and we'll handle cellar door between us. And I can work Musk from my base at Daylesford, it's only 6 kilometres away!'

When it became apparent that I'd made a gigantic rod for my own back with the marriage break-up, to my relief and to her credit, Sue never said, 'I told you so!'

Meanwhile, Julien was occupied with her career as a social worker and associated projects—the skate park (behind which I had thrown my weight and that of a couple of friends I'd made over the years, friends who were keen to help their community; we made it work); the swimming pool sports complex; and the various intricacies of social life among the dysfunctional families with whom she was concerned in her work. Cam was studying in Melbourne, so it was possible to see him, but to see Jesse by appointment on access visits when I had spent father and son time with him on more than 300 days a year was not going to be easy for either of us.

In planting Musk I was allowed the luxury of paying a contractor to drive in the posts, for Passing Clouds had borrowed money for establishment costs. I'd marked it all out and ripped it along the vine rows and put some lime/super mix into the rip lines. The posts were duly ordered and thumped in, not a demanding job as the soil was so friable and free of rock. The actual spacings gave me some grief. Conventional wisdom would have it that close planting in the French manner would be appropriate, but I was still convinced that the important thing was buds per acre rather than vines per acre. Anecdotal wisdom had it that there were usually heavy rains from thunderstorms around Christmas and it seemed to me that, given the quality and nature of the soil, my problem could be excessive vigour, so I decided on a wide spacing. This also meant that we would have a greater degree of ground cover and therefore less compaction by tractor work and fewer erosion problems on the steep slope.

I had seen in Richard Smart and Mike Robinson's *Sunlight into Wine* a photograph of a trellis system in New Zealand that

controlled excess vigour. This was a two-tier system, virtually turning one row of vines into two or, if vigorous enough,
four, and incidentally (although importantly to me) leaving a
2-metre wide strip under the vines, which would receive no
traffic and thus resist compaction. Richard Smart came out
and had a look, suggesting that if I adopted that system I should
initially use one tier, then add a cane to make another arm for
another tier if the excess vigour required it.

I needn't have bothered. It was still a local joke eight years
later that they hadn't had a proper summer rain since Graeme
Leith planted his grapes on the hill. I thought I could get away
without irrigation if I used 'grow tubes'—triangular plastic tubes
that fit around the young vines like miniature hothouses—in
the first year, and with installation of these over the vines they
fairly rocketed up, until those tender shoots poked out the top
of the grow tubes—and the wind hit them and their tips shriv-
elled. After their cosseting in the warm and damp microclimate
of the grow tubes, they did not like the real world at Musk! I'd
planted a row of shelter trees on the southern boundary, but
they wouldn't become effective for at least five years.

I gave the vines another year but the rate of growth was
still poor, so I then decided to put in a trickle irrigation system.
I'd had a bore put down by then and it had been successful,
with superb water in an aquifer. The drill had gone through
about 90 feet of topsoil then struck some scoria rock and finally
at about 100 feet, a quartz plate or reef, and through that lay the
aquifer of crystal clear pure water. I installed a small Honda
motor and pump on that, so now I had water available, and
it remained only to hook up to 6 kilometres of dripper tube
into mains and sub-mains, sectioned off so 25 per cent of the
vineyard could be watered at any one time by manipulating the
taps. But the vines didn't respond satisfactorily, so the next year
I put an extra dripper on every vine, as it seemed that due to
the porosity of the soil the water was going straight down, not
spreading out to cover enough of the root system.

Years later, in 2009, I put 1000 litres per vine on a section of
the vineyard twice, a month apart in the growing season, and

was barely able to detect any difference. But that was more than ten years on and several crops had been picked by then, so I'm getting ahead of myself . . .

Bed and breakfast

As mentioned, back in 1989 at Passing Clouds we started the B&B run by Cliff and Marg, the idea being to bring in some extra money selling more wine at the cellar door and generally amplifying the awareness and reputation of the label. It all seemed to work. But Cliff told me later, after their retirement from Passing Clouds, that although initially keen on the B&B idea, he would never run another one. He later bought Duncan McKenzie's vineyard, one we had previously bought grapes from, and he still runs it now with Maureen, his current partner, as Burnt Acre vineyard in recognition of a fire they had there once.

After Cliff and Marg left, Fay Roberts, a great cook and hostess, moved into the house and ran the B&B. Her daughter was the partner of a hiking and fishing mate of mine and when they brought Fay up to visit and she found there was a job going, running the B&B, she was very interested. She'd been raising children in the suburbs and reckoned she needed a change. She'd been brought up with some back-to-nature people in Nimbin and relished the idea of living close to the bush, growing some veggies and being hostess to paying guests interested in wine and food.

Her husband was supposed to live at Passing Clouds with her, but he was more wedded to his suburban lifestyle, so she left him to it. I'd often see her in the mornings and ask her how things were going. She'd often reply, 'Oh, just another day in paradise, really, Graeme.'

The population of Kingower increased by one when a chap named Clark came to live at Fishlock's, a pretty much ruined cottage over the road from the Gilmores' hotel. Clark had been a jockey but his inability or reluctance to endure the constant rigours of weight loss before races entitled him to the epithet of 'the fat jockey'. He had obviously done some other things before coming to a life of anonymity at Kingower. As he needed work, and I needed a lot of holes dug for the footings of a new shed to cater for our increasing stocks of wine, I employed him part-time as a labourer, and he helped me in the winery as well. One morning I was working in the winery, waiting for Clark to come to work, but he didn't show up. From the winery I thought I could see his dog over at Faye's place, so I went over and knocked on her door. She answered and I asked if she knew where Clark was and she professed not to know. I looked pointedly at the pair of boots on the ground outside the door. 'Well, his dog's here and his boots are here, would you mind going inside and looking under the dining room table and if you find him tell him to come to bloody work!' He turned up a little bedraggled, about ten minutes later.

One week he became quite agitated. He kept looking from the winery up the road to over at his shack, and I asked him what was up. It transpired that an old acquaintance of his, who had just been released from jail, was under the impression that Clark owed him something and might come looking for it.

A couple of days later, returning from town in the orange ute, I observed a car outside Clark's place and a physical altercation being conducted under the verandah. I diverted and pulled up at Clark's. Coincidentally I had just bought a new pick-handle, among other things, and thought I might take it with me and join the discussion. Clark was being shoved around pretty seriously by the big guy who, when I approached, pick-handle at my side, decided that the odds had turned against him and retreated to his car, yelling threats at Clark, including that he'd be back to get him. Clark told me later that police in Melbourne had apprehended the man with a rifle in a sugar bag, but he had managed to get himself into a psychiatric institution and, when the heat was off, discharged himself.

In any case he reappeared in Kingower, but by then his target had gone to live at a mate's place elsewhere in the district. I saw the grey Valiant cruising around and made sure my rifle had bullets in it. That night Geoffrey Graham and his family were disturbed by what sounded like gunfire between their place and ours, and rather than investigate they sensibly rang the police, who found the burned-out Valiant crashed into a tree. It had caught fire and those 'gunshots' had been its tyres exploding! The man, fortunately, was never seen again by any of us at Kingower.

However, Clark and his mate used to reappear, sometimes after having taken something recreational, and they'd terrorise Faye to the extent that she rang me at Daylesford very early one morning to say they were at her house and wouldn't leave. I drove up there as quickly as I could and dealt with it. But Faye was spooked and soon relinquished the B&B, moving to a little cottage at nearby Rheola that was quieter (at least until Faye got there).

Jill Bartlett was the next to run the B&B. She had wanted a break from the city where she had a house. She also had a block of land at Euroa, where she was planning to build a house later on, so she was getting a taste of country life in a similar geophysical area. Again we all became good friends, and again, because the house was dedicated to the B&B, when I overnighted there I slept in a caravan behind the tasting room so I had access to toilets and hot water.

I was sometimes joined by the family during vintage. One night as we sat around the campfire by the caravan, we saw a car entering the driveway. The driver, having seen our fire, had come to us distraught, for a ute had run off the road and hit a tree in the bush; the engine was roaring and the lights were still on but he could not see the driver. I drove up to the crash site and stalled the motor of the wrecked ute and looked around, finally finding the body of our neighbour and good friend Merv Gilmore, husband of Bev and father of Mark, Karen and Narelle. It was an awful tragedy; he must have swerved to avoid a kangaroo and lost control on a bend there. It was a sad funeral, indeed.

Merv had been a friend for a long time and, as an accomplished storyteller, he had often regaled us with humorous anecdotes of the old days of Kingower. Once when I was pruning and miles from reality in my mind, I was startled to see a movement beside me in the vines. It was Mervyn. He looked at me seriously then said, 'I want to shake your hand.' Perplexed, I held out my hand. 'All these years we've been laughing at you— we didn't think you could do it. But you've proved us wrong.' He tilted his head towards me and walked away.

Expanding production

It was about that time in 1996 that I decided we had better expand production, finish with the B&B and concentrate on winemaking. So that was where Greg and Paige came in. During 1998, after their year in barrel and year in bottle, we sold the '96 wines but still only got wages out of it, so that was when I let Greg and Paige go and returned to Kingower to take over the winemaking again, spent some borrowed money on better equipment to reduce the labour input, and tried to upgrade the quality to the point where we could raise prices and make the place produce more than wages.

We invested money in a new press and two new variable capacity tanks, known cynically in the trade as 'variable catastrophes'. This is because the moveable lids are sealed with a large tube like a giant clear bicycle tube, and if it inadvertently leaks and air gets in, the CO_2 escapes unnoticed and the wine becomes oxidised and ruined. There's a pressure gauge on them, beside the pump, and it's a good idea to check them every couple of days—it's cheap insurance. We had to build a concrete ramp and platforms for the new tanks. Then, having been fortunate enough to get, for virtually nothing, a truckload of experimental industrial-type concrete tiles, we painstakingly cut and laid them.

Cameron and his friend Mick helped during school holidays, learning tiling and other skills. It was hard, dusty and unpleasant work. When finished, however, to us it was a thing of beauty, and at last I had a winery to be proud of. (The original winery, having been extended piecemeal according to the demands of the various vintages, was not a pleasant thing to behold. In fact, it was a corrugated-iron blight on the landscape, and I was glad to be rid of it. Most of it is now sheds at Bill Ricardo's place.) We even built a sturdy catwalk 3 metres high which enabled us to work at that high level with pumps and also clean the tanks safely from above, although for stubborn tartrate deposits someone still had to crawl through the manhole and stand up inside on the floor of the tank to perform manual cleaning, aided by the trusty Karcher pressure cleaner, or 'Karachi' as it was dubbed by one of the student clowns who was doing part-time work with us. (The same evening he was blowing his French horn among the vines—Mozart, a hauntingly beautiful sound.)

Later, we bought a barrel washer that fits onto the Karachi. It has a fixed spray-head that rotates two ways and effortlessly cleans the entire inside with hot or cold water as required. Before that, we had to raise a barrel on the forklift, bunghole down, and perform repeated washings with the Karcher spray lance. In 2002, our endearing and valuable assistant, Miwako, had done most of that work so she was delighted with the new toy the following year.

In 2003 Miwako shared the barrel washing and other chores with Marian Fitzgerald, who had started working with us. I had done a Passing Clouds tasting at a venue in Sydney and was approached by a young woman who wanted to learn winemaking, work for a small winery and also study the subject academically. I was going to need an assistant after Miwako left and we needed more help during vintage, so Marian joined us. She was an articulate and intelligent team member who lived at Kingower for many months with her boyfriend Sam, and we all got on well together, particularly as she had a great sense of humour, of fun, part of the deal when you work at Passing Clouds. Sue was delighted, for she had another female companion whom she could lure from the winery for conversation and gossip.

At about that time, towards the end of the vintage and after Miwako had returned to Japan, Marian was away visiting her parents. I had organised for two people to come and work at the winery. But I received a phone call from them; they were sorry but car trouble meant they were stuck in Ballarat, 140 kilometres away. They couldn't come to work for me, so it looked as if I was in serious strife. I would have to transfer the contents of two fermenters to the press by bucket and then press it out, impossible without labour.

I was contemplating my dilemma when I observed two cyclists approaching the winery, a very unusual circumstance, Kingower being so far off the beaten track. They happened to be a winemaking couple from Canada who were bicycling around Central Victoria looking at unirrigated vineyards and, as it turned out, would be delighted to bucket grapes into the press for me all day in exchange for a night's accommodation. They stayed two nights. We worked hard and had a lot of fun, and enjoyed good meals and wine. We talked all the last night and the next day off they rode into the sunset. It seemed that the Angel had flown in again; they were certainly Heaven sent.

As a postscript to that vintage, when we are bucketing into the press we usually put on some 'bucketing music'; at that time it was Johnny Cash. Our Canadian friends must have decided to broaden my horizon a little, for a couple of months later I received a Merle Haggard tape from them. Thus for the next couple of vintages he shared the airwaves with Johnny. Marian Fitzgerald later incorporated the *Oh, Brother Where Art Thou* and *Pulp Fiction* soundtracks into the mix, and in 2004 Susie McDonald added Seaman Dan and Johnny Jones, cementing the eclecticism of the Passing Clouds bucketing experience.

The perils of pinot

In 1999, old friends of ours, Bruce and Mary Jones, who many years before had planted grapes at Upper Beaconsfield, had some grapes for sale at their lovely vineyard at Narre Warren East. Passing Clouds was not really in a position to buy them, so I shared the cost with two friends who were establishing wineries near Daylesford. We made the wine at the winery of one of those couples, Graeme and Jenny Ellender. The other couple was Ken and Miranda Jones, friends of Julien's whom I had assisted with the purchase of a house and land, later to be known as 'Big Shed' wines.

Winemaking was new to both couples but having planted vineyards they needed to learn quickly. The process was to be as simple as possible, with no intervention to affect the result, for I wanted a basic assessment of these grapes. So we threw them into a stainless-steel fermenter, added some yeast and foot-trod them twice daily until ferment was finished. They were then pressed and put into a barrel, there to remain for a year before bottling, without clarifying or filtering. A year later the result was impressive; the wine seemed to me to have more of the desirable 'Burgundian' character than Yarra Valley pinots I'd tasted.

So we were hooked, and decided to go ahead with the scheme, sharing everything three ways. I thought of the name—Three Wise Men—and registered it as a business. In the next year we made the 2000 vintage, which was very good, but being split three ways was of insufficient quantity to enter in shows. If I recall correctly it was actually split four ways, for I think I shared my one-third with Bruce and Mary Jones, who had decided that, as well as growing the grapes, they would like to become involved in the finished wine.

Thus, four wise men being one too many, we disbanded and a new partnership was formed between Passing Clouds and Woongarra, Bruce and Mary's vineyard. The plan was that they would supply the grapes and I would make the wine; we would share the cost of barrels, while I'd pay for winemaking costs, bottling, corking and labelling. We would take half each of the finished product and sell it as we saw fit, for they were intending to develop a cellar door on their property.

It seemed necessary to have some new barrels and we shared the cost of some new Australian barrels made by Heinrich coopers in Adelaide from French oak. I felt I had a good handle on the making of this variety by now. Over the two years I (we)

had used several techniques in the production of this wine—
pre-fermentation soak with and without sulphur, different
yeasts, foot-stomped, destemmed, whole bunch, and mixtures
of these techniques, all in their different barrels, being tasted
and assessed during maturation.

Ken and Miranda took their half of the previous vintage,
and I put all of ours (or what was to become ours and Bruce
and Mary's) into sterile plastic containers and barrels and took
it to Kingower for further settling and ultimately bottling,
having gained a good idea of what I'd like to do with the next
vintage. And by the time the 2001 vintage was ready, so was I,
with what I reckoned was the best yeast, the new (previously
mentioned) barrels and some good French oak barrels I had
previously used for chardonnay, likewise Australian made. All
that remained was to wait for a year in barrel and a further year
in bottle to see if it had worked.

At about that time my oldest son Sebastian heard of a
married couple, Robert and Vanessa McKernan, who had a
good little vineyard at Coldstream, an elevated site in the Yarra
Valley. We met them and, convinced of their integrity, skills
and thoroughness, arranged to buy their forthcoming crop.
Thus began a mutually beneficial business relationship that
lasted until 2008 when parts of the Yarra Valley were declared
phylloxera-infected areas and, although there was no phylloxera at the McKernans' place, we could no longer transport
their grapes to Kingower.

The friendship remains, however. Robert, being an engi-
neer, had done the computations for our winery catwalk in
2002–03 and would always bring a seafood feast when they
came to collect wine and taste the new batch. He was always
keen to help in the production of their own wine, the grapes
for which come from their vines, pruned by Vanessa. Vanessa's
sandwiches are always a triumph, and their combined cleaning-
up skills on the Queen's Birthday wine release are legendary.

Another pinot noir irony is that, of all our range, the
Passing Clouds Coldstream Pinot is the wine our distributors
find easiest to sell; they are constantly asking us for more than

we can supply. The 2002 was rated above the Coldstream Hills Reserve at the 2004 Melbourne Wine Show.

But a more delicious moment was at hand, for at the 2003 Victorian Wines Show, held at Seymour, the Three Wise Men was entered as well as my Passing Clouds wines, so I was competing against myself as well as everybody else! I had labelled wine in the new barrels as 'Reserve', supposing it would be better than the remainder in the other barrels, and I entered it in the pinot noir section. When I sent the samples to James Halliday for tasting, I had written in my winemaking notes that the only difference between the 'standard' wine and the Reserve was the oak barrels used. In his write-up he questioned this, suggesting that there was another factor involved. Years later, to my embarrassment, I read the vintage diary and realised that the Reserve had been picked a week later, so was a little riper, something that had not escaped Halliday but had escaped the winemaker!

Bruce Jones was with me at Seymour and we sat down on a bench, frantically thumbing through the results sheet, not knowing where to look first. Then, having found the appropriate class, fearing to look up to the winners, I disciplined myself to start at the bottom. We were not in the also-rans, but we were not in the Bronzes, either. My eyes crept up the printed lists, heart thumping, into the Silvers—top-scoring silver, Three Wise Men . . . Yes, and incredibly, in the Golds and second from the top, Three Wise Men Reserve!

I punched Bruce on the knee so hard it must have hurt him. He was not as excited as I was; it was almost as if he had expected it. I was elated, ecstatic, over the moon!

Once more, we were pipped for the trophy by half a point. This time it went to Lindsay McCall of Paringa—to be expected, as he is, if medals are anything to go by, Victoria's leading pinot noir maker. Lindsay uses barrels made in France; I was using barrels made in Australia. One can't help wondering, for it's generally accepted that French barrels are usually made from better quality or better matured timber, and all serious pinot winemakers use them.

But what a result! It should mean, among other things, that we should have a wine in the $50 retail bracket. We might even make some money at last. The Passing Clouds Pinot was a top-scoring bronze, so we had four medals from four wines, three of them pinots, plus a top bronze for the ever reliable Graeme's Blend shiraz cabernet, against all those people making all those pinots! All those winemakers who travelled the world attending pinot noir seminars, all those who went to France each year to unlock the secrets of pinot noir, all those teams of winemakers employed by companies who would throw as much money as was required into their search for the holy grail, and the ageing boy from the bush, maker of cabernet and shiraz, Graeme Leith, had won the second top gold and the top silver medal!

It was heady stuff, indeed. David von Salden, then wine-maker at Waterwheel, said years ago when we won the gold for the '82 Shiraz Cabernet, 'That is the stuff that dreams are made of!' And so to me, on that day, it was!

Sadly, the dream went sour a few years later when Bruce and Mary, having trouble selling their half of the wine, discounted it, despite my pleas, thus damaging the reputation of the label and, in some quarters, mine as well, for now wine that I was selling at $20 wholesale could be bought online for $20 retail! So that was the end of that. All that work wasted; I had done quite a bit of sales work in Sydney and had built a trusted clientele for the wine. I sent their next batches of already-made wine down to Bruce and Mary, and we had no trouble selling our share of it, labelled as Passing Clouds Reserve, over the following years and at a good price, for they were wonderful wines.

The year 2004 looked like being a good vintage. We would have fruit from all over the place, apart from our own crop which was restricted due to encroaching drought. There was again shiraz and cabernet from Wedderburn, and shiraz from Axedale, which had certainly proved its worth. I was first asked to make wine from there in 2002, for the directors of the company wanted some wine made for their own purposes and, as their previous contract had not been concluded happily, it was suggested that I should do it. I agreed. It was another vineyard from which to make wine, always an exciting challenge, and contract winemaking puts a bit of money in the bank more quickly than waiting for your own wines to mature in barrel and bottles before sale.

It was successful. I made some for them and some for me, until the company changed hands, after which we purchased for our requirements. There were some tense moments with the first 2004 batch, which was machine harvested. The magnets on the harvester that pluck any foreign ferrous metal object from the picked fruit must not have been working because heavy-duty vineyard staples came through the crusher and into our beautiful must pump below, seizing it when a staple jammed between the housing and the lovely sculptural form of the stainless-steel lobe that rotated and forced the must into the hose and then into the vats. We reversed the pump and fished it out, now a grotesquely shaped staple, leaving a scar on our beautiful machine, but before long another staple followed.

Brian White, the vineyard manager, who had stayed behind to help us before collecting his bins and returning to Axedale, rang his crew to inform them that they must have a problem with the magnets on the harvester, but it was too late for our batch and we had to painstakingly sort through the bunches on the slide between the bin tipper and the crusher, finding a couple more in the process.

As well, we had fruit from Zonnebeke, 5 kilometres down the road from Kingower, and some from another grower nearby, Richard McHardy at Wiela. Marian and Miwako had worked the previous vintage but they were both gone. Miwako was working at a winery in Japan. Marian and her boyfriend Sam, who had come to live with us and spent six months in the writer's garret above the garage while attempting the great Australian novel, had both returned to Sydney.

But the Angel flew in again. Susie McDonald, my wife Julien's niece, lived down the road, opposite Phil and Ann Adam at Zonnebeke in Ross and Dorothy Reading's old place, a house on 40 or so acres, and she used to come up to visit. She and her boyfriend Dominique were both involved with cooking and catering, and had cooked the last Queen's Birthday meal at Passing Clouds, a traditional thing we do to coincide with the release of the new wines. (The 'Ugly Uncles' come out to sing and to play their great music, we have wine tastings and barbecue fires, plus we serve 120 or so meals cooked in 'the big pan'. This is actually the cast iron end of an old boiler, saucer-shaped and able to cook an enormous amount of food. I think they did a cassoulet in 2003. I've never met a chef who has laid eyes on that pan and not wanted to cook something in it.)

Susie McDonald was a qualified Chinese medicine practitioner and needed a workplace. As it happened, Sue Mackinnon and I had bought a house over the road from the Kingower vineyard, directly opposite the entrance to the tasting room. It was a small place, about twenty years old, that Una Richardson had lived in until her departure to a better place in 2003. The bank agreed to stake us and we bought it for about $40,000 at auction. We were motivated to buy it because the idea of 'ferals' moving in did not appeal. There were some people in the area who tended to drive around in old V8s with bad exhaust systems during the night, then sleep most of the day at each other's houses if the recreational medicine had overwhelmed them. They also had a habit of driving the cars into the ground and leaving the expired carcasses at their houses. We couldn't have that at the entrance to our beautiful tasting room.

Anyway, the house across the road had been virtually empty for about twelve months and fitted the bill perfectly for Susie. We had the floors sanded and lacquered and some nice lighting put in. Susie installed the massage table and ran her practice from there for a couple of years. As her hands began giving her increasing trouble, her thoughts turned to winery work. Being an asthmatic she thought she could not work in a winery: some years earlier, when visiting a winery nearby, she had inhaled some sulphur fumes when sulphur was added to some white grapes being crushed. This is actually quite a hazardous practice because such fumes can be toxic. But after setting her mind at rest that Passing Clouds had no need of such methods, she decided to give the winery a go, and she took to it like a duck to water—except for eating and sleeping and emailing, for the whole vintage Susie was hardly ever out of the winery.

Winemaking is very much like large-volume cooking. Provided the basic foodstuffs are of top quality and everything is kept clean, the timing of all subsequent operations becomes critical, and perhaps that's the difference between a great chef and an ordinary one—and so with winemaking. Susie fitted neatly into the system and we became virtually a three-person team—Susie, Bill and me. Despite the age difference of about thirty years between Susie and me, we worked well together, developed a rapport and enjoyed each other's company, often carrying on like teenagers. This was just as well because it was at about this time that my wife suggested I leave Daylesford, so I appreciated support.

Thus I stayed at Kingower, working for the whole vintage, going to Musk only to net the vineyard and repair and maintain it as necessary, which was a continual burden. But grapes came thick and fast at Kingower; the quality was good, we had a good team, and we went for it. Who knew, we thought we might even turn a profit down the track in 2006 when the wine—after its one year in barrel and one year in bottle—was ready to sell.

That vintage we were to make sauvignon blanc from Zonnebeke and pinot grigio from Franklinford, as well as char-donnay from Wedderburn and our own vineyard. All these batches had to be fermented separately, all picked and crushed at the appropriate ripeness which, being dependent on the weather, was a matter of speculation. Sometimes rain would dilute the juice in the berries, particularly with pinot and char-donnay, which have a shallower root system than shiraz and cabernet, and at Kingower were showing more stress than the other varieties. Phil and Ann at Zonnebeke had some water available from their very large dam; it was beginning to lower now, but there was enough to keep the vines healthy, for they are planted on heavy granitic sand and need water. The Axedale fruit is also lightly irrigated and dedicated people, Brian and Sally, with whom we have cooperated for some years, keep the vines in perfect condition. They had some testing times when the drought broke in 2011 and some of their vineyard was swept away in the ensuing flood. They didn't need any irrigation that year!

A changing of the guard

In the years 2007–08 my ageing body was showing signs of deterioration; my knees had to be replaced with titanium ones, and various other bits and pieces needed repair. So it was decided that I should attend to these things and that my second son Cameron who, perhaps to his surprise, had caught the winemaking bug, would take a significant winemaking role. He was accepted into the Melbourne University oenology course at the Dookie Campus and showed an enthusiasm for learning that had been largely absent during his days at Ballarat Grammar School. Thus Passing Clouds was to continue and I was to pass the baton.

Tess Graham, the daughter of Geoff and Jan up the road a bit, was keen to work in the winery. Over the years she had been picking grapes on her family's vineyard for us, and had been a member of the (nearly) All-Girl After-School Pinot Noir Foot-Stomping Team. Tess was employed in the winery, and so another Leith male with a female assistant became the Passing Clouds winemaking duo.

I was fortunate enough to be cared for by my friend Jane Buck—she who had married my old mate Michael in England all those years ago. I lived with her at her house in Castlemaine, more or less between Musk and Kingower. So as well as having a friend in need and an expanded group of friends in Castlemaine, I could work at either place after the various recuperations.

Most of the work at Musk involved the tractor, so that when I was able to climb aboard the faithful Ferguson it wasn't too onerous, although attaching the various implements was often challenging. Cam and Tessa were going great guns with the winemaking at Kingower and I was only an hour's drive or a phone call away when I was occasionally required for advice or help. So we muddled along pretty well, the wines showing the traditional and desirable Passing Clouds characteristics.

As Sue Mackinnon's house was only 100 metres or so from the winery, we winery people were always toing and froing from there, and Cameron was learning more and more from Sue about the running of the business, for she did much of that from her home 'headquarters'. Sue's muscular condition had been declining over the years and she had taken to using an electric tricycle to get about. She would occasionally come over to the winery on her trike to be part of the winemaking. She loved being there and we always treated her like royalty.

This trike was becoming more complicated as Sue aged and her muscular atrophy insidiously stole her physical capacity. So that was another thing Cameron had to learn—Zen and the art of electric tricycle maintenance, which was becoming more demanding as time went by. The tricycle had been added to and modified to such an extent that it was like a sort of agricultural Ferrari, capable of great things but as temperamental as anything. If it wouldn't go up or down or sideways or backwards or forwards, then Cameron or I had to be summoned from the winery, or else Ray Smith, an electronics whiz from down the road. Sue referred to we three assistants collectively as the Dodgy Brothers. We lived in dread of the phone call to tell us that the trike was misbehaving and prayed that we could fix it, particularly if Sue was on it at the time, giving panicked and generally unhelpful suggestions. Launch time at Cape Canaveral was probably less stressful.

We had engaged the services of a bookkeeper, Jeanette, to help Sue with the increasingly onerous and time-consuming work attached to the previously simple business of running a small winery, now mired in bureaucratic complexity. Sue was having trouble in more ways than one, and had her sister Jill not been there, sharing the house and helping her, things would have been grim, indeed.

I wondered if anything more sinister was lurking because she seemed to be losing weight and seemed distracted at times.

I worried that she might be starving herself, so I went to see our friend Max, Sue's doctor, on some pretext and while there conveyed my fears to him. He didn't tell me what was wrong with Sue, but I left the surgery with the conviction that Sue had cancer. Our mutual friend and neighbour, Robin Hardiman, was soon to be diagnosed with pancreatic cancer and in fact was to predecease Sue, but hers was terminal also. Her life had run its course—there would be another eulogy to write.

The disease overcame Sue quickly, so that when death came it was a blessed relief. She died in peace, without her wonderful mind being obscured by the darkness of dementia, or her body racked with untreated pain. On the night before she died, our dear friend Karen Sloan (née Gilmore) and I sat on her bed and talked with her for a long time. Due to her painkilling medication Sue was not completely rational, and it seemed to Karen and me that she was unnecessarily distressed about something. It was as if she had some secret that she could not divulge, some fact that tormented her and wouldn't let her go. As gently as we could we tried repeatedly to make her see that whatever it was didn't matter, that she should forget it and escape the torment.

I said my goodbye to Sue, and as I left Karen took my hand. 'You just told her that it was all right to die now, didn't you, Poon?' I hadn't realised that I was doing that. Karen waited there with Sue for Jill, who'd been out visiting. At 3 a.m. Jill heard her dog Ridley howl and in the morning when she went to Sue's room, her soul had departed. She is buried in the Kingower cemetery next to her old friends John Sendy and Robin Hardiman, a stone's throw from where lie the ashes of Ondine and David, and of Vosje and Vosje's mother, who had requested her ashes be flown to Australia and buried beside those of her daughter and granddaughter.

An old friend of Sue's wrote to her on 10 April 2009, nineteen days before she died:

It looks like farewell to an exemplar of courage for
a great spread of friends (R.H. is going to beat you
to the exit though!). How well I remember your

amazing, searching eyes, and the beauty that has not
left your face—for a magnitude of years of physical
distress never did erase it. Thank you for all the caring
and witty friendship over the years. We are losing a
unique and treasured spirit. I hope that that Sweet
Sister Morphine lays a cool, cool hand on you (as
the Stones once sang). Goodbye, dear person, Roger
Dunn.

Mohammed to the mountain

Meanwhile, in the years leading up to 2010, the drought was
tightening its relentless grip on the Kingower vineyard and
those of our neighbours. It seemed to be approaching the
severity of the Federation drought, which lasted ten years,
breaking in 1908, and I was reminded of the theory held by
my late brother, the scientist Ian, that there was a seven-year
cycle of drought in Australia and that seven times that cycle
had produced a much worse forty-nine-year drought.

I thought back to my childhood, rabbit shooting with
Dad more than fifty years before in the drought-stricken
paddocks near Daylesford, where there seemed to be nothing
but dust and rabbits. I had read, also, of the breaking of that
Federation drought when, after ten years of declining rainfall,
there were ten days of intense heat followed by flooding rains
of such magnitude that dams burst and the watersheds of the
Campaspe and Loddon river systems were joined, something
that was to be virtually repeated in 2011.

Ten years previously Sue and I had had a bore put down
at Kingower in the hope of drought-proofing ourselves, but
the resultant water, although clear and tasting good to our
optimistic palates, proved too saline to be risked on vines.
However, in desperation we flooded the vineyard with our bore
water in 2004; although this initially seemed successful, later
the burning of the leaf tips from salt established that we could
not continue with this regime, so we kept hoping for rain.

The vines at Kingower were deteriorating, trunks were splitting and the Eutypa disease, which atrophies the leaves and canes, was encroaching on our vineyard and on that of our neighbours at Blanche Barkly.

Cameron and I began to toy with the idea of abandoning the Kingower winery and moving the winemaking operations to Musk, a bold and challenging prospect indeed, but one that had to be addressed if we were to continue running the business. It was unlikely that Cameron could continue to live at Kingower with his girl in Melbourne, and unlikely that I could maintain the winemaking and run the business at Kingower.

So we decided to take Mohammed to the mountain, to build another winery shed at Musk and move everything there. Much money and sixteen semitrailer loads later it was done, me avoiding most of the hassle of the actual moving by going to Bali for a month on the pretence of recovering from my final knee operation. The work was left to Cameron, Bill Ricardo and the unstoppable truckie 'Jungle Jim' Poynton, who as a youth years before had, at the Rheola Hall, uttered Hanrahan's immortal words, 'We'll all be rooned.'

But there were black clouds on the horizon, too. For many sleep-starved nights, worrying about (among other things) the disintegration of my family and the loss of my beloved Daylesford family house had a few years earlier begun to manifest themselves as the early stages of chronic depression. Some dark years followed but I managed to crawl slowly from my pit of despair and rejoin Cameron at work. I had not been completely idle in those depressed times and was still doing some winery work, and together we did some extensive building modifications to the Kingower house, a couple of times with Jesse working alongside us.

I had, for years, wanted to make some modifications to the house, putting in some French doors and changing a few doorways, but it was going to be challenging as the walls of the original were rammed earth, not an easy material to work with, and more than half a metre thick. Then one night something happened which stirred me into action.

For some weeks the pressure pump had been turning itself on at times when no water was being used. It seemed that water was escaping somewhere but no trace of a leak could be found. It was all very mysterious. On the night in question I'd had friends over for dinner. It had been a late night and I was sleeping soundly when I was rudely awoken by a sound, as if someone had tipped a gigantic wheelbarrow filled with earth and rocks through the door. Alarmed and frightened, I reached for the bedside lamp and in its light observed that the bedroom wall had turned largely to mud—and collapsed! My boots were floating in it! I turned the light off, rolled over and went back to sleep, relieved. Now I knew where the leak was.

In the morning I rang Cameron to let him know that we had another building project coming up, and asked Pete the plumber for a quote on replumbing the whole house, and started measuring up the new doorways.

The idea of my retirement vineyard at Musk had always embraced the idea of a cellar door and maybe a small cafe, so we set to after the winery was established. The first addition was a cellar door facility designed by my old friend and architect Simon Reed, and built by Simon the builder.

Simon Reed was always something of a jackdaw and knew where there were some doors available from a demolition site, doors that we would find useful for our new winery, so we took my white ute to Melbourne to collect them. We were halfway home with our load of doors on the tray when I stopped for petrol at Woodend. Simon offered to drive, as he liked driving utes and I could get on with some work on the laptop. Twenty minutes later something made me look up to see Simon asleep at the wheel and one of the largest eucalypts in the world looming up at 90 kilometres per hour. I managed to wrench the steering wheel to the right, missing the gum tree but not by much—the passenger side mirror exploded as we grazed it. Simon was apparently under medication for a heart condition and the medication, I later found, sometimes made him sleepy in the afternoons. The heart condition tragically killed him in

January 2013. Had we hit the tree, the 250 kilograms of doors on the ute's tray behind us would have sliced us both in half. Perhaps the Angel had tapped me on the shoulder.

When I got home to Jane's place that night, I said, 'You almost saw me on television tonight.'

She asked, 'Was it some winemaking do?'

'No, nothing as glamorous as that.'

Family matters

As someone once said: 'Family is not an important thing. It's everything.' I know how true this is, as I am blessed with three fine sons. As I wrote earlier, the close bond I have with my eldest son, Sebastian, and with my two younger sons, Cameron and Jesse, means everything to me and now, with three grand-children, my cup overfloweth.

We have many things in common, including a shared passion for the sport of fly-fishing for trout. I have fished with all my sons, but only once have we joined forces in a family fly-fishing expedition. A few years ago we all managed to get together and take our four-wheel drives to the Tasmanian Central Highlands, driving in on the perilous track to the remote Pillans and Julian lakes, high up in the Great Western Tiers, where we set up our base camp. Cameron, Sebastian and his partner Tania, and our friends Rod Whiteway and his daughter Tania, headed off with their packs and hike tents to explore and fish some of the remote back-country lakes, leaving Jesse and me to fish the waters near our base camp.

At one point Jesse spotted a huge trout and expertly fished for it. It took the fly and Jesse lifted the rod, but a little too powerfully, and the trout headed off like a torpedo with the fly in its jaw but now disconnected from the line. Had Jess landed that fish I think he would have become as dedicated as the rest of us, but it was 'the one that got away'. Instead he has recently purchased a motorcycle and gets his thrills riding it through the winding roads around Daylesford.

Sebastian, now aged forty-nine, lives with his partner Tania in Footscray, in Melbourne. Seb is not involved in the wine business, having made his career in agricultural chemicals and fertilisers. He and Tania have given me two beautiful and lively grandchildren, Mackenzie (six) and Ella (four), who love their 'Grandpa Beard' and delight in playing word games and ball games with him. I usually see the family when I am in Melbourne (last time we went to the zoo), and it's good when the family visits Musk or Kingower. Mackenzie bears the same name as a creek in the Grampians where Seb and I sometimes fished for trout. I cherish a photograph of a young Ondine and Sebastian standing in front of the MacKenzie Falls.

At twenty-eight years, Cameron is now the winemaker, and Passing Clouds is in good hands. Under him, this year's 2013 vintage is a triumph. The Musk vineyard is now fully mature after fifteen years. We have refined our vineyard management practices for this site, and we've enjoyed a good warm season. Cam has honed his pinot noir-making skills over the last few years and it's a pleasure to watch him and the winery crew put them into practice. Perhaps my greatest satisfaction is to taste the wines he has made and discuss their development with him. Cam and his wife Marion live at Hepburn Springs, not far from the Musk vineyard and winery. As I write, Cameron and Marion are expecting their first child—a third grandchild for me to love and the start of a life of parenthood for them.

My youngest son Jesse is working with me and Cameron at Passing Clouds now, running the sales and cellar door, a job at which he excels, for he sells wine to satisfied customers. When people leave that cellar door they are likely to know more about wine—certainly more about the wine they have purchased—than they did when they entered. Jesse, aged twenty-three, now lives at the old family house overlooking the lake at Daylesford, renting from his mother, my ex-wife Julien, who now owns it. I have been introduced to some lovely young girls by Jesse over the years and am the better for it!

So that's a snapshot of my immediate family as of the year 2013. Our futures promise to be just as diverse and interesting.

I'll probably sell the Kingower property and build a house at Musk to be closer to the action.

Why do we do it?

The cellar door at Musk is working well, so well in fact that now, at the time of writing, in the winter of 2013, we've sold out of chardonnay and pinot noir and have taken a small crusher to Coldstream and taken advantage once again of those wonderful McKernan grapes. We'll probably release them mid-2014 while we leave our cooler climate pinots and chardonnays to rest a little longer in the bottle.

Our traditional full-bodied reds are still being made to the old tried and trusted formulas: 60 per cent shiraz and 40 per cent cabernet for the Graeme's Blend, matured mainly in American oak; 90 per cent cabernet for the Angel Blend with the addition of 5 per cent each of merlot and cab franc, matured in French oak; and the Reserve Shiraz, made from riper fruit and matured in a mix of barrels—French from different forests, or fine-grained water-bent selected American barrels. All expensive, but to make the best wine possible the best ingredients and components must be used.

Several of our traditional growers were, like us at Kingower, experiencing difficulty getting large enough quantities of perfectly ripened fruit so we have been taking increasingly large parcels of fruit, microscopic in the overall scheme of Australian viticulture, from Zonnebeke at Rheola, from Axedale near Bendigo and, more recently, from the Turner's Crossing vineyard at nearby Serpentine, the cabernet from there showing the characters we require for the Angel Blend. Thus the adventure continues—our big reds live on, as does the name of Passing Clouds.

Why do we do it, though? What makes it an ongoing adventure is probably hard to explain. What makes us work with an almost fanatical zeal, for long and often inconvenient hours and for little financial reward when we could be doing something else—something less taxing on our minds, our bodies, our relationships? It is a constant journey that really has no end, for it is a succession of journeys, from vintage to vintage, each one promising something different from the one before, sometimes better, sometimes worse, but always different and always with the enticing, tantalising possibility that we can make a wine that is better than any we have ever made before, perhaps better than anybody has ever made before.

Just as a landscape gardener may never live long enough to see his plans reach glorious fruition, so winemakers (elderly ones, at least) are making wines they will never live long enough to see reach maturity. But still we do it.

Are we seeking some sort of immortality in a bottle? Probably. We seem to approach each new vintage with hope tempered by trepidation, for every one is a new challenge to be met. Sometimes when vintage approached, I used to relate myself to a line in Banjo Patterson's *The Man from Snowy River*—'And the stockhorse snuffs the battle with delight.' Vintage is a battle, always.

But vintage is more than merely a battle, for the winemaker must orchestrate the whole operation from grape picking to bottling. Indeed, he or she is like a conductor of an orchestra.

The instruments are assembled—the picking buckets, the trailer, the tractor. At the winery, awaiting the arrival of the grapes, the crusher lies in readiness like a giant bassoon asleep but about to wake and unleash its sound. The press is a torrent of brass restrained. The fermentation tanks are ready, waiting to be filled, the press crouches hungry, too. The barrels, freed of last year's vintage and now cleansed, lurk in the shadows.

The musicians are assembled—the pickers with their snips and buckets, the men to collect the grape-filled buckets, the winery workers waiting to receive them, and the winemaker about to weave his magic—or more accurately perhaps, to assist nature in the wondrous alchemic process that turns the prosaic grape into the poetry that is wine. When the hydrometer, in consultation with his palate, tells the wine-maker that all is ripe enough, then the baton is flourished and vintage commences. And there's no stopping it until the last grape is fermented.

Vintage is an exciting and all-consuming time, and when the last strains of the music fade and the winery floor is cleaned for the final time, we return home to reconnect with our trun-cated lives, hoping, selfishly, that our family is still there for us. We may have been away from reality, as it is generally known, for some months, but we weren't counting the days.

10

Making wine

Vintage

Winemaking, or vinification, is the production of wine, starting with selection of the grapes and ending with bottling the finished wine.

Vintage (the harvesting of wine grapes) is one of the most crucial steps in the process of winemaking. The time of harvest is determined primarily by the ripeness of the grape as measured by sugar, acid and tannin levels, with winemakers basing their decision to pick based on the style of wine they wish to produce. The weather can also shape the timetable of harvesting with the threat of heat, rain, hail and frost, which can damage the grapes and bring about various vine diseases. Spraying the foliage and bunches against the likely infection of mildew becomes a significant and time-consuming chore throughout the season; winemakers practising organic or biodynamic viticulture have a particularly stressful time of it during conditions that are favourable to disease.

At Kingower, grapes are usually harvested in about mid-March, and at our cooler-climate Musk winery as late as the first week in May. For us, vintage usually lasts about two months.

As vintage time comes around, we order in the yeast, along with some tartaric acid in crystalline form in case the wine requires additional acid. This is usually the case with very ripe fruit, because as the sugars in the grapes increase the acid falls away.

Ironically, perhaps, the tartaric has often been extracted from the residue of vintage, from the by-product 'marc'—the leftover pips and skins. Being so cool, our Musk vineyard does not require the addition of acid to the crushed grapes ('must'). There is plenty of it retained and it is one of the reasons why the vineyard is where it is, for naturally occurring acids seem to be superior to added tartaric. On the other hand, super-ripe shiraz may require 2 or more grams of tartaric per litre to ensure that the wine is not flabby or flat on the palate. The acid also has the virtue of being a preservative and explains the longevity of, for instance, cool-climate pinots and chardonnays compared to those from warmer climes.

In preparation for the harvest, as vintage time approaches, we clean our fermenters and move them into position inside the winery shed.

Our friends, the fermenters

Fermenters come in all shapes and sizes, from the humble but effective 'large saucepans' to the high-tech rotary fermenters that receive the grapes in one end and after several days of slow rotation—providing maceration without the need for plunging bulk or pumping over—eventually emit fermented must (the pulp of crushed grapes) out the other end, ready to be poured into the press.

At Passing Clouds our fermenters are all old stainless-steel milk vats of differing shapes, open (without lids), acquired over the years. They were all given girls' names, a more informal and pleasant way, we thought, of identifying and referring to them than numbers.

Anna, the largest, takes about 3 tons three times each vintage. Thus over the years—since 1980 when my partner Sue Mackinnon drove to Shepparton in the Telecom ute and brought her back to the winery with half an hour to spare before she was put into service—Anna has probably fermented 180 tons of grapes, or 108,000 bottles of wine, or comfortably more than a million dollars' worth(even at $10 a bottle).

In all, Passing Clouds uses twelve fermenters. As well as big Anna, there are Beryl, Claudia, Dionne, Esmé, Francine, Gertrude, Harriet, Ina, Marilyn, Olivia and finally Pamela, so named because she is such a masterpiece of the stainless-steel craftsman's work that I could not bear to cut her outer sheath off and remove the insulation as we had done with the others. There was a curvaceous and beautiful television actress named Pamela Anderson, and our new fermenter had beautifully rounded and voluptuous curves on her interior that conceal the cooling pipes within. On her flanks was a plaque showing that she had been proudly made by the Anderson Company. So, inevitably, Pamela.

All the open fermenters (except those that may be in use for whole-bunch foot-stomped treatment) are hand-plunged twice daily to force the floating 'cap' of skins down into the liquid wine beneath. The plunging tool we use has a shaft, or handle, welded to a stainless-steel plate, with an additional small handle set halfway up the shaft and at right angles to it, to allow for extra purchase.

Then, in 2002, we acquired two new 5000-litre variable capacity upright tanks. These can be used for either fermentation or storage so they are pivotal to our operations. As they have a water jacket they can be hooked up to the chiller and the ferment can be cooled. We can even wrap them in insulation and take the temperature down to sub-zero for cold stabilisation prior to bottling.

Our dedicated Japanese assistant at the time, Miwako, named them after the oldest women in Japan, 105-year-old twins with the Japanese equivalent names of Silver and Gold. Finally, Jill Burdett, from Old Loddon Wines at Bridgewater, lent us two other variable capacity tanks, hence they became Jill and her daughter Alisa. Although they are holding tanks, Silver, Gold, Jill and Alisa can also be used as fermenters if required, as they often are.

As noted, Anna is the largest of the open fermenters, holding almost 3 tons, and the other girls hold 1.5 tons down to about a half a ton in the case of Ina and Francine.

All of them can be moved with a forklift, so they are brought into the winery shed for the two-month vintage period. Then, when no longer required for fermentation purposes, they are taken back outside and parked under the peppercorn trees for the other ten months of the year, to allow the vacated part of the winery to be used for barrel storage.

The used barrels are thoroughly washed with the highly sophisticated barrel washer, a wheeled implement attached by hose to a large pressure washer. A rotating nozzle, slender enough to fit into the bung hole of the barrel, is inserted and the machine energised so that the nozzle turns, powered by its electric motor, every which way inside the barrel. The jet of water thus released can be varied in temperature from cold to steam and the force of the jet is powerful enough to dislodge unwanted tartrate crystals from the wooden staves of the barrel which then wash out of the bunghole of the upturned barrel. It wasn't always like this; in my early winemaking days I cleaned them using a piece of plastic pipe with slots cut into it at various angles. This was attached to a water hose inserted into the barrel and jiggled about, which was then rolled over on wooden rails and drained. This process was repeated until the water ran clear, but it was always an imprecise procedure, even later when we had a forklift and could raise the inverted barrel to a respectable height and insert the pressure washer lance. After washing, the barrels are then given some form of sulphur treatment (we burn sulphur rings inside them) to protect them from spoilage.

Selecting barrels for purchase is a complex business, as there are so many combinations and permutations: French, American or Hungarian? Barriques, hogsheads or puncheons? No toast, partial toast or full toast? Australian or French made? One-, two- or three-year air-dried timber? What forest—Vosjes, Limousin, Troncais, Missouri? How much are you prepared to pay?

You generally get what you pay for, and an extra tight-grained French oak barrel made by a reputable maker costs a lot. We are now in the age of the 'celebrity cooper'!

From berry to bottle

After the decision to harvest has been made, the grapes are usually hand-picked into plastic buckets then tipped into half-ton plastic or wooden bins and transported to the winery on a trailer or the back of a ute. In the case of mechanically harvested fruit, the harvester pours the grapes into the bins, travelling along beside it on a truck or trailer.

Usually, the grapes are lifted up with the forklift in half-ton boxes onto the bin tipper 2.3 metres above the ground. They are then tipped and raked out onto the stainless-steel slide and so down into the crusher/destemmer below.

We have had several crusher/destemmers over the years, of increasing sophistication. For instance, our current one can be adjusted to crush and destem in various ways. For basic wine-making it can be set so that the grape berries are fully crushed and the stalks are flung out the end by a series of paddles, like an Archimedean screw with arms. But its internal workings can be altered so that the grapes can be only partially crushed, or not crushed at all if whole-berry ferment is required. If whole-bunch fermentation is required—that is, the bunch goes into the ferment fruit, stalks and all—then we usually put the buckets onto the trailer instead of tipping them into the half-ton bins, and at the winery pour them direct from the buckets into the press hatch. This is a time- and energy-consuming business, but necessary if we want delicate treatment of the whites; so we usually do this with chardonnay.

For whole-bunch fermentation of pinot, we tip the grapes from the picking buckets directly into an open fermenter, say, Beryl or Dionne, and possibly leave them there for a couple of days under a plastic sheet lid and a protective CO_2 cover, for what is called a cold soak. They are usually given a dose of sulphur to eliminate any potential nasty bugs, then fermentation occurs naturally with wild or indigenous yeast or with the addition of one of the commercially available cultured yeasts.

As fermentation begins, the grapes—either whole-bunch or destemmed, depending on the winemaker's preference—are normally foot-stomped once or twice a day by people with very clean legs and feet. At Kingower the 'All-girl Foot-stomping Team' would get off the school bus, wash their feet and legs, then stomp away to the music on the ghettoblaster delivered by the bands or singers of their choice—as years went by, it was the Seekers' 'Georgie Girl' then, eventually, Aqua's 'I'm a Barbie Girl'. Foot-stomping is a traditional and gentle way of crushing the grapes, and still perhaps the best, especially for pinot noir. Large wineries with an eye to ultimate quality have alternative mechanical devices that replicate the work of the stompers.

If the grapes are being crushed/destemmed, then the must falls into the must pump below, under the crusher that delivers them into the various fermenting vats via a large hose. When each vat is full enough, or when changing batches, the hose is swapped over to another vat.

As with the crushers, we have had several presses over the years to press out the must after fermentation or, in the case of whole-bunch treatment, before fermentation. We began with a basic basket press, consisting of a cage or basket made with wooden slats sitting on a metal base, with a large threaded metal rod rising from the centre of the base onto which was placed a wooden lid. Then a very basic and very heavy metal ratchet device, with the aid of the handle, would be progressively cranked down as the juice was squeezed out into the stainless-steel tray beneath—a process that would take an hour or two until it was considered that enough tannin and colour had been extracted. The pressure would then be released by reversing the mechanism and cranking it up, at which time the two halves of the basket could be separated and removed, leaving a solid cake of skins and pips that could be pushed or forked onto the trailer to be taken out to the vineyard and spread beneath the vines as mulch. (In France, the skins and pips are often re-fermented with the addition of water and the resulting poor quality wine distilled into cheap brandy, or for the ubiquitous *marc de Bourgogne*.)

We finally ended up with three of those hand-cranked presses but our production became too much for them, so we purchased a second-hand Giaguaro Press that had a much larger basket and a hydraulic motor to force the lid down via a powerful ram. We really felt ourselves to be in Rolls-Royce country as the press automatically went about its work.

Later again, when we began harvesting serious quantities (for us) of chardonnay from Musk and began purchasing more red grapes, we bought an airbag press with a 1500-litre capacity. This meets our requirements, although even it is stretched at times, with the press—and the boys feeding and emptying it—being flat-out during the 2013 vintage at Musk.

The airbag press works on a simple principle and consists of a large horizontal drum, perforated on one side to allow the juice to run out. Within there is a large bladder or bag which lies deflated while the press is filled, either from the must pump or the buckets. The hatch is then closed and locked and the pressing cycle begins. This can be manually or automically controlled after the timer is set to the winemaker's requirements to take over the operation. From then on it cycles in a similar manner to a domestic clothes-washing machine; it rotates then stops with the perforated side facing down and begins to drain. The bag then inflates to force more juice from the pips and skins within. After the predetermined time, the bag deflates and the drum rotates, rolling the contents around for the set period; then it stops again and the bag inflates to a higher pressure and so on until the operation is complete. Towards the end of the pressing cycle, the winemaker observes and tastes the wine, now a trickle, and decides when to call 'full stop'. It is a truly wonderful machine. Comparing the resulting wine to that from the basket press we have no reason to prefer the basket-pressed wine with reds, and with whites the airbag press is, to our minds, definitely superior.

As fermentation progresses, if the temperature begins to rise towards an unacceptable level, the stainless-steel cooling coil is inserted into the must through which coolant is pumped from the moveable refrigeration unit, the 'gelati machine' as it is known here, for it makes things very cold and is made in Italy. In earlier times we had a little crusher/destemmer that just sat across the vat and we fed the buckets into it directly from the trailer as it arrived from the vineyard. Silver and Gold both have cooling water jackets built into their sides so the cooling unit hoses are connected to these, and this small but very effective machine can control fermenting temperatures in them as well as in the open fermenters. If required we can wrap the fermenters in insulation and cold-stabilise the whites and pinots down to –2 degrees Celsius. If this cold stabilisation is not carried out, then the bottled wine can drop crystals of tartrate—not harmful but not aesthetically pleasing to some.

Prior to bottling, the white wines are 'fined' or clarified by the addition of various clarifying substances, from isinglass (gelatin) to milk, most of which, perhaps surprisingly, have been used for centuries. At Passing Clouds we fine our reds with egg whites, which also soften the tannins.

Our Big Daddy is T1, a 13,000-litre holding tank where we put finished wine (blended in the tank if required) to be readied for bottling. Silver and Gold are usually put into service in their other role of holding or blending tanks at this time, as are Jill and Alisa, often Bertha and Little Silver. Cameron has recently purchased some more, so now we have Tessa and co. as well. The bottling and labelling is done by the contract bottling company, Portavin, which uses a semitrailer packed with high-tech machinery and conveyor belts—a veritable factory on wheels. After this the bottles are put into cartons, which are then folded, closed and pushed through the taping machine, after which the description of the wine is spray-painted onto the side of the carton. It then goes down the gravity roller conveyor to be stacked onto pallets on the ground, then wrapped and forklifted to the warehouse shed.

The full-bodied reds—the Graeme's Blend, the Angel and the shiraz—are not labelled, capsuled and cartoned until they get closer to the point of sale some years down the track. The exception is the ever-increasing amount of screw-capped wine, the bottles of which are laid down on specially designed plastic nests to avoid damage to the capsules.

It is an accounting nightmare, but we're not here for the 'quick quid'; we're here to make, mature and finally sell wine— wine as good as we can make it! Indeed, it could honestly be said that we're not here for any sort of quid at all. As James Halliday once wrote: 'A winery is a black hole into which you continually shovel money.'

On the rare occasions when people ask me about the financial aspects of the business, I cheerfully tell them: 'We don't make money, we make wine.' This is true. Sue and I have never paid ourselves more than a labourer's wage and, had I not sold my Melbourne house years ago to finance Passing Clouds, and had Sue not sold an investment property she was paying off, we would have been financially better off than we were as wine producers. But then we wouldn't have had the wonderful and exhilarating rollercoaster ride that the vineyard and winery took us on.

Sue was very proud of our achievements, that we had built it all from virtually nothing. Some criticised Sue's brother Hamish for not giving Sue money from Kaladbro, the Mackinnon family property on the Victorian–South Australian border. I once overheard a conversation between Sue and one of her visiting friends.

'You should get money from your family. Your brother lives like an Eastern potentate and you can't afford decent clothes!'

Sue replied, 'I've never done anything for Kaladbro. I don't need their money, they do.' And, indeed, Passing Clouds became better known than Kaladbro; no longer did people say to Hamish, 'Oh, you're one of the Mackinnons from the Western district.' It was more likely to be: 'Oh, your sister is a partner in Passing Clouds, isn't she?' However, she apparently did receive a small stipend from the family but I never knew what she did with it; I guess it went into her 'Going to Greece money' bank account which she used mainly for charity donations, though once she went into a syndicate with friends and bought a racehorse! Hamish at one stage managed to talk her into mortgaging her house for Kaladbro; perhaps that was why she thought they were poverty stricken.

Corks—Portuguese roulette!

We calculate the litreages and order the appropriate labels, capsules and corks. We used natural corks for many years but when I found myself referring to bottling time as 'Portuguese roulette'—for about 5 per cent of the bottles would be cork tainted and therefore spoiled to a greater or lesser extent, from having a slight unpleasant odour and taste, to being foul-tasting and undrinkable—we, with many others in the industry, sought alternative closures. It is more than annoying and frustrating to make the wine carefully and conscientiously, nurturing it through its various rackings, treating it like a baby, only to end up with about 5 per cent rendered unacceptable for drinking. This travesty is promoted by whacking pieces of cork bark into the bottles. Unfortunately, some of these corks are contaminated by a mouldy smell, 2,4,6-Trichloroanisole (TCA).

This travesty would be, of course, unacceptable with any other food product. Imagine what people would think if 5 per cent of their favourite cola had to be thrown away! It is as well that the Portuguese don't make brake pads for automobiles, or artificial valves for human hearts, where the 5 per cent failure rate could be more than embarrassing. They're lucky that cork taint does not kill!

According to the Portuguese the actual source of cork taint is still, amazingly, open to speculation. But the problem is certainly mould that exists in some of the bark before it is punched out into corks. I don't know how the Portuguese can get away with claiming they haven't worked it out yet! When a beagle dog at an airport can detect an apple in a suitcase or some cryopacked marijuana in a handbag, and the cork producers can't detect a foul odour in their own product, you have to wonder, don't you? You could write a PhD thesis on it. I wish someone would!

We have used screw caps since 2004, and also another product called Diam—still cork, but ground fine—bombarded with CO_2 in an autoclave that removes the taint. This cork powder, for it is apparently little more than that, is then moulded and compressed into a cork shape and colour. You then have a natural cork product that has no taint and, because of its uniformity, is less prone to leakage. For some years we have found them to be spot-on (so far, so good). My only regret is that the Portuguese are getting some money out of it, having cost us so much over the years. At one stage our American marketers asked for screw caps but the next year they wanted cork, as the fashion had changed, so we use Diam for them always.

Cork taint is really expensive for the industry. Often the consumer doesn't recognise or identify cork taint but rather assumes that a wine is badly made, or is just not nice to drink, and will not be buying that one again, thank you very much. And this, when the winemaker's only sin was using natural cork!

This is the reason, of course, that natural cork closures have largely been replaced with screw caps. The French are not immune from the curse, either—many wine waiters both here and in France have had to pour some very expensive French wine down the sink because of cork taint!

Bottles and labels

As bottling approaches, Diams and/or screw caps are ordered some months in advance, and these often have to be printed. You might have to order 30,000 to 50,000 to get a good price. Labels have to be printed for the new vintage year, alcohol levels established so that they can be stated on the label, and any other additions included. For example, 'fish products used' if isinglass (a dried product made from the swim bladder of the sturgeon) has been used for fining, or 'egg products used, traces may remain' if egg whites have been used for fining and tannin removal.

Bottles are ordered by the tens of thousands and are kept out of the sun even though they are plastic-wrapped when they arrive and washed by us before filling. Once we had a lot of bottles that were badly made—misshapen—and we had to abort the bottling until the men in suits came up from Melbourne and tried to get out of it as cheaply as they could, even offering to sell us the bodgie bottles at half-price. I told them, among other things, that I couldn't see the logic in that.

But usually it goes well, although in 2004 we had two boxes of Diams go missing. When they didn't arrive the carrier tracked one to Adelaide and a week later the other box to Brisbane, having a holiday in the sun—very difficult to bottle at Kingower when 5000 of your corks are in Brizzie! Susie brought the message back from headquarters that they'd been located. I rang to ask Sue what had gone wrong and, with typical Sue wit, she quoted from a Tom Lehrer song of the 1950s: 'I make ze rockets go up, but where zey come down, is not my department, said Werner von Braun.'

The operators of the bottling caravans have become friends over the years, but none of the original operators is still in operation. Even the Victorian chief Ian Matthews has sold his interest in the bottling line and now works as an adviser with the new company that took it over. However, he continued to visit Sue, always bringing a bottle of Sauternes; after dinner he would sit on the end of her bed and they would talk for hours while they sipped the unctuous nectar. If they didn't finish the bottle, he'd cook her breakfast in the morning and serve the remainder with it, insisting that it was the perfect accompaniment to that meal, before going back to work in Melbourne.

The hours are long and hard for the operators. When bottling or labelling for us is completed, they clean up, pack their gear, hook the 3-ton caravan onto their huge American utilities and go off to the next job—Rutherglen, Mornington Peninsula or wherever. Our loyal bottling crew—four for a bottling and five for a labelling—were locals. Kim and Jude used to come with their baby girls, who are now both mothers, and Kim and Jude still work with us, sometimes with their daughters Shae Maree and Zoe. The Collies, Ian and Barbara, were always there, as were Bill Ricardo for reliable backbone and Rohan the Ratbag to provide constant levity. The whole team was loyal and devoted to Passing Clouds, and if one couldn't work for some reason or other they'd find someone else to fill in. If we needed another couple of hours so that the operator could finish and move on to the next job, they always voted to work on even though they were almost exhausted after handling up to 20,000 bottles. They are the salt of the earth and we could not have done it without them.

In earlier days, before we could afford all the concrete required to use a forklift, we used to borrow a tractor with a fork attached. It was a terrifying thing to use, because from the glass-louvred cabin it wasn't possible to see the end of the forks, and we were glad to dispense with 'Mad Max' when we poured concrete slabs and could use a conventional forklift. Unfortunately, bottling often has to be done during vintage and that can mean that a winery crew and bottling crew have to work from the same location. That calls for some fine-tuning. We try to pick a lull in vintage proceedings but that's difficult when you are looking many weeks ahead, so sometimes we get caught with a forklift serving two masters, the picking crew and the bottling crew. When that happens, it makes for interesting times!

Pitfalls and pleasures

The 2004 vintage was the last really substantial vintage before the drought tightened its grip on us. In 2005 we bought more grapes as our own crop diminished, and an even greater proportion in 2006, and so on until we felt we had to call a halt to grape purchases in 2009. For, instead of *growing* $50,000 worth of grapes we were *buying* them in, and quality was becoming the major issue as our neighbouring vineyards fell victim to the drought.

We were still buying good quality fruit from the Adam family at nearby Rheola and some great shiraz from Axedale, located between Bendigo and Heathcote, and so kept the Graeme's Blend to a high quality standard. But the drought persisted, debilitating the vines at Kingower to the extent that the trunks on the harder soils were splitting and withering, and some vines were actually dying. By the end of the 2007–08 season, it was obvious that sections of our Kingower vineyard should be removed—it was simply not worth pruning, spraying and netting the remaining vines.

The bird prevention measures alone are always demanding, but the predations of kangaroos are becoming annually more troublesome, too. Their numbers used to be controlled by amateur shooters, as undesirable as that may be. But they were, and are, protected and it has become increasingly difficult for the young men to gain a shooter's licence unless they live on a farm and/or can establish that the firearm will be used to control pests. In 2006 I took to doing a kangaroo patrol before bedtime and again at 3 a.m. but they kept coming; there was nothing to eat in the bush. Carcasses on the road became more common, and at present cars that have run into kangaroos are the mainstays of the rural panel-beating industry.

The Musk vineyard, despite being deprived of that best of fertilisers—the master's foot upon the soil—has been producing more fruit annually, although the cost in terms of labour and stress are great. We kept a tractor and spray unit and slasher at Musk, but as I could no longer live in nearby Daylesford it meant a 100-kilometre trip each way from Kingower to spray or slash at Musk. We didn't have a proper shed there for many years, just a shipping container; the rest of it had to wait until the niceties of property settlement had been completed.

For all that, we hope and cheerfully anticipate that the 2013s live up to the great expectations we have of them in the barrel, and that we can continue to get excellent grapes for our big reds.

What the critics are saying

Here's a selection of reviews of our 2012 wines.

The Angel 2012 'Cabernet cannot get much more elegant than this without losing its mojo; the finesse of this wine is magical, as is its purity and balance. Enough to please a pinot drinker.' 96 points – James Halliday

Graeme's Blend Shiraz Cabernet 2012 'Yet another major success from 2012; blackcurrant and blackberry fruit play tag with each other on the bouquet and palate alike, the oak integrated and balanced, the gently savoury tannins doing no more than providing structure.' 94 points – James Halliday

Macedon Syrah 2012 'Standout wine in a bracket of Victorian Shiraz (or Syrah, if you are so inclined). Blackcurrant, cracked black pepper, violet perfume, grilled meat, touch of vanilla. Medium bodied, clean acidity, lovely silky tannin, some raspberry peeping through and a fresh finish. Delightful!' 94 points – Gary Walsh; Trophy – Best Shiraz, Macedon Ranges Wine Show

Kingower Vintage 2004

Diary of a typical year
by Graeme Leith (with Susie McDonald)

Tuesday, 23 March

The day dawns bright and clear. The Burdetts' fruit seems to be ready. It is grown at Bridgewater on Loddon, 15 kilometres away from Kingower. We buy some of the grapes outright and others we make up for the Burdetts to sell under their own label, Old Loddon Wines. The grapes are always good—Russell is a skilled and conscientious viticulturist and his wife Jill is a great supporter and organiser. Our tests show what experience has taught us is the correct level of ripeness for their varieties, merlot and cabernet franc, both at about 13 degrees baumé. We've been expecting the Zonnebeke sauvignon blanc to come in first but it stopped ripening at its predicted rate, probably due to a little stress from the heat, so it's the Burdetts' merlot and cab franc that are the first cabs off the rank.

Their first trailer-load arrives at about lunchtime. We forklift them onto the bin tipper, start the crusher, and with a person each side of the bin tipper slide, armed with rakes to drag the bunches down, we're away! Vintage proper has commenced!

Two tons go through the crusher uneventfully and the must is pumped into Jill and we make up the yeast culture right away—the sooner it's fermented the better.

The afternoon pick usually comes in at about 5.30 p.m. The grapes will be too warm from being on the vines in the sun, and we will leave them to cool down overnight because to add the yeast at this temperature would create an explosive situation—it would take off like a bushfire and be as hard to control. We don't like using Jill as a fermenter for it's hard to drag the pips and skins out of her when the free-run wine has been removed. She has a cooling jacket on her, useful for fermentation, and it looks as if we're going to need a lot of fermenters fairly quickly as, apart from the sauvignon blanc, everything is ripening fast in this hot weather.

A quick motorbike trip 5 kilometres to Phil and Anne at Zonnebeke and a tedious picking of single berries for a 300-berry sample taken for baumé across the vineyard reveals, on return to our laboratory, that it is now ready to go. As Phil and Anne have friends staying with them as house guests and potential pickers, they are ready to start picking, so we set it up for the morning. Phil brings his trailer up while we're crushing the last of the Burdett merlot and takes some half-ton boxes and bags to pick into.

We clean up the winery and get ready for the whites. We're often not sure how we will make this until we see the fruit come in, then we have to decide on whole-bunch pressing, crush/destem, or crush only into the press. If healthy, the stems or stalks don't detract from the quality of the wine and during pressing the stalks assist in draining. Then we add sulphur, to avoid oxidation spoilage, and also some specialised enzymes to assist separation of the solids and juice and, later, clarification. Whichever way it goes, we are going to need the cooling machine hooked up to one of the large tanks, with a cooling jacket—either Silver or Gold. The cabernet franc has cooled down to an acceptable 17 degrees Celsius and is now ready for yeast inoculation so that the cooler comes off Silver and goes on to Gold.

The Burdetts' afternoon pick fruit comes in at about 5 p.m. We unload the bins into the winery with the evaporative cooler on; we will crush them in the morning when they've lost some of their heat load.

Wednesday, 24 March

Comes the morning and we decide to crush the Burdetts' fruit without destemming, with a good dose of sulphur straight into the press through the big 100-millimetre hose, and away we go. There is still some warmth in the grapes in the middle of the bin, but it will average out okay. Refill the press and begin immediately to press out and pump into Gold, under cover of inert CO_2 to prevent oxidation, and when the level rises high enough in the tank to be influenced by the cooling jacket, we set the gelati machine into action.

'Woolly' Graham comes in with some pinot noir grapes from his block up the road. The Grahams have been growing grapes for us for many years and, although Kingower pinot noir fruit is now passé for pinot (we've moved to cool-climate fruit for our pinots), we'll take it and make it into rosé. It's ripe, so they get the go-ahead. ('Woolly' has had a cancer scare and chemotherapy, so has become bald. The local wags now call him 'Shawn'.)

Bill Humphreys comes in with samples of his merlot and cab franc and it's ripe, too, so he also gets the go-ahead. It's all about to happen—fast. We've cleared the skins and stalks from the first sauv blanc pressing and the second press is draining when the Burdett merlot comes in. We wash and clean up the bin tipper slide and crusher and put them all through, pumping the must across to Beryl, who is soon full. There's a bit too much for Beryl, so half a ton also goes into Francine.

We have a quick dinner then it's back to the winery to clean up in preparation for the morning, leaving Beryl to cool down a bit overnight.

Thursday, 25 March

The morning reveals the sauvignon blanc in Gold is down to 5 degrees Celsius; we'll leave it at that with the sulphur, but wrap it in an insulating blanket of foil-backed mat. Jill is bopping along nicely, starting to ferment well, but we have to keep an eye on her temperature. We add the yeast to Beryl and are ready for the first batch of the Humphreys' merlot, which comes in at about 11 a.m. and is crushed, destemmed and pumped into Claudia. We've just got that done when the Grahams' pinot arrives and we decide we're not going to have time to muck around making rosé, so we crush and destem it—it'll be a Kingower cleanskin pinot. Their cab franc is coming in next; they're picking it already.

Friday, 26 March

Crush and destem the rest of the Humphreys' merlot into
Dionne, and the Grahams' cab franc into Marilyn. Phil brings
in some samples of the Zonnebeke merlot, rejected five days
ago as it was down in baumé, but has now rocketed up—it's
13 degrees so they'll have to pick as soon as possible. We've got
to keep Anna free for the first shiraz so will crush into Olivia
(she holds 1.25 tons) and surplus can go into Esmé then Ina.

Jill has reached the danger point of fermentation as the
amount of yeast cells is at a maximum, so we put the cooler
on her to control the temperature before it takes off. We give
Gold another couple of hours cooling before changeover. We've
added some bentonite to help her clarify and drop some lees
sediment and clean up the juice prior to ferment, and we'll
soon rack her off into Silver. Somebody told me of a new yeast
strain that works well with sauv blanc so I've ordered some of
that; it's the most sauv blanc we've made so we may as well give
it every chance of success.

Saturday, 27 March

Zonnebeke merlot comes in early afternoon. The morning
is taken up with testing samples from our home vineyard,
Zonnebeke cabernet and Richard McHardy's shiraz from Weila
just down the road. Normal winery duties are taking up quite
a lot of time now; every vat is hand-plunged for ten minutes or
so, then temperature, pH and baumé taken and recorded on
the whiteboard, so that we can track the rate of fermentation of
any particular batch at a glance.

We crush the Zonnebeke fruit and do the afternoon
plunging, then have a quick meal at the house and go back to
the winery to clean up. I stay back alone in the winery after
Susie has gone home. I love to have a glass or two of wine in the
company of the vats, listening to the murmur of the ferments,
hearing 'the girls' whispering to each other, luxuriating in the
aromas and, less enjoyably, worrying about where we're going

to fit everything when the shiraz comes in. Apart from the open fermenters, we can ferment in Silver and Gold, which will take more than 4 tons each and have the advantage of being able to be pumped over—that is, connecting the inlet hose of the pump to the lower valve, opening it up and pumping the cooler unoxygenated juice from the lower section and spraying it onto the cap of the ferment above. This was a perilous business at one stage when we had to do it from ladders. But now we stand on our wonderful new catwalk and do it in safety and comfort. The 2-inch pump we use creates enough force for the wine to break through the tough skins, making hand-plunging unnecessary. I've been comparing the wines resulting from both the hand-plunged and the pumped-over for years, and at this stage can see very little difference. This is gratifying as it's a lot easier to turn on a pump and hold a hose than physically force the cap under with the plunging tool.

Plunging can require considerable effort or weight. One morning years ago, my then assistant, the diminutive Winifred, called to me for help; she was trying to punch a cabernet ferment with particularly tough skins and couldn't break through the cap, so was bouncing up and down on the plunging tool like a kid on a pogo stick. I lent her a bit of weight and we both had a good laugh. China Gleeson, on the other hand, who worked for many vintages, used to love plunging; it was the one time of the year he got to lose some fat and put on muscle.

Sunday, 28 March

All the merlot and cab franc are in and start fermenting, all is under control, normal winery duties proceeding, things looking good. After plunging we go to the Grahams for a barbecue.

Monday, 29 March

All still appears to be under control and God is in his Heaven. Then while we're having coffee after the morning plunging, there's a huge bang up near Gold and Silver and a resounding clang as if giant stainless-steel cymbals have been struck. We drop everything and rush up. There's a lovely smell of fermenting sauvignon blanc. The wild yeasts have decided that they can dominate my sulphur additions and my cooling, and have taken off in Silver. I'm sure this wouldn't happen in a more professional place. The lid had a solid silicon bung in it and as the carbon dioxide was produced and the pressure grew, the silicon bung resisted it, but the silicon tube around the variable capacity lid could not—it proved too powerful for the tube and let go, sending that 2-metre wide metal lid flying.

No damage is done except to the tube, which is shredded, so we decide now is a good time to rack from the custard-like bentonite lees into Silver, ready for further fermentation, which hydrometer readings confirm is well underway. And I still haven't received my special expensive sauvignon blanc yeast! If it comes in time we'll put some in anyway, and although it won't dominate the wild yeast it will at least work with it—harmoniously, we hope.

Tuesday, 30 March

I'm awoken at 3.45 a.m. by Bruno running around the house whining and barking; he can hear a thunderstorm coming, or senses it. I can hear or see nothing so I suppose he senses it. I try to comfort him but he is trembling, clearly distressed. I'm glad I didn't let him out last night. Last year at Daylesford he took off prior to a thunderstorm and mercifully was found the next day by a considerate neighbour who had a hunch and looked in the old change rooms by the lake where he found Bruno, hiding in the corner, long after the storm had passed. I suppose that golden retrievers go to earth in storms for reasons best known to themselves.

Too late to try to sleep again, so I go over the dry creek to the winery with Bruno on a strong chain—a novelty for him. The sauv blanc is sitting comfortably at 12 degrees Celsius due to the ministrations of the cooling machine. All other temperatures are good so I plunge the reds or pump over according to the vessel, and by the time Bill gets to the winery at 7.30 a.m. we are clear to get everything ready for pressing the Burdett merlot out from the tank that Jill Burdett has lent me. But we decide after an hour's bucketing and carrying to the press that she (now named Jill) is not a good fermenter for red wines. It's just too hard to get the skins and pips out; the sides are too high to remove them from the top and the hatch is too small to successfully remove them from the bottom. But Susie and Bill pitch into it with goodwill and humour and we have the press loaded and running by eleven. I've done some calculations and booked the pickers for tomorrow, Wednesday. I have to go to Melbourne today via Daylesford so I'd better leave at 12.30 p.m.

More than an hour to Daylesford. I get there, shower, change then collect the things son Cameron wants dropped off at his lodgings in Russell Street in Melbourne. Surfboard I can find, likewise wetsuit, but I can't find the didgeridoo or the runners. Quick phone call to Cam, who's fortunately not in class, and we sort that out. I find the didge and the runners.

Vince Tallarida is modifying some draining screens that I bought from him for Silver and Gold; they don't work properly on our unirrigated fruit. Susie has washed the shredded tube from Silver and put it in the ute. I want to show it to Vince for fun and ask for my money back, tongue firmly in cheek. Get to his factory in Brunswick, close to the city, and have to wait a while before Vince can give me his attention. I collect the modified screens and show Vince the exploded tube. I had noticed a pleasant and fruity aroma in the car on the way down and vaguely wondered where it was coming from. Vince could smell it on the tube and said, 'You've been making something nice and aromatic in that tank. Sauv blanc, perhaps?' Spot on, Vince!

I'm due at the Windsor Hotel for the annual Stonier International Pinot Noir Tasting which I feel I need to attend every year, despite it being held during my vintage, because there we can learn more about the elusive pinot noir, tasting and discussing the best from around the world.

Through the traffic to Russell Street, give Cameron a call on the mobile as arranged, to Victoria Hall where he meets me and takes his stuff, a quick chat, and then off to the Windsor. Get a park dead opposite the entrance, charge the meter and I'm inside by 5.40 p.m. for enrolment, a glass of bubbly and a couple of nori rolls before filing in.

Say hello to James Halliday, leading wine judge and writer, who says, 'You must be pleased with your '02s.'

'Yes,' I agree smugly, 'particularly the Coldstream Pinot that beat the Coldstream Hills ones.'

'Do you mean the Three Wise Men?'

'No,' I explain, 'the Passing Clouds one—made from fruit I purchased from the McKernans just down the road from your place.'

Len Evans is there and James begins berating him for not having acknowledged the case of Reserve Coldstream Hills Chardonnay James had sent him. He defends himself on the grounds that he thought someone else had sent it. For two senior gentlemen they have a lot of boyish fun.

The tasting is as good as ever. Grant van Every is our table captain, and when he asks to talk on the first flight of five wines, I suggest that in order to save time we try to knock out the ones we clearly don't like due to supposed faults and concentrate on the others. Each 'flight' consists of five glasses of wine identified only by number. The idea is that the tasters will evaluate and rate the wines during discussion with the others at the table. The provenance of the wines is revealed later.

Grant suggests I start with one, so I have a go at number three that to me seems to clearly have a fault. Grant says, 'Yes, brettomyces.' (Wine with brett tastes 'dirty' to most people.) However, Chris at the table says he likes it. Later Grant told me that one of the wineries represented here has had its problems with 'brett' for years and that could be it. When the wines were unmasked later it turned out to be from that winery, and surprisingly (to me), because I can't abide the smell or taste of brett, gathered some conditional approving comment from the panel.

The guest panellist, Jean-Pierre De Smet, chose French wines as his preferred. One Australian wine got a hammering from everybody, particularly Halliday, for over-the-top ripeness; the winemaker was not there so everybody could get stuck into him in his absence. The judging panel made thought-provoking and sometimes controversial comments. Len Evans has always liked to provide a contrary point of view, as he considers structure more important than other qualities; he may well be right, and he gets everyone thinking. Can't help but admire their palates, wine memories and perception—that is why they're judges and I'm a mere winemaker, I suppose.

Gary Baldwin, winemaking consultant, comes up to say hello after the tasting and agrees that number three has problems and commented that some people don't see some taste aspects of 'brett' as a bad thing. At any gathering of wine people you always learn something and it's often something you don't expect to learn.

A buffet meal, mostly salmon for me, then out into the night where the wind is blowing hard at 9.30 p.m. I think of Musk where the wind will be twice as strong and decide to take the Ballarat Road rather than the Calder Highway. If I take the Calder I then go to Daylesford on the Woodend–Daylesford road past Musk and will not be able to resist the temptation to drive in and look at my nets, knowing that if they're blowing off I'll be trying to lash them down in my suit in the darkness and the gale. Fool on the Hill, indeed! No, better wait until morning and repair whatever damage there may be in the daylight when the wind has abated.

I drive up to the family house at 11 p.m. to see the white Magna in the driveway and the bedroom light on. Julien is home—is this good or bad? It's bad.

'I thought you were staying in Melbourne,' she says. 'Jesse said so.'

'No, I told you the night before last that I wasn't. In any case I wouldn't have left Bruno overnight in the backyard without running it past you.'

Wordless and furious she dresses, goes out to her car and drives off to somewhere. I drink a lovely little stubby of Heineken and go to bed on my side of the now-deserted marital couch. I don't need the guest room.

Wednesday, 31 March

Son Jesse, 14, wakes up in the morning expecting to be greeted by his mother, does a double-take and says, 'Hello, Dad.'

Jess is off to school. 'Will I make your sandwich?'

'No, buying lunch today, Dad. Have you got $5 on you?'

'Okay. How was yesterday's sandwich?'

'Dunno, didn't eat it.'

'Why not?'

'Forgot.'

'Okay, get it out of your bag and put it on the table. I might have it for lunch today, and if it's too far gone Bruno can have it.'

A quick goodbye hug then Jesse's off to the school bus and I go to Musk where inspection surprisingly reveals no damage, and then it's on to Kingower, not fast for once.

I haven't heard from the winery crew, so assume that everything must be okay. Susie and Bill are pressing out so it's a relaxed drive, and as I travel I speculate that this is probably my 3000th or so trip from Daylesford to Kingower. For the first three years or so, I often did it on the motorbike, the mighty Honda F1 750, and sometimes in the car. But as I increasingly had a dog or a case of wine or more, sometimes twenty cases, the motorbike fell into disuse and the Alfasud would do many punishing trips at speeds up to 180 kilometres per hour. The Alfa finally succumbed to electrical gremlins and odometer fatigue, although it still looked good to me and was still fun to drive—maybe like an ageing girlfriend with whom you've had many good times. So the first of the Hilux diesel utes was purchased and the Telecom ute left unregistered and relegated to vineyard use only. The return trip is 200 kilometres per day, so in three years that's about 150,000 kilometres. Then for the next nine years or so I stayed overnight at Passing Clouds sometimes, especially in winter, so would then see the family every day, breakfast one day and dinner the next, probably averaging two-and-a-half trips per week, or 500 kilometres. Nine years at 25,000 kilometres per year, or 225,000 plus 150,000 = 375,000 kilometres. RACV research shows it costs $1.40 per kilometre to run a medium-sized diesel four-wheel drive, or $500,000 over twelve years. That's a lot of money and time to go to work! But then a contributing factor to the demise of my first marriage was my failure to change the location of our family.

I arrive back at Kingower to find everything working like a German band—Susie and Bill pressing, pickers picking, good cabernet coming from our own vineyard, very ripe but no shrivel yet, very healthy bunches. Our neighbour Mark Gilmore picked his cabernet in his vineyard, adjoining Passing Clouds, on Saturday, at 13 degrees baumé. Ours tasted riper, his soil a little hungrier and drier with some stress showing. Ours is now coming in at just over 14 degrees baumé. In the old days everyone seemed to pick at about 12.5 degrees baumé, but over the years we've steadily moved it up a per cent or two, as have most other people. The wine risks losing a little varietal and regional character, but seems to be compensated for by increased colour, tannin and mouthfeel due to the higher glycerol associated with the higher alcohol. Six pickers out there in our vineyard. They end up with 1.6 tons for the day, as they started on the sloping side of the vineyard where the fruit is small and light in weight.

Richard McHardy comes in with samples of his shiraz that has miraculously jumped from 13 to 15-plus baumé in the week. This is not possible! On questioning, it turns out that the previous sample was from the Scott Henry trellised section that hadn't seen as much water as the VSP (vertical shoot positioned) which, maybe due to the extra water and consequent additional healthy foliage, has ripened faster. I ask Richard to get some pickers into the VSP ASAP! I don't really want a lot of 16 per cent alcohol monster shiraz—a little, maybe, for our microscopic share of the American market, but certainly not for the Graeme's Blend.

Have Jesse's sandwich for lunch. Not bad. Thanks, Julien.

The pinot grigio is fermented almost to dryness; we will give it a bit longer before stopping the fermentation and leave it with a tiny bit of sweetness to enhance the flavour. Lesley, the grower, won a medal with it last year and that's why she wanted us to make it again, but making small batches with somebody else's precious fruit is a great responsibility. The sauvignon blanc is at 4 degrees baumé and tasting delicious.

The pickers go home, we continue crushing, and the battery-powered bin tipper stutters to a halt. Between the bin tipper and forklift it looks as if we have battery problems. I ask Bill to slip into town and buy a couple of new ones. We finish the crushing and clean-up, and Bill installs the new batteries. 'Hey, boss, do you know what year you bought those batteries?'

'Well, yes, Bill, probably 1998.' My parsimonious Scottish heritage coming back to bite me!

We finish the plunging, Bill goes home and Susie and I taste the thirty-one barrels I've laid out on the concrete, ready for their final racking prior to their ultimate blending and bottling sometime down the track. Sue will book the bottling caravan and order the bottles and corks when we give her the estimated quantities. Susie and I have some biscuits and camembert and share a bottle of the '03 Narre Warren East Pinot Noir, our first taste since bottling about three weeks ago. We taste it with some apprehension for there were a few green berries in the crush although the baumé readings were spot on. We're happy with it. It doesn't have the seductive cherry liqueur character of the 2002; it's a little more vegetative but certainly not green. It's early days yet, so all's well and, anyway, I think I heard somewhere that the most famous pinot in the world, the Domaine Romanee Conti, shows a tiny touch of green in its youth!

Later with dinner we try one of the 15.6 baumé shiraz that I contract-made for a couple of chaps two years ago, but it overpowers the steak and we only have a glass each. I'm not happy with these monster shiraz we make these days in terms of where they fit with food, particularly those that have some residual sugar. I wonder what's the point—to me, they're neither fish nor fowl, neither savoury nor sweet, and who needs that much alcohol anyway? It means a glass or two less of really good, lower alcohol wine you can drink in your life. However, they can be very seductive and people's eyes often widen with surprised delight when they are presented with one of these big wines in the tasting room.

Thursday, 1 April

Richard McHardy's shiraz keeps arriving—he only has a small trailer so he brings it one half-ton box at a time. I don't know about the logistics at the other end but it works for him and for us as well, for we unload his box, he goes back with an empty one, and we crush when we've got 2 tons or so. This enables Susie and me to fine, with egg white, the laid-out barrels of last year's shiraz. Our big tanks are all going to be spoken for, so we rack each barrel off lees (sediment) and into a clean one with the beaten egg whites and restack them.

The truck arrives with new barrels and Bill gets them off, but we find that there are only ten instead of eleven. The forklift is running erratically so I get Bill to clean the spark plugs while I get on the 'dog and bone'. We've got some pickers coming tomorrow and Vanessa Buck is arriving soon for her annual working pilgrimage to Passing Clouds; we'll need her again this year. The cooling unit (the 'gelati machine') is working flat-out as we move its cooling coil from tank to tank to control temperatures. In the old days during a hot spell I would sleep in the garage (for that was what the old winery then was) and set the alarm for every two hours or so. One night Halley's Comet went over when we had a houseful of pickers, and they all got up at some stage through the night to have a look at it and thought that while they were up they might as well go to the toilet. The pressure pump for refilling the toilet cistern did that thing that pressure pumps noisily and incessantly do, cutting in and out, and it was in the winery shed, very close to my 'bed' on the floor, so I didn't need the alarm clock on that best-forgotten night.

Dinner tonight—flathead that Vanessa has brought up, as arranged, with Susie's special vegetables and a couple of bottles of reisling that I 'home made' from a few vines we have here. It's surprisingly good. And I then spoil us with a bottle of the 2001 Gold Medal Three Wise Men Pinot, which is spectacular and provides a unique experience to some—not everybody gets to drink gold medal pinot noir.

The weather report tells me there's a gale warning for Port Phillip Bay—therefore strong winds at Musk. Can't be helped. As Jesse said to me recently, 'Don't worry about anything that you can't change, Dad.'

Friday, 2 April

Beautiful day dawns bright and clear, a good team ready to go. Hugo, family friend and uni student, came up with his mother Mary last night. He's a good strong lad and also has a killer wit which endears him to me—a good addition to the team. We've got Kim, Jude, Barb, Ian and Rohan the human gramophone out there picking. Hugo and Vanessa have dropped the picking bins out and then they're away on the creek block shiraz.

Some years ago I had a lovely young Englishman named William Wolseley working here and staying with me. He was obsessed with pinot noir, and while pruning, whenever he'd find a gap in the shiraz, he'd stick a pinot cutting in. Against all odds they prospered and so when the first load of grapes arrived it was disconcerting to see some very overripe pinot bunches among the shiraz. My first inclination was to remove them, a time-consuming business on such a busy day. I think I'd read somewhere that the legendary Hunter Valley winemaker

Maurice O'Shea had once made a wine, later to become famous, from this unlikely combination of pinot and shiraz, so we left them in. William left Kingower in 1983 with his car carrying the canoe he'd made in the tasting room on the roof rack and the boot full of shiraz and pinot cuttings, to establish his own vineyard, which he did, on the Bellarine Peninsula. I haven't been there to visit him yet, but I will!

I've got to go to Wedderburn to check the ripeness of Beau Foster's fruit—it's a 30-kilometre trip so I jump on the motorbike. The fruit's good, and ripe enough, so I give him the go-ahead; he's got pickers ready. Coming back I open the throttle and, as the speed rises, something strange and frightening happens—at 160 kilometres per hour there's a bang, a shock and the bloody bike starts violently shaking its head. I am going to die. My life flashes before me—all the close shaves I've had on motorbikes or in cars—and now they're going to scrape my remains off this lonely road. Then as suddenly as it started, the violent shaking stops. I am to live!

I halt the bike and examine the wheels and brakes. All is in order, so I slowly ride back to the point where it happened and there's the culprit, a pothole about the shape and size of a large pudding basin.

This motorcycle is a Honda 250 CBR. It is a street racer and accelerates at a phenomenal rate, but is not a country-road high-speed tourer and it doesn't have a shock absorber for the steering. Cameron (who is overseas right now) and I more or less share the bike. He was living in the city at the time when I got it and, as his work was about 5 kilometres away, he needed something that would accelerate from 0 to 100 in nanoseconds to get to work and open up the bar. When Cameron returned from overseas, I said to him, 'Cam, this thing's a widow-maker on country roads, we've got to sell it to somebody in the city.' But he didn't believe me and it was only when he hit a bump mid-corner at high speed and had a similar experience that he actually agreed. And so we sold it.

Soon Beau Foster arrives from Wedderburn with his huge trailer loaded to the gunwales with shiraz, most of which had been picked last night. There'll be a few more loads before the weekend is over. Some cab sauv comes in from Bill and Margaret Humphreys from their vineyard just down the road. He's a good operator and I don't have to worry about his fruit quality. He's nicknamed Billy Merlot for that is what he mostly grows, with some cab franc and some cab sauv, part of which we buy and some of which we make up for his own label, Hallmark.

The weighing machine begins to give crazy readings. These electronic devices are anarchic and evil sometimes, and the bane of my life. This one, I'm beginning to conclude, only works with a fully charged battery. If I had another battery charger I could probably hook it up semi-permanently, but the battery charger is required to top up the bin tipper battery.

So the shiraz keeps pouring in—it is load, unload, tip them onto the chute, rake them into the crusher, crush, destem, change the hose over to the next fermenter, get rid of the stalks. It seems to go on ad infinitum and always with the added spice that something might break down any time!

Bruce Jones rings, wants to pick Wednesday but will confirm tomorrow. Presumably he needs to organise pickers—he uses the Cambodian crew, who turn up by the white van full and are generally considered more reliable than part-time Aussies, and everybody probably needs them at the same time. He's expecting about 6.5 tons of pinot for the Three Wise Men.

Robert McKernan rings from Coldstream; he, too, would like to pick soon but the baumé on his pinot is not quite high enough for us—a compromise might have to be reached. He's got a whole season's work hanging on the vines, increasingly vulnerable to mildew as it's too late to spray them again because we are well into the withholding period.

The team is still working like a German band. I offer Susie a couple of days off but she won't take them, thank the Lord. Bruno, ever the retriever, appears with a pair of panties in his mouth; nobody seems to know where they came from.

Saturday, 3 April

All still happening, the roar of the crusher the dominant sound
in the winery—our fruit, Richard McHardy's, Beau Foster's and
a bit from the Humphreys. Weighing machine still playing up.
Finally get chardonnay racked from Bertha into barrel ready
for Zonnebeke.

Sunday, 4 April

An 8.30 start for pickers. Bloody weighing machine playing
up. *Okay, machine, if you like high voltage, I'll give you some!*
I measure the voltage that the battery charger gives out, it's
18 volts, much higher than the 12 volts that the machine is
supposed to require, but I hook it up direct to the charger and
it works perfectly.

PS (and for the rest of vintage): I am buying some grapes
from that really good vineyard at Axedale. I know it's good for
I have made some contract wine from there for the owners.
Stefano de Pieri and I have decided to make a wine to be sold
exclusively at his restaurant and I reckon these grapes will
fit the bill. A large wine company tasted some of the wine
I made, did a trial batch of their own last year, and are now
purchasing the bulk of the grapes for one of their prestige
labels. The fruit is machine-harvested and, as they're not
going to crank up the machine for our pathetic few tons, we'll
have to take ours at the same time, so I've got to ring Vinni
the vineyard manager soon.

We start off by working through last night's backlog of
grapes. Vanessa working like a Trojan. Susie and I start on
emptying Silver into the airbag press, never an easy job. The
big pump has to serve two masters, the press and the crusher,
so the crushing has to wait a while. Things are starting to look
a bit frantic when the Angel flies in to help: Richard's picking
crew has been reduced to four so that'll take some pressure off.
(There must have been a big party last night at Korong Vale,
where his pickers live.)

Bill comes in after lunch, having returned from shopping with wife Marion who doesn't drive, and brings with him a new battery charger—our worries should be over! Susie's neck is bad; she didn't have much sleep last night but she elects to stay, so we rack T2 to barrel and the balance into Jill to give us room for the Angel Blend and we're all fined and cleaned up by 6.30 p.m. Yeast into Silver, now with about 4000 litres in her. As we move barrels out, we put Olivia in place ready for the next onslaught. Bruce and Robert both phone again, worried about ripeness.

Oldest son Sebastian calls me about coming up to Kingower on Friday. He usually comes up to help his old school mate, Mark Gilmore from next door, during vintage. It gives him a chance to catch up and work with his other Kingower friends and stay with his old 'Da'. I look forward to this. It'll be good to spend some time with him. Youngest son Jesse rings; I had called earlier to ask Julien if she'd take Jesse out to Musk to check nets. Jess reports one rip repaired and birds driven out. This might be so.

Monday, 5 April

Trying to talk to Vinni on the phone with Hugo's licorice sticking my teeth together. The panties that Bruno found had disappeared but now are returned. We wash them and hang them on their stick for Susie's friend Domenique to see; for some reason they seem to annoy him so we keep doing it. He brings a sandwich along for Susie's lunch but doesn't comment. Marian, who used to work and live with us with her boyfriend Sam while he wrote the Great Australian Novel, has driven from Cobram to help us. Great to see Maz again. She has brought with her a huge zucchini frittata thing, which is delicious and so doesn't last long. Susie and I keep nipping over to the house fridge and eating large slices of it while the other's back is turned.

Vinni rings back to say he thinks Monday next week will be okay for our shiraz. If we manage a big pressing on Sunday, we should be clear—we've got a lot of ferments going now and some should be ready to come out by the weekend. Bruce Jones calls to change picking to Thursday—grapes should arrive at 8 p.m. in a temperature-controlled truck. Robert McKernan rings, very disconsolate and verging on panic; the latest weather report is very bad for Yarra Valley and he doesn't think the grapes will hold out over Easter. If it does rain heavily as forecast, then the sugar levels will drop and we'll be worse off than we are now, so I suggest a compromise: pick two-thirds before Easter and leave one-third on the vines in the hope of a bit of Indian Summer that we often get at this time of the year. We'd better go for it. Can he pick Friday and Saturday? Do Cambodians observe Good Friday?

I do some calculations: we'll need more fermentation vessels than we have, so I ring and order a batch of Fermenta bags, large plastic bags in which wine can be fermented. They only hold a half-ton each, but we'll need them, and I've always wanted to try making some pinot in them. They can apparently produce good results; you simply fill them up with must, or even whole bunches if they'll fit through the orifice, add some yeast culture, screw the lid on with its tube sticking out the top to allow the carbon dioxide to escape and no oxygen to enter, then leave it to its own devices. If you want some post-fermentation maceration, then you just leave the must in the bag for as long as required. There's even a cooling jacket on the outer skin through which cold water can be circulated if needed.

One of Susie's patients, a local farmer, has hurt his back, so even though she has told people that the clinic is closed for the duration of vintage she takes pity on him and nips over the road to her clinic to treat him. Vinni rings back from Axedale; the large company has done its tests on the Axedale fruit and insists that they be harvested Friday and Saturday, so that means ours, too. Susie returns an hour after she left to find that all has changed in that hour. We are looking at all our fermenters being filled to capacity and more than 20 tons of fruit arriving over Easter. We've got to hope that those Fermenta bags arrive on time or we're in serious trouble, although we can start pressing out Dionne and Esmé on Friday. Bill won't be here but Vanessa and her friend Vicky should be here Friday afternoon, and maybe Jesse as well, if he can get a lift from Daylesford.

Richard McHardy's car has broken down towing its penultimate load and is stranded up the road a bit. Mercifully I'm able to fix it and he's away again. I'm tiring now. I feel physically tired and emotionally drained and we're hardly a month into vintage. I think enviously of my Burgundian friends, whose picking is spread over a mere ten days. Fortunately, Susie is thinking ahead, getting malo-lactic cultures into the still-warm wine in barrel and monitoring the ferments, leaving me to worry about fermentation space with Jesse's words ringing in my ears: 'Don't worry about anything that you can't change, Dad.'

Tuesday, 6 April

I wake early, having had my first good sleep in a month, from 10 p.m. to 6 a.m. The winery reveals temperatures rising. We had the cooler in Dionne all of yesterday afternoon and she's down to 22 degrees Celsius, but Esmé, Claudia and Anna are all rising. So we plan to put the cooler into them in that order but it doesn't quite work out like that. It's only been in Esmé an hour when we see that the cap on Silver is rising above the fermenter like a muffin top, so of course the temperature, too, is rising, fast. We disconnect the hoses from the cooling coil and connect them to Silver, not daring to agitate the must, for that will increase the rate of fermentation. It's necessary to remove some must from Silver, now beginning to trickle down the sides, so Susie and Hugo set to with buckets and get some of the surplus into Sanai (the emergency green bin), while Gelati goes about his ministrations. It feels pretty warm, and it is. At 26 degrees Celsius, Silver's gone up 2 degrees since 8 a.m. I decide we'd better get the old inefficient cooler from the shed and see if it still works. We've got to lower the temperatures in Claudia and Anna.

The old cooler looks like a heap of neglected rubbish but I manage to coax it to life. It works on a separate circuit so it doesn't overload the one we're using, and we leave them both running flat-out while we go about normal winery duties, keeping everything crossed, for if one of them fails, or we have a power outage, I could ruin some of the best shiraz I've had in my twenty-four years of winemaking! Nothing goes wrong, and by 12.30 p.m. the temperature in Silver has fallen to a more comfortable 24 degrees Celsius. Whew, a close call!

We've unpacked the cellar bags, large plastic bags for storing wine, for the sauv blanc; it's fermented almost to dryness so we rack it into the bags from Gold, leaving her ready for the next onslaught of McKernan pinot on Friday night or Saturday morning. The Fermenta bags arrive with the courier 'just in time' but with no instructions for assembly. However, it transpires that the Fermenta bag instructions arrived with the cellar bags.

Jesse and his mate Will arrive—Julien must have driven them up but she doesn't like to come over to the winery when I'm working with those people whom I once foolishly referred to as 'my other family'. Vanessa's sister Vicki, husband Serge and possibly daughter Jessica are due to arrive tomorrow after-noon also, after calling in at Musk on the way to take some photographs. We'll run out of beds so there'll be some air mattresses on the floor. I think I've organised enough food.

The Jones's fruit arrives from Narre Warren after an uneventful trip so, being cool and sulphured, is forklifted off and put in the winery ready for tomorrow. The grapes are from three different vine clones, mainly MV6, with a smaller amount of the 114 and 115 clones. We continue pressing out, so the press is hissing and roaring all day.

Wednesday, 7 April

Wake at 2.30 a.m. not sleeping too well—a few things on the mind and not all to do with winemaking. Start in the winery at 3.30 a.m.—want to get temperatures in order and readings done before Susie arrives so that we can get cracking on the pinot. Temperatures are finally under control so when she gets here at 8 a.m. we set up our new Fermenta bags in their bins and we crush/destem a couple of tons into Marilyn and Beryl. Vanessa and Vicki arrive, and we decide who's cooking what and when, then we deal with the rest of the pinot—some into the Fermenta bags, some into vats for foot-stomping, and some destemmed and only lightly crushed. The small amount of 114 and 115 clones are crush/destemmed and kept separate. I make up yeast culture. I'm not risking wild yeasts; I can't trust them and, besides, they take longer to ferment so they tie up precious fermenter space.

A horrible grinding noise signals the arrival of Jesse and Will in the Telecom ute, the front suspension of which they have comprehensively wrecked. They have a prepared speech, of course—how it wasn't a very big ditch that Will drove over and they weren't going very fast. The front wheels pointing in different directions tell the true story so they cop a good telling-off and skulk away, to return later and apologise, Jesse not having to think too hard to decide on the best course of action to take with Dad. I have some lunch and a couple of glasses of pinot, shower then off to bed, leaving the rest of the crew to continue pressing out.

Half-asleep I hear lots of sounds of excited children's voices; the Grahams must have arrived with their grenache and their jolly retinue of pickers and kids. I arise, we crush the grenache and we add the yeast culture to the pinot, Susie doing the vats and me the Fermenta bags (although I miscalculate and the last one gets only about half the dose).

Everyone has assembled for 'Pino'clock'. Work's finished by about 6 p.m., so I rat around in the 'cellar' under the stairs and get out some golden oldies—the 1997 Bronze Medal Pinot that Greg Bennett made from Kingower fruit, the original 2000 Three Wise Men experimental one, and some 2002 Coldstream, as well as a few early shiraz cabs of ours. It's a tradition to open a few of these old beauties during the pickers' weekends; they appreciate being able to taste them and it gives me a chance to look at them without bottle remnants going to waste. Of course, drinking a bit of wine also makes people happier than they would otherwise be.

Vicky Scotland has made a delicious stew; we remove the pieces of meat for the vegetarian, Will. Young Daylesford vegetarians don't seem to be all that fussy anyway, and I'm sure the meat juices will be good for him. We have a great meal, tell lots of jokes and go to bed early.

Robert McKernan has rung, he's definitely picking tomorrow—which means more than 5 tons arriving tomorrow night. It's not much for him; he's changed some of his pruning and maybe that's caused a lighter crop.

Thursday, 8 April

Wake at 5 a.m., before the alarm goes off, turn the big outside light on ready for the truck to collect our bins to take to Axedale for the mechanically harvested fruit. Hear the truck coming down Billygoat Hill and Stuart arrives at 6.01 a.m. Give him a coffee after we load the bins on, and off he goes to Axedale, more than an hour away. Vanessa is hand-plunging, we unload the press, and try out my new trailer to take the skins and pips from beneath the press (needs a little modification).

Someone has mislaid the key for the big pump control box; they must have decided someone was going to steal it. City people! It turns up later in somebody's pocket as I'm getting the angle grinder out.

Reload the press and start pressing—but hey, there's wine overflowing from the press sump! The beautiful new pump has failed, it won't respond to its 'fat controller' remote, so I hastily grab the old small pump and get it sucking, but we've lost some good wine. What's the point of a brand new pump with a 10-metre lead and remote control if it doesn't work? It's Easter, no good ringing the supplier, so I open up the beautiful new waterproof remote control and there it is, quite simply, a loose wire on the start button. I tighten it, cursing the person whose job it was to do it at the factory.

Brian White arrives with the Axedale fruit, unfortunately with some vineyard staples included. Serge, Vikki and daughter have arrived and we're having a great barbecue, awaiting the truck with the McKernans' Coldstream fruit aboard, which arrives at dusk. I unload it (twelve bins) and suggest to the driver that he go over to the house and get something to eat and a strong coffee.

He returns to the winery: 'You want another coffee, Wally?'

'Nah, thanks.'

'What time do you think you'll get back home?'

'Depends when you finish with the boxes.'

I can't believe this. 'Do you mean you want to take the bins back?'

'Yeah, Rob could only borrow them overnight; didn't he tell you?'

The reality dawns. We've got to crush twelve bins tonight, in the dark.

I go over the dry creek bed to the house and make the dreaded announcement. Everybody using their glasses or plates puts them down, including Serge, Vikki and Jesse. There is no discussion, they are all coming over to help. At least everything has been made ready for the morning so we can make an immediate start.

We don't have lighting over the crusher so set up some temporary floodlights. I raise the first bin on the forklift to slide it into its frame but to my horror it doesn't fit—these bins are about an inch wider than the standard ones! By manoeuvring the forks and pushing forward, I jam the first one in. I don't like this as the whole structure of the bin tipper flexes and bends in protest, but I have no choice. Everybody is at their station, one each side of the slide, armed with rakes, one at the big pump control, another at the crusher to deal with the stalks, and two at the hose end to spread the must evenly and change over into a new vat when required.

More people than we normally require, but not everyone is familiar with the process and everyone wants to be part of it. So we progress, me sick at the prospect of breaking something. But somehow we battle through it, the job is finally done and the driver goes back to Coldstream with his over-sized bins. I had enough labour to be able to fork a couple of bins into a vat for foot-stomping, so it's pretty much where I wanted us to be, just earlier. As I go back to the house I reflect on the instinctive will of my friends to help. I suppose that's mateship.

We finish our feast and the surprise wine of the night is a 1987 cabernet, a cool wet year when I picked early for I was going organic then and was afraid of powdery mildew. It is restrained, of course, but elegant and complete, almost in defiance of the stated 11.2 per cent alcohol on the label. Very Bordeaux-like, really.

Friday, 9 April

Shiraz into new barrels, normal winery duties—plunging, foot-stomping, taking readings, cleaning up. Bill's back at work tomorrow so will have to spend some time working on the bin tipper mountings. I've loosened them where they were bolted into the concrete during last night's pushing and shoving.

Saturday, 10 April

Just when you think the war's over! Bruce Jones rings to say he's picking 3 or more tons on Thursday—shoot, I'd clean forgotten that extra picking. He's short of bins, of course; nearly all of them are here. Can't have a truckie travel a 500-kilometre return journey with a few bins. Maybe the regular freight people can take them to Melbourne then transfer them to Narre Warren. When in trouble, handball to Sue!

'Sue, do you think you could possibly . . . ?'

Robert McKernan arrives—he wants to work in the winery on his own grapes. Robert, Hugo, Shae Maree, the trainee back from wherever, Susie and me, Vanessa and Vicki—too many people, unfamiliar sounds coming from here and there.

Dionne's temperature rising, also Esmé's. We put the cooler on them. Then Gold, with the Axedale shiraz, starts blowing her stack—heaps of H_2S, the smell almost overwhelming the perfume of fermenting wine. Susie is up on the catwalk feeding in DAP (diammonium phosphate) for nitrogen, also yeast nutrients. How can it still be producing H_2S? There's plenty of nitrogen in the ferment and we don't want it to carry excess nitrogen into the barrel because of the possible consequences, but I don't want to be adding copper later, either, to cure the problem. We connect the cooler to Gold to bring her down from 25 degrees Celsius. Get her down to 22 degrees. And then Silver's cap starts to rise! It's just too hot in the winery. Someone's been listening to the radio—it's the hottest April day for forty years or something. Then I discover the thermometers built into Silver and Gold are both reading 5 degrees too high according to our electronic probe and glass thermometer. How can the Italians make a tank with thermometers reading 5 degrees too high, and why? Is some Italian factory worker now choking with mirth on his tagliatelli?

Rob makes lunch as planned with the seafood he has brought up—prawns and oysters—no bread, no salad, just prawns and oysters. The afternoon becomes like the Mad Hatter's Tea Party. People fumbling with hoses, splashes of wine everywhere, people saying 'sorry, sorry', and Susie and I trying to supervise. Too many people, too much wine, even my desk is wine-splashed and hemmed in with barrels and bins containing Fermenta bags. In the heat Robert speculates that he could have left the grapes on because the forecast rain has bypassed the Yarra Valley—too late now, and I'd made the call.

Foot-stomped pinots progressing well. Male visitors to the winery seem always to bring up that old observation when they see people foot-stomping: 'I thought you had to have virgins for that job, haw, haw.' Hugo sticks his head in the winery and yells, 'Tell Graeme that the virgins he ordered have arrived!' I look out and there, walking towards us, framed by wattle and eucalypt and holding hands, are two of the sweetest, most innocent-looking twelve-year-old girls imaginable, obviously daughters of parents who are visiting Sue. Good one, Hugo!

Sunday, 11 April

Phil Adam from just down the road at Rheola has some shiraz for us—maybe it will suit the Two Mates, the wine I'm making in concert with Stefano for his restaurant. In any case we'll keep it separate and see what it tastes like when it's fermented. We crush it between pressings; it means changing the big pump over again, of course, and somebody dropped the inverter control box for the big pump and there's something rattling inside it. Will open it up and have a look when I get time.

The Fermenta bags are getting warm but our cooling's pretty well occupied with Silver and Gold. Thank God for the 'gelati machine'! We could not have coped with the old cooler, still beavering away at the open fermenters. The ambient temperature is still summer-like; serious Indian Summer this year. Susie can't get enough liquid out of one of them for a test sample—the one I put insufficient yeast into. Salacious jokes are made about them with their orifices and chimneys, and the one that's slow to get going is now referred to as Sister Maria after an old joke I used to tell. All the pinots are going crazy. Me, too. Press flat-out. I'll have to cancel my trip to Musk, too much happening. I ring Jamie Kinnear who has a tiny vineyard near there and is a good man with a hydrometer and he agrees to go to Musk and take some readings for me. We're running out of storage space. Sue orders more Fermenta bags by express post.

Monday, 12 April

Press out McHardy shiraz from Beryl and Beau Foster's shiraz from Claudia. Two foot-stomped green bins of pinot are put into new French oak hogsheads at 1 degree baumé. Narre Warren fruit arrives (nine bins). Sue must have organised it. I noticed that the bins were gone, Susie knew about it—secret women's business! It looks like rain. Susie moves the bins into the winery but it doesn't rain, so after lunch we move them back to the crusher and deal with them. Sister Maria decides to join the party and is gurgling and frothing away. I've ordered a tanker of water for the winery but it hasn't arrived yet and we run out in the middle of cleaning up. Ring the water carter who offers to be out at 6 a.m. Gunga Din very busy this Indian summer.

Jamie rings and reports a brix reading of 18 degrees, but also of net damage—there are birds in there. To paraphrase the Japanese haiku poet Basho, 'Oh what a game it is to set, Currawongs loose beneath the net.' I'll have to go to Musk.

The nets cover 10 acres like an aviary. At first we netted them in the conventional manner, covering a few rows and draping them down to the ground, where they were secured by pegs and wires. But the cunning old crows, with the benefit of an absentee landlord, found that they could cling to the nets and insert their beaks through them to attack the fruit. Thus it seemed necessary to cover the whole vineyard—a demanding task indeed, for it requires a length of net to be run covering a few rows and secured to the ground on the outside of the outer row, then another run has to be made over the next few rows, which means another trip 250 metres up the hill paying out the net from the roller attached to the tractor. Then the two nets have to be stitched together up the length of the row.

Last vintage we used conventional plastic net hooks for this job. These, however, proved inadequate to cope with the fierce southerlies roaring over the high point of the Great Dividing Range only about 300 metres from our most southerly and highest vines, so many of them broke or stretched open and let go, leaving great gaps in the netting. So this vintage saw

Cameron, Jesse and I get a little production line going on the back verandah at Ruthven Street after school. I made up a small metal jig to allow us to turn short lengths of high-tensile 2.5-mm wire into compressed 'S' shapes and we made up 3000 of them to replace the plastic ones.

I've planted trees along the southern boundary of our property but it'll be a few more years before they provide an adequate windbreak. Brother Greg suggested a wall of hay bales, which was a good idea but the cost seemed prohibitive— it would be like a piece of the Great Wall of China, in hay.

We get a lighter crop and less ripening on the upper half of the vineyard so the current positive thinking is to harvest that section at about 11 degrees baumé with huge natural acid for a sparkling, and the lower section at, say, 12.5 to 13 degrees baumé for the still chardonnay and pinot.

Originally I had planned a little cafe for Musk where we could serve an inexpensive tank-fermented chardonnay so I planted more of that than pinot. But it looks as if the cafe is not to be, so it's been back to the drawing board. I've ordered more pinot rootlings to plant before next spring so that we'll have more pinot to play with in 2011–12. More vines, more work, more trellis, more wires, and on a yet unproven site—no wonder I am completely uninterested in conventional gambling, there's enough of it here!

So it appears that Bruno and I are going to Musk for a few days for some netting work. Bruno is invaluable for driving the birds out from the nets; although a retriever, he rounds up the birds like a kelpie rounding up sheep and drives them to the corner where I have opened the nets to allow them to escape. I'll leave Susie in charge of the winery, and this diary, which she can't wait to get her hands on. She'll be disappointed to find it's nearly all about winemaking! We have a great seafood dinner and I prepare to head off in the morning.

The Bhagwan goes to Musk by Susie McDonald

Tuesday, 13 April

Water arrives 6 a.m. Crush remaining shiraz and two bins of pinot into Beryl and Pamela respectively. Hugo poncing away being a catwalk model on our catwalk where he's supposed to be pumping over Gold. We press Esmé, Dionne and Ina into cellar bags that I collect from post office after Sue tells me they've arrived there. Huge truck and trailer arrive with road gravel. Don't know what to do but the driver does. He apparently did the last load four years ago. Bhagwan forgot to tell me about this. Fermenter bag ladies are pregnant, bloated and burping. Sister Maria has a burning ring of fermentation. H_2S seems to be under control in Gold but there's some in the pinot in Claudia so I add some DAP (see lab book for quantity). New barrel racks arrive and I get bogged on forklift. Graeme at Musk unfortunately. Phone him and miraculously get him on mobile. He tells me towing chain is on the tractor ready for Susie getting bogged on forklift.

Afternoon. The pipes are calling; chimney music. Now the winery is silent, free of ear-battering machines, black labradors and golden retrievers, the chimneys sound like an enormous Hopi Indian ear candle sucking wax out of a very hot nun's ear. At 8 p.m. Sister Maria explodes! She must have got a blockage in her chimney and, when it let go, sprayed a good deal of wine about the place.

Wednesday, 14 April

Good fresh morning and the convent is quiet! Robert and Hugo depart today but first we will press out green bin shiraz and Claudia, with my friend Domenique assisting today. Perhaps Hugo and Robert will stay to unload and press out Silver, too. Yes, they do; Robert insists on staying till the end. Russell and Virginia appear with a bottle of champagne for Graeme and me. No Graeme, so more for Susie! I ask Hugo if he'd like to leave a note on the whiteboard; the whiteboard must have reminded him of the bookies' chalkboards at racecourses because he's written, 'Claudia, Race 5, Rosehill, 3 to 1.'

Thursday, 15 April

Press Harriet, then Francine, sleep. The Bhagwan returns, having fixed some nets, shot some crows and liberated some pied currawongs.

Friday, 16 April

The chess game with barrels, tanks and cellar bags. Jill Burdett visits and helps set up for taking Angel 2003 off finings for bottling this Friday. McHardy shiraz from Bertha to barrels. Jill stays for lunch—garden fresh salad from the winery veggie garden (baby zucchini, delicious sweet tomatoes, purple beans, olive oil and lime), Polish sausage Graeme has brought back from Istra at Musk, and . . . Cruskits! Tonight it's a big roast dinner at Newbridge Hotel for Dionne's and my birthdays. Great bash, then back to change the cooler from Pamela into Claudia. We find message from Sue: corks for Friday's bottling have arrived but we're two boxes (5000 corks) short!

Saturday, 17 April

Press some Axedale shiraz into Bertha and three 'out of space' bags *avec* Jill B. who didn't get one drop of grape juice on her all day! Picnic lunch on upside-down bin, courtesy of Cassie and Ross, now staying at Sue's. Clean winery's tiled floor, finally. Poor Bill the council worker raking driveway gravel with love. Angel off finings into Silver with sulphur addition. The other two boxes of corks have been located, one in Melbourne and the other in Brisbane; they were all part of the same consignment, from Adelaide! Lots of transferring—Graeme's Blend off finings into Gold and Silver, having transferred Angel '03 to T2. Using big pump for all this shuffling. Add sulphur and tartaric. Graeme's Blend into T1, leaving Gold and Silver free again so Silver can take the Reserve Shiraz from Alisa and three hogsheads, all on finings. Over to Silver to await bottling on Friday/Saturday. All in all, 28,000 litres of '03 wine pumped and ready for bottling.

Also rack the Axedale '04 shiraz that had H_2S, not wanting to leave it in barrel. Suspend a little bit of copper wire in it to make sure it's clean and then it's into Gold while she's empty. Back to clean barrels. Press out Pamela into Alisa and bucket Zonnebeke cabernet out of Marilyn into Esmé to create room by clearing out all the now unnecessary vats. So bye-bye Anna, Ina, Marylin, Olivia and Pamela. Enjoy your ten-month holiday under the peppercorn tree! Now we can work on storing new wine in barrel in some order. For lunch, we have hock and *Kaiserfleisch* soup made last night—three-quarters in pot, one-quarter on ute floor.

Dinner at Sue's with Ross and Cassie; Ross, as usual at this time of the year, making and bottling chutney and jam. Cassie cooked delicious chicken with two quartered oranges stuffed inside with one cinnamon stick, orange juice, half a jar of whole-seed Dijon mustard and marmalade. Sticky date pudding for dessert. Fantastic meal!

By Graeme Leith

Sunday, 18 April

Late start after dinner last night and a good sleep. Shae Maree working today, comes in even later because: 'Dale left his car keys in Nathan's car and Nathan went to Ballarat, didn't he?'

I'm now able to move some of the fermenters out of the shed with the forklift to create some much-needed space for barrels. There are barrels full of wine everywhere, including in front of the big warehouse shed where the bottling caravan will have to park tonight ready for tomorrow's bottling. Second out is Pamela. She is used as an emergency back-up, and if I have to use her, I trickle water through her cooling pipes to cool her down, a necessary inconvenience as I wish to leave her intact.

Harriet's already gone; every year I swear I'll never use her again and every following year I run out of fermenters and she gets pressed into service again. She's too tall for her width, and because of her depth someone has to get in to bucket out the remaining must when no more can be removed from the top with buckets and scoops, and the floor is diabolically slippery. Cameron hurt his back in there one year and I, of course, still feel guilty about that.

Anna is the last to go outside. She is of such length that she cannot fit through the door sideways so she goes out with me on the forklift on one end and the girls pushing the other end on the trolley jack. (It was early '80s when we got Anna from Kyabram; Sue drove up in the Telecom ute mid-vintage after we had obtained measurements over the phone and established that she'd fit in the back, which she did, just, with some of her sticking out the sides and quite a bit out the end.)

At last, half of the barrel room is now clear of fermenters and we can start to collect the barrels on racks scattered all about the place and stack them in order in our beautiful newfound space. This clears the area around the bin tipper so we can begin to crush the Zonnebeke shiraz that has been sitting in bins since last night. Jill Burdett is here, and Shae Maree and Susie, with me on the forklift and between times doing my share of those other jobs around the crusher. So these Zonnebeke grapes go into Claudia and Beryl which we pressed out this morning. Baumé 14.8 degrees, fruit in perfect condition, no need for any more sulphur. Susie makes up the yeast culture and goes over to her clinic to do some Chinese doctoring she'd optimistically booked in some time ago. I add the cultures but forget the stainless-steel pots they're in and they sink into the must to be discovered by Susie when she hits them with the plunging tool in the morning.

I'm living hand-to-mouth with the clothes washing again now, just getting off the line what I need after the shower. Very warm and humid tonight, could be a bad moon rising! Patrick arrives with the bottling trailer, unhitches it and goes to Bendigo.

Monday, 19 April—Bottling day

I'm woken at 5.30 a.m. by rain on the skylight. Quickly out to the line in the raw to get some clothes off it, cursing a little— so often it won't rain for months then rains on bottling day! Intermittent drizzle continues; if it starts raining hard the forklift might bog. Get the bottles onto the concrete, it's just light enough to do so.

Patrick arrives and soon steam starts to emerge from the caravan as he gets his hot water happening. I make us a strong latte each from the 'laboratory bar and grill' and go over to the house to get us some toast. The lights go out and the toaster dies. I look out the window to the caravan and its lights are out, too, and from a separate power supply. Looks like a power outage on bottling day!

Power outages sometimes occur these days when rain falls after a long dusty period—the electricity tracks down the wet dust to earth and trips the whole system. In the old days, under the good old state-owned State Electricity Commission (SEC), they used to advise us that they were going to clean the insulators on such and such a Sunday and we should be aware that we'd have no electricity between the hours of 8.30 to 12, or whatever. But somebody had a better idea. And so our electricity distribution network has been sold to overseas people, who need to make money out of it to pay the high interest rates at which they have borrowed to get the money to buy the bloody thing and to give their shareholders a good return, so they cut down on maintenance, people like me are inconvenienced and lose money, and some people die agonising deaths in bushfires caused by poorly maintained powerlines falling, while electricity prices will soon go through the roof, but at least the unions got a whacking, that'll teach them to try to look after themselves! Thanks, Jeff Kennett, enjoy your pension!

Jan Graham drives down to see if our power's out and goes back to ring the electricity company. I've already tried—their lines are predictably busy. Our bottling crew arrives in their separate cars, disconsolate because they can't start work. Then after another twenty minutes, 'ping', and the lights come on again. We have to wait a bit until the water heats and we're finally away.

Susie puts some shiraz back into barrel, Vanessa arrives at about 10.30 a.m. so that gives us three people to man the line while the crew is having smoko so that we can claw back some time. Patrick has to leave us tomorrow night and go to Rutherglen for his next job. When this happens I usually take the job of removing the bottles from the washing carousel and passing them to the conveyer belt going to the bottling filler. I revel in the mindlessness of it. It's not necessary to look at what you're doing—catch bottle with left hand, invert, pass to right hand, place on conveyer. I stare at the caravan wall ahead and try not to think of my low regard for the cork industry.

Bottling is successfully completed, we have a beer with the bottling crew and they go home with their wages and some of the newly bottled wine. It is wine they could never afford to buy and they treasure it. Increasingly as years pass they open up some of their older ones and have come to see the joy in, and the beauty of, good red wine. The gift doesn't do their self-esteem any harm, either, and increases their already strong loyalty to Passing Clouds.

This vintage we've bottled 500 dozen Angel Blend, 722 dozen Graeme's Blend, and 425 dozen Reserve Shiraz—or about 29 pallets all up.

The Fermenta bags have concluded their gestation period and we can press them out whenever we like, for they are immune to the deleterious effects of oxygen while they stay in their bags, so we decide to taste them now. It's always intriguing how the same grapes in different fermenters can produce different results and, later, wine from the same ferment in different barrels likewise. So we pipette some wine from the five bags into glasses. The results are surprising, for all of the wines had identical origins and treatment before they went into the Fermenta bags.

1 – Fresh, berry cherry on nose, clean, fresh on palate, lovely flavour, great finish.

2 – Deep, rich, great mouthfeel, long finish, more concentrated than 1.

3 – Neutral on nose, seems in concentration to be between 1 and 2, good rich finish.

4 – Nose deeper, bit of a not unpleasant (in fact, nice) pong, no cherries or strawberries, more floral or perfumed, good finish.

5 – Good fruit, touch of straw, deep rich flavour, more plums and roses. No cherry berry, good finish.

Jamie rings: three weeks ago he cut some bunches off our Musk vines and let them fall to the ground so he could observe the difference in ripening of the vines with the full crop and the ones with the depleted, or thinned crop. His readings are consistent: Chardonnay full crop, 9.7 degrees baumé; thinned crop, 11.5 baumé. Pinot noir full crop, 10.6 baumé; thinned crop 12.5 baumé. As most of the crop is not thinned, we have a way to go, but we're getting there!

Tuesday, 20 April

Press blue bin Three Wise Men. Foot-stomp batch.

Wednesday, 21 April

Coldstream from Silver into barrel. Early finish tonight.

Thursday, 22 April

Brian rings from Axedale, he's got a couple of tons remaining unsold, do we want it at a reduced price? It's about 15 degrees baumé and he will deliver to us. Yeah, why not? It arrives a few hours later and we crush it and clean up.

Friday, 23 April

Press one Fermenta bag of Coldstream pinot and Sister Maria, both look good. I have to go to Daylesford to be with son Jesse—a good opportunity to take a trailer-load of fruit boxes and picking bins to Musk ready for the harvest there, whenever that may be. Can't find the spare wheel for the trailer; halfway down I realise that we must have lent it to Richard when he shredded his trailer tyre. Too late now, but our tyres look good anyhow. Meet up with Jesse as planned at Ruthven Street. He's sick, doesn't want to go to Musk, even with the rifle. Must be sick.

I'm surprised when the tyre loses its tread just out of Daylesford, but perhaps I shouldn't be. I'd been going very fast on the back roads between Kingower and Maldon and it's becoming apparent that the Angel doesn't like Musk! Tyre service place is closed, so leave trailer outside the cemetery and go looking for another wheel. Can't get onto one, so go back to Jesse and make some dinner for us. Julien is away which is why I'm staying at the house to be with Jesse. I nip out to the cemetery at 6.30 a.m. and the trailer's gone, despite this being a well-travelled road day and night. Report to police, leave message on answering machine, go to Musk and take samples, return to Kingower for we have to crush remainder of McKernan fruit arriving early this arvo, which it does. Susie's parents Karin and John arrive. A couple of peaceful days are anticipated.

Saturday, 24 April

Freezing windy day. Neighbour from Musk, Brian Wilson, and son Scott arrive with their chardonnay. Musk is about an hour and twenty minutes away with the big trailer behind. They're exhausted and Brian's hand is still frozen almost solid. They've been picking in the snow, for today is the day they had chosen and, as his pickers are friends of his and Scott's who all have to be back at work tomorrow, it had to happen today despite the weather. Brian never allows anything to defeat him but I think today tested him severely. 'It's too hard,' he said. 'It's just too hard.' But they've managed about 2.5 tons of grapes and that's a lot of bunches with frozen hands. They're not quite ripe enough for still table wine and it's going to cost a lot of money to get it turned into sparkling. Brian's young wife seems to be leaving him and it looks as if he's going to lose the property that he's put all his money, heart and soul into. After we make up the base wine, we'll put it into cellar bags and see what transpires with the wine and the marriage.

Our grapes at Musk, at a slightly higher altitude, will need a little more time to ripen, so we joyfully anticipate stripping the nets off, packing them away and taking our team of pickers from Kingower down to Musk. I ring up Castlemaine Hire and book a Porta-loo, but am unable to give him a firm date—it all depends on the ripening gods.

PS

A year later, almost to the day, I was driving to Musk past the cemetery from where the trailer had been purloined. There were some people there by the side of the road, chainsawing up a fallen tree and loading the cut pieces onto a trailer, which, although of a different colour, bore a striking resemblance to my trailer. So I stopped and investigated. My trailer was not your normal trailer, having, among other things, mudguards made from chequer-plate steel, not the usual tin. There were other unique features as well, so I knew that it was my trailer.

The people loading the logs tried to ignore me; they appeared to me to be European, perhaps Yugoslavian.

'Where did you get the trailer from?' I ventured. The men ignored me and kept working.

A woman replied, 'Fromma de Sunshine market.'

'That's interesting, it's my trailer.'

'We bought im fair and square from de Sunshine market. You can'ta prove anyting.'

So I rang the Daylesford police station and informed them of my dilemma and the duty constable drove out there—generously, I thought, for he was on another case and had a naughty girl he was taking to her home in the police car with him.

His assessment of the situation was that, even if it was my trailer, I was unlikely to get it back. The welded identification numbers had, as I had previously observed, been ground off and it's very difficult in the circumstances to establish ownership. But he was sympathetic and we arranged to talk the next day.

I quickly drove back to Daylesford and returned with my camera to find the people still there. Rather ostentatiously I took various photographs of the trailer, including some from beneath, thinking that would keep the pressure on them. I spoke to the constable the next day and he reiterated that I was unlikely to get it back but he agreed to go and visit them at their nearby property with a view to hopefully pressuring them some more.

He rang me late that afternoon: 'Is it all right with you if I hook your trailer up to the police four-wheel drive and bring it to your house at Ruthven Street?'

'How did you get it from them?' I asked, surprised.

'Well, they say they didn't steal it, but they want you to have it back!'

Now that's what I call good old-fashioned country policing. I could hardly wait to see Bill's reaction when I returned to Kingower the next day, for I knew that he would recognise the trailer as soon as he saw it. The look on his face when I drove in towing the trailer was worth the wait.

PPS

Brian Wilson lost his house and subsequently, after a jaunt to the Philippines, most of his remaining wealth. These misfortunes were later compounded by the tragedy of the death of his beloved son Scott, who was accidentally killed when chainsawing down a neighbour's tree in the US, where he was then living.

PPPS

The Passing Clouds Reserve Shiraz 2004 was rated in the highly respected *Jeremy Oliver Wine Annual* (2007) at 96 points, which placed it above the current release Penfolds Grange at 95 points, the Grant Burge Meshach at 95 points, the Hensche Hill of Grace at 91, the Rockford Basket Pressed Shiraz at 93, and the Wolf Blass Platinum label at 95. During subsequent rackings and blendings, the small batch with the few overripe pinot noir bunches was combined with others and I don't know whether the final barrels selected for the Reserve Shiraz actually included that tiny percentage of pinot noir. I'll never know, but I sometimes wonder!

Musk Vintage 2013

Diary of an exceptional year
by Cameron Leith

Leading up to vintage we spend a lot of time in the vineyard, ensuring the canopy is open enough, that there is enough leaf but not too much—essentially that the vines are in balance and will be able to produce the best fruit possible.

My father Graeme does most of the spraying for mildew these days. Fortunately, because of the warm dry weather, we did not have to do too much spraying this season. In fact, 2013 is turning out to be an extraordinary year because of its predicted continuing warmth.

Wednesday, 30 January – Sunday, 17 February

Dad did a sulphur and copper spray then grabbed a couple of days off and went fishing in the Snowy Mountains. To his surprise, when he returned, he found that Luke and I had built a brand-new deck over the dam in the anticipation of it filling eventually.

The dam had been built many years ago but didn't hold water successfully due to the porosity of the soil, so fairly recently we had it lined with bentonite mat. This was quite a project, as it requires a lot of earth to be taken from the bank, then huge rolls of thick bentonite 'carpet' to be laid with the aid of the big digger that feeds the spools out. They are then covered over with the removed earth and so lie there, concealed. As the contractor Brian Williams said, 'You've spent a lot of money making it look as if no money's been spent!' But now the dam holds water, which is fed to it from the windmill via our old Furphy tank that we mounted on a big pipe so it sits above the projected high-water mark, and the water pours or trickles, depending on the wind velocity, into the dam. It is unlikely to be full by the end of vintage, but it's getting there!

Monday, 18 February

Vintage approaches with more pace than last year due to the unusually dry and warm weather. We do not net for birds at Musk as we used to, due to the high winds and unusual trellising system. Instead we employ a bird-scaring device. A little beyond veraison (when the berries begin to accumulate sugars and the colour of the pinot berries changes from green to red), the device has to be set up and got running. It is a complicated system requiring the erection of large poles to hold the radar scanners. These are set up at either end of the vineyard and energised with solar-charged batteries. When a bird flies through the radar beam, it alerts the other pieces of electronic equipment to bring into play various scaring mechanisms. These include speakers situated in different parts of the vineyard that, when alerted, emit the distress calls of various birds.

There is also an inflatable 'scary clown' who rises up and waves his arms about, and a gas gun can be connected to the system to emit a loud bang. These things are all randomised so that the birds don't become familiar with the pattern and generally it works successfully, especially with crows (that is, ravens) which, being intelligent, are more or less easily frightened off. On the other hand, the pied currawongs are stupid and are not so easy to discourage, and it is often necessary to patrol the vineyard with rifle in hand. We fire blanks at them, or occasionally ratshot, which doesn't reach them but sends them packing for a while. This becomes increasingly tedious as ripeness approaches and it is necessary to mount dawn and dusk patrols.

We are quite familiar with the erection procedure of this device by now, and the job takes a surprisingly short time. This year we have Luke and Darren who are working with us as casual employees over vintage. Luke is with us today and, after some tense moments when the radar is hoisted on posts 5 metres high, the thing is screeching away and the scary clown is popping up and waving his arms around when there's any bird activity. Our nearest neighbours are about 500 metres away but if the wind is in the right direction they can easily hear the distress call. Some of them don't mind it, but a couple do. We know this because we've received a few phone calls over the years—unfortunately anonymous, so we don't know who we are annoying.

Tuesday, 19 February

Plans are underway to go to the McKernans' vineyard at Coldstream in the Yarra Valley and to process some pinot noir there. We have had much success with their pinot over the years and are keen to make it again. Due to the discovery of the vine-root sucking louse, phylloxera, in the Valley, we had not been able to take their fruit for some years even though there was no phylloxera on the McKernan property. However, we are able to crush the fruit down there and bring the resulting must back home to our winery for fermentation. I had been in discussion with the Department of Primary Industries and it was apparent that we could bring the must back in sealed containers, provided certain conditions were met at the Coldstream vineyard and at our end. After inspections by the DPI and an incredible amount of paperwork (that was subsequently proved to be largely unnecessary), we were given the go-ahead, and so the operation was planned.

It appears that vintage is going to be early due to this spell of warm weather, so bottling and labelling have to be rescheduled to an earlier date to free the winery for fermentation. Lids needed to be made for the bins to contain the plastic bags in which the must would be transported, and Luke, a handy man with timber, was able to do this. Our crusher was too large to be transported so I hired a small one from Melbourne and the night before picking Luke and I go to Coldstream to have all in readiness for an early morning pick—and have a good evening meal with Robert and Vanessa McKernan.

Monday, 25 February

Upon arrival at the McKernans' the first thing I see is the hired crusher. Its size is of grave concern, looking like it was built for hobbyists, not someone about to crush at least 4 tons in a day. The rep had claimed it would do the job, but the look of it results in an interrupted sleep for me.

Tuesday, 26 February

This morning Luke and I go straight down to the vineyard, pick a bucket of grapes as the sun rises over the vineyard and push it through the mini crusher. With sighs of relief if goes through quickly, and we know we'll be able to keep up with the fourteen pickers.

The Cambodian team had been organised by Robert and away they go on a day which unfortunately turns out to be 35 degrees, and of course much hotter in the sun. Even the Cambodians are apparently feeling the heat for they aren't working as fast as I had hoped and there are some communication problems. However, the day had started off well in the meticulously groomed McKernan vineyard as hot air balloons drifted overhead at the 6 a.m. start.

The system is worked out; beautiful fruit is coming off thick and fast. My mobile lab (some instruments set up on the back of the ute) informs me that the figures are looking good, and the juice tastes and looks superb. Some hours later in the day I receive a telephone call from Bendigo Wine Estates, from whom we are purchasing some shiraz grapes as we normally do. However, we aren't expecting them for at least a week. I had been so busy looking at the weather for Coldstream that I had neglected to check Bendigo. A storm is brewing and the call has to be made. Do we get the shiraz off now, or risk our luck and hope the storm misses the vineyard? I tell Brian I'll call him back in five and make the decision while getting the next bin of buckets into the crusher. In the five-minute break between loads I call Brian back and tell him to go for it. He says he will and that the truck with grapes onboard would be at our Musk winery in the next four hours. Dad is hastily called—can he be there to forklift it off the truck? Yeah, good old Dad can do it; he probably didn't have a date tonight anyway! (Actually he did, and he was quite pissed off. And she was teed off. GL)

Luke and I get to Musk at eight o'clock that night, cover and gas the shiraz with CO_2 ready for the morning, crack a beer and wait for the truck from Coldstream to arrive; it had left some time after us because it had to be pressure-washed in accordance with DPI instructions.

The grapes from Coldstream duly arrive about an hour later and the 500-kilo bins unloaded. Most were inoculated, but some were not as the heat had encouraged indigenous fermentation to begin already.

Wednesday, 27 February

Up early to process the Axedale shiraz. Then a quick coffee and begin plunging for the season. Spend remainder of the day getting all equipment in order.

Thursday, 28 February

Crazily trying to finish bottling prep for the 2012s. Everything is out of barrel and in tank now, ready for final sulphur checks. Looks like we will have a lot of fruit coming in before bottling— space is at a premium.

Friday, 1 March – Monday, 4 March

Off to Serpentine to check fruit as Paul thinks it's getting close. Must have picked something up in the tyre at the vineyard— bad flat tyre coming back on the Serpentine–Bridgewater Road. Kelpie pup Nillo watching as we change it in the blazing sun, perhaps wondering why we humans bother with such complex lives. Serpentine shiraz looking good again!

Tuesday, 5 March

Things are starting to happen pretty fast. A couple of tons of Serpentine shiraz arrive. We had trialled a bit last year and found it excellent. It has an amazing colour, almost inky black, and a structure to die for. This wine ended up showing such fruit intensity and power that we kept it separate throughout the winemaking process and intend to take it out of barrel (after eighteen months) to be bottled as our Reserve Shiraz.

Simon and Emily Smith rock up with a half-ton bin of shiraz for their own label—not as much as they were expecting. Very glad they turned up when they did; we were needing to use the crusher anyway. It's painful to have to clean the crusher when only half a ton has gone through it.

Wednesday, 6 March

The Coldstream pinot has finished ferment. Press directly to barrel. Lots of plunging now as the winery begins to fill.

Thursday, 7 March

Axedale shiraz now finished ferment. Had to press direct to barrel as not a single tank free. Final sulphur adjustments for 2012s to be bottled. Bottling line arrives; manage to get it in place—just (again).

Friday, 8 March

Luke and I at the winery well before dawn so we can get the plunging out of the way before the bottling crew arrives. I do the ferment checks as Luke plunges. One final rack of a 2012 wine and we are ready for bottling. Crew arrives and the line is clinking away by 8 a.m.

Saturday, 9 March

Another day, bottling as as yesterday. The clickety-clack, clickety-clack of the bottling line might be soporific in more benign circumstances. The bottling crew people are working seamlessly and apparently tirelessly. Mordi from Vaughan Springs wants to pick tomorrow. Needs to pick up the bins tonight.

Sunday, 10 March

Vaughan Springs shiraz being picked today. Mordi arrives with the fruit at about 4 p.m. It is much less than he expected (estimated 3.5 tons, got 1.8 tons). This means I am going to have to buy some more shiraz from somewhere to fill demand. The season has been unusual and very dry, so those of us using historical data rather than picking and weighing sample bunches right here and now end up being, well, less than accurate.

Dad goes off to Kingower to look at the Zonnebeke crop of shiraz which, in most years, becomes our single vineyard Bendigo shiraz. The kangaroos were beginning to attack the crop and there were some losses due to their depredations, so a little less fruit than estimated there, also. The grower Phil Adam is frustrated; having spent about six weeks keeping the cockatoos off his pistachios, he's now got kangaroos in the shiraz. While we'd had trouble at our Kingower vineyard from kangaroo damage for many years during the drought, this is the first time for Phil, and we assume it was due to the kangaroo population being so very high and the fact that, incredibly in Bendigo, the 2013 growing season was drier than the driest of years through the drought, with no rain being sighted from November to March.

Tuesday, 12 March

The Gilmore grapes arrive from their Kingower vineyard; we are making the wine for their own brand, Both Banks, a nod to the fact that their vineyard is planted on both sides of the rarely flowing Kingower Creek, and also their dealing with the money variety when purchasing the property. On his way there Dad passed their truck in almost exactly the same place as he did last year.

Wednesday, 13 March

The Serpentine cabernet is arriving today. Financially things were tight so we had dropped our order from 7 tons to 6 tons in January, for every ton of fruit not only needs to be purchased (and this is not cheap for premium fruit), but also needs barrels, and they are expensive! However, the Serpentine vineyard's scales had broken and they had to estimate the 6 tons. When it arrives we weigh it at 8.257 tons! But Paul generously refuses to charge us for any more than we had ordered. He will, of course, be getting a few cases of the resultant wine!

Now space is really tight in the winery, requiring me to do some more logistics work with a forklift. Half the winery is taken up with packaged wine and barrels, the rest with open fermenters. It's the same old adage—a year after you build a shed, it's too small. We think longingly of our lovely empty sheds we'd left behind at Kingower.

As all of this is happening, we are eagerly attending to and watching our home vineyard at Musk. Ripening has been happening at a pace and the beautiful pinot noir and chardonnay bunches are now in superb condition with not a hint of rot or mildew.

Thursday, 14 March

Luke and I arrive at Musk this morning and soon realise that the bird alarm isn't working. It is quickly established that someone had vandalised the unit—the wires to the speakers have been cut and the scary clown stolen. His base holding the fan unit is still there (although bent almost horizontal) but his suit, which was inflated by the fan, has gone. It appears that one of our anonymous callers had visited in the night. We are able to join the wires and get the speakers working but we hold off on ordering a new clown until we call the police. Senior Constable Ian Wallace comes and investigates and takes the old clown base away, considering the unlikely possibility of it having identifiable fingerprints. Ian is the same policeman who recovered our stolen trailer in 2004 with some inspirational detective work, so it is no real surprise to us some days later when he contacts us, saying, 'We've got a crook.' We'd ordered a new scary clown by then and had it up and running.

Friday, 15 March

Phil Adam rings from Zonnebeke to say the crop loss is becoming significant due to kangaroo depredations. After taking some final measurements and tasting the fruit at the vineyard, we are surprised that the baumé and flavours have jumped to an acceptable level. This was a not an uncommon occurrence in 2012; one vineyard jumped 1.5 degrees baumé in a week (0.5 is about the norm). We push the go button for Phil and Anne to pick next Saturday. As their crop was diminished we ring Brian at Bendigo Wine Estate to see if we can purchase another couple of tons of shiraz, and luckily they have some for us.

Saturday, 16 March

Axedale shiraz arrives. I want to experiment with post-fermentation maceration so that goes into Olivia, and when fermentation is complete she is covered to prevent oxidation and I wait for the cap to fall. (After a month the cap still hadn't fallen, but the wine was tasting superb with plenty of depth and a very attractive tannin structure.) I talk to Dad and straightaway ring Ron Laughton of Jasper Hill, who is familiar with this winemaking technique, and discover that Ron goes off tannin structure (among other things) regardless of what the cap is doing. Luke is set to work getting the press ready and it is pressed this afternoon.

Sunday, 17 March

Today the Zonnebeke fruit arrived, 3.6 tons, and in the following days Fontanella pinot grigio, Goodwill wines with more pinot noir, and Max and Susan Haverfield with yet more pinot! We are producing a lot of pinot this year and it is absolutely fascinating to see what these sites produce—all remarkably different in their own way. Pinot is arguably one of the hardest varieties to make; there are so many options for the winemaker—whole bunch, whole berry, cold soaks, post-ferment soak, oak treatment, the list goes on—and there are percentages to determine for all of those options.

Monday, 18 March

Pressing day. Serpentine shiraz from the 5th March picking has fermented out to dryness and is looking great, so that is put through the press and into settling tanks with the free run wine. Likewise the Vaughan Springs shiraz, which has also decided to finish its ferment today.

Tuesday, 19 March

More pressing, plus pinot coming in from Kilmore for two contract clients, more for Goodwill wine, and some for Fontanella also. On the phone with another contract client in Mornington. Doesn't look like they will get the fruit off in time for us to process tonight. Manage to talk him out of driving down tonight—and arriving at 1 a.m.!

Wednesday, 20 March

Mornington fruit arrives at dawn—he must have left at 1 a.m. Inspection shows white bunches interspersed with the pinot. Looks like he must have been given some pinot gris rootlings mixed in with his pinot noir, apparently colourblind pickers!

Decision is made to process it together as the quantities of white bunches are so small.

Thursday, 21 March

It takes us until lunchtime to plunge and do ferment checks. Once we finish, we almost have to start again. Raoul's help is called for. He's a great bloke who works in hospitality. He'd done some work for us previously but had never heard of the scary man, and upon hearing all the talk of the scary man he wanted to know where he lived! Or did we keep him chained up somewhere? Of course we teased him and kept the joke going for as long as possible.

Friday, 22 March

The season is advancing, the pied currawongs are becoming more aggressive, and misty rain and heavy dews mean spraying against mildew is becoming a more constant chore. Due to our trellising set-up, it is difficult to apply spray inside the canopy so we'd had a framework made up attached to the spray unit that carried arms with a nozzle attached to spray inside the canopy. However, the arms and/or nozzles were constantly getting caught up and breaking the welds, and that meant a return to base for rewelding, as profanities were muttered or, as the day progressed, yelled. After much trial and error, Dad eventually replaced the arms with flexible plastic ones which finally solved the problem, but it is still a nerve-wracking three or four hours on the tractor every ten days or so.

We have previously had Natalie, the 'three-quarter sized Dolly Parton', and her crew out to 'shoot thin', taking out all unnecessary vine shoots and thereby limiting the crop and allowing better penetration of sprays, sunlight and air.

We are determined this year to do everything possible to produce a perfect crop so are baffled when we find some berry splitting. Then we realise that it is only on one side of the canopy and that the culprit must have been hail. After speaking to a neighbour, it was confirmed that there had, in fact, been a short sharp hailstorm on the night before we observed the splitting—one of the tribulations of share-farming with God! Damaged berries later shrivel, dry and largely fall off, so it appears that we have no loss of quality.

We have Natalie and crew out again to leaf pluck, a tedious and expensive job, but one that we feel we have to do in the interests of quality.

Saturday, 23 March

The time is fast approaching for our first pick of chardonnay for our sparkling base wine (which seems to be about three weeks ahead of last year), so I'm monitoring it daily.

Sunday, 24 March

Today more plunging, and pressing out some of the contract pinot—which is looking brilliant.

Monday, 25 March

More plunging, more pressing. Testing of the chardonnay grapes reveals that we can expect a perfect flavour and a perfect set of numbers in a couple of days, so Natalie and crew are called for once again. More contract grapes arriving. Last year's contract wine, now bottled and packaged, being collected. Five rows of chardonnay picked for sparkling base. Now the waiting game for the chardonnay and pinot to fully ripen for our still wines.

Tuesday, 26 March

Get everything ready for harvesting the sparkling-base grapes tomorrow. Buckets cleaned, tractor fuelled, secateurs found, etc. etc.

Wednesday, 27 March

Crew arrives early and we get started. Fruit coming off beautifully. Almost half a ton per row. I am in the winery, while Dad, Luke, Raoul and Darren handle pick-ups and help to hand-load the whole bunches into the press. A big day, but looks like we will have some impressive base wine.

Thursday, 28 March

We are having constant trouble with the bird scarer—it keeps going off whenever a car comes to the cellar door or a truck comes to the winery. We relocate one of the radar posts to a new position. Now it goes off whenever the motorbike goes past it! This is pretty often, as we're doing constant patrols to keep the currawongs at bay. Contact with the bird-scarer people informs us that there is new software available to allow the unit to discriminate better between birds and vehicles. Money is so tight that we don't even ask what the cost would be.

Dad is doing some dawn and dusk patrols in his little Fiat Cinquecento cabriolet because he can stick a rifle out of the sunroof. He took it in for a service at the pretentious Melbourne Fiat dealers the other day, who were unimpressed at finding spent .22 rifle shells under the seats—apparently it's supposed to be a city car.

Friday, 29 March

Fontanella pinot grigio comes in. Big day of pressing.

Saturday, 30 March

Pinot noir is showing an uncharacteristic ripening, some perfectly ripe berries and some green berries on the same bunch. This is troubling, but suddenly the green berries start ripening at an accelerated pace, and it looks as if it's all going to come into balance. Baumé steadily and slowly creeping up, the chardonnay beginning to show the awaited golden colour on the skins, and flavour developing. We've stopped spraying now. Hope with all the work we've done that the crop is adequately protected.

Sunday, 31 March

Looks like that's it for fruit coming in from the Bendigo region now. We just have to look after all the ferments and get them safely housed in barrel.

Monday, 1 April – Sunday, 14 April

Things have finally started to calm down a bit. Still doing bird patrols. Dad sleeping at winery some nights so he can do patrols and take some of the pressure off us. In the last fortnight we have been pressing out the Bendigo reds as they finish fermentation. We're working through the wines in settling tanks, racking them into barrels which we wash to free them of their sulphur protection, for the wine in them must go through its desirable malo-lactic (sometimes referred to as the secondary fermentation) and any sulphur will inhibit or prevent that.

Only the extended maceration experimental wine remains unpressed, quietly stewing in its own juice while we monitor the chardonnay and pinot, tracking their agonisingly slow journey to ripeness.

Monday, 15 April

Pinot baumé hits 12.8 degrees and the flavours are ripe! Dad and I high-five each other and we ring Natalie to organise picking. We're going to use all the Burgundian tricks that have worked for us in the past on this vintage. The pinot is a little riper than the chardonnay, so we'll pick it first.

Wednesday, 17 April

Natalie and crew arrive, and the job is on! Fruit sorting before destemming, then pre-ferment cold soak a portion of whole bunches—these little babies are going to get the works. The pinot is measured by the hydrometer at 13.1 degrees baumé, pH is 3.35, no time to do a TA (titrateable acid test, to see how many grams per litre there are) but it is looking perfect at the moment.

Our Musk vineyard was planted at this altitude according to the proposition that the best wines are made in a warm vintage in a cool climate, and awareness that the best DRC wines (of the Domaine de la Romanee Conti itself) come from the last vineyard of the domaine to be harvested. We will find out in a year or two whether or not it has worked for us at Musk, for it's a warm year and it's certainly a cool climate!

Friday, 19 April

The pinots are fermenting and the chardonnay has reached the desired level of ripeness. Natalie is alerted when we receive a weather report—it's going to rain seriously on our projected second day of picking! Can she do the impossible and double the number of pickers? She'll see what she can do. She's an organisational genius. If anybody can do it, Nat can.

Saturday, 20 April

The next morning at dawn the cars start rolling in. How do these people do it? On short notice they're here for us. They must have been up since 5 a.m. in Malmsbury and Kyneton, more than 30 minutes' drive away, and they're going to try to get our crop of chardonnay off in one day!

Before long they're in the vineyard going for it, a whole football team in number. Dad is on the tractor collecting the grapes. Me, Luke, Daryl and Raoul are in the winery, and my younger brother Jesse is even lending a hand on pick-ups in between his cellar door duties. We are whole-bunch pressing this year and didn't have the money to set up a chute for the press so the grapes have to be manually loaded into the hatch of the press and the cycle started. It's hard work and the press roars and hisses all day and into the night.

While the press is doing its cycle, one of the winery crew goes out on the trailer behind the tractor to collect the buckets and load them into the bins on the trailer and redistribute them up the rows ahead of the pickers. No sooner do we unload than we're back for another load. If the press is being loaded, Dad grabs one of the pickers to pour the grapes into the big bins. As the pickers start to tire, Natalie asks if she can have Darren back in the vineyard. Dad suspects he's her Stakanovite; she wants him there to set the pace for the other pickers, so we let him go.

By lunchtime they're halfway through the vineyard. We might make it yet, as the storm clouds gather. It's almost half-past five when the last grape is picked. One of the pickers punches her fist at the sky: 'We came, we saw, we conquered!' These people are truly the salt of the earth. What have we done to deserve such loyalty?

Those pickers who want a glass of wine are welcome to it. They sit, talking at the tables outside the tasting room, sipping their glasses of Graeme's Blend, their preferred tipple. Some go down to the business end of the winery to watch the fruits of their labours being pressed. As has become the custom after picking, Dad joins them and shares the camaraderie, they take their presentation bottle of wine, payment is made, and they depart into the late dusk.

'Thank you for the work,' they say as they go.

'No, no,' protests Dad, 'we should be thanking you!'

We'll see them next at an end-of-vintage dinner at a Kyneton hotel that Natalie is organising; we are all to dress up, and there's to be a prize for the best-dressed person. They have braved the elements and worked like Trojans; their financial reward for the day is less than the amount a lot of people spend on lunch.

Back at the press we are still working. I am by the press, monitoring the flavour and taste of the juice, before deciding when to shut it off. Luke and Raoul are busily cleaning the buckets and bins and removing the pressing to the compost heap as the light fades.

We'd been having issues with the Karcher pressure washer all vintage and had discovered how vital it is to the winemaking operations—after all, winemaking involves a huge amount of cleaning up. Anyway, it had to be sent for repairs for three days. It finally expires again at 9 p.m. but Dad, the electrician, has gone home by then. The boys grab the hoses and I struggle with the problem, knowing that if we can't get it going then clean-up is going to take a lot longer. Eventually a dodgy switch is isolated and is able to be bodgied up to get us through the night. (Of all the times for this to happen, of course it happens on the busiest day in vintage!)

Sunday, 21 April

Luke and I are back at the winery early this morning to rack and inoculate the chardonnay and put the higher quality batches in barrels.

Monday, 22 April

Things finally start to slow down in the winery as the chardonnays are the last of twenty-five batches to be processed and the tally is added—70 tons in more than twenty-five batches is a lot to keep in one's head, particularly when it is considered that there are batches within all the batches, whether they be yeast trials, indigenous versus cultured yeasts, cold soak, whole-bunch percentages, and so on!

Tuesday, 23 April

Luke had brought a spit along early in the piece and we had been enjoying throwing some cut of meat on in the morning and enjoying a beautiful warm lunch once a week, and then having excellent sandwiches for the rest of the week. Our families had also been enjoying coming out for these occasions, as it was a rare thing throughout vintage for Luke and I to sit down and have a meal with them. Even then, we would always have to get up and check the press or unload a truck.

So we take great pleasure in finally sitting down to the spit we had been planning all vintage—venison wrapped in lamb wrapped in sausages. This keeps the venison beautifully moist and rare, and is a perfect way to finish off vintage with all the Passing Clouds team and their families. Accompanied, of course, by a few good bottles from Dad's 'cellar'—a couple of potato boxes turned on their sides holding special bottles dating back to 1980, five years before my birth!

Although we will still be working seven days, our hours will return to almost normal now, and batches can be tasted and minor adjustments made if required. It is also possible to get the first real indication of the quality of the vintage, although it's hard to generalise with so many wines from so many sites generally showing a real depth of flavour and colour with powerful fruit and structure.

But vintage 2013? It looks like being a cracker.

PS

Passing Clouds was awarded two gold medals at the Victorian Wines Show on 18 November 2014—one for our Fools on the Hill Pinot Noir, made from the fruit from our Musk vineyard, the other for our Bendigo Shiraz, made from fruit from three vineyards, including the Axedale grapes that Cameron wrote about in his diary on 16 March 2013.

Winery dogs

I seem to have always had a dog at Passing Clouds, at Kingower or Musk. Some of them were purchased and others just happened. A winery doesn't seem to be complete without a dog, man's best friend.

Protos

The first vineyard dog was Protos, whom I inherited from my friend Vicki Barclay. She had received him as a gift from her friend Basil Efthamidias, hence the Greek influence suggested in the name—as in prototype, the first.

Protos was a cross between an Afghan and a standard poodle and shared the best characteristics of both breeds. He had grace, a natural haughtiness, an elegant and streamlined frame and long hair from his Afghan side but lacked a certain amount of concentration. From the poodle side he had intelligence, cunning, loyalty and black colouration. He loved to chase things, which did become a concern during his last months in Melbourne when his attention turned to postmen on bicycles. One of these must have aimed a kick at him at some stage because he had to be called off a couple of times when frenzied barking from down the street revealed Protos in pursuit of the inedible in uniform. Derelicts, too, aroused his ire, and it can be assumed that one of them had aimed a kick at him at some time, so any shabbily dressed shuffler copped a good barking.

Protos was probably past middle age when Sue and I first started going to Kingower, and he spent his last years there as a permanent resident. He was an amazing dog and had earned something of a reputation as a free spirit in Melbourne during the early 1970s when I was working the electrical contracting business, Carlton Lighting. He was never on a lead or chain as he considered them undignified and dog-like, so he was left to roam.

At one stage, we were engaged in some fairly extensive wiring work at Lazar's restaurant in the city, in King Street. I was living in North Carlton at 453 Canning Street, next door to Susie Palmer. Protos could always calculate how long the job would take, within reason, and wouldn't venture far from the van if a screwdriver and pair of pliers were the only tools taken onto the job. But if it was a full toolbox and some fittings, he knew he was okay for a lap or two of the block. If the pair of steps and ladder came off the van, he knew he was set for a bit of decent adventuring. So he would leave the job at Lazar's for longer and longer periods. This may seem irresponsible of his owner, and it certainly was. The owner has no excuse except to say it was a different world then.

Anyway, one day it became apparent that Protos was returning from somewhere late in the afternoon, shortly before knock-off time. Where from, who knew? Then Susie next door said to me one evening, 'You came home for lunch today—I saw Protos on your doorstep, but I didn't see your van.' I had not been there for lunch, but Protos had. Three kilometres through the busiest part of the city, crossing maybe fifteen sets of traffic lights to go home. Just because he could! And then to return to be back in time to get into the van and go home again!

In his whole career, Protos was never picked up by a policeman or dogcatcher although he thoroughly deserved to be. When he was younger and I lived at 330 Drummond Street, opposite the Pram Factory, a noted test route for learner drivers, he would indulge himself by lying on the road and yawning lazily. If 'L' drivers approached, he knew they wouldn't run him over. The distraught instructors would sometimes have to resort to knocking on doors if he didn't want to budge. It was always on Saturday afternoons or Sundays that these anarchic events took place, so little traffic built up behind the learner drivers, but it was often enough to create a minor gridlock in front of the police station, a few doors away.

Once, Sue and I were expecting friends at her place, 28 Carlton Street. The friends were a few minutes late and explained that there was a small traffic jam up the road, outside the Lemon Tree Hotel. When Richard got out of the car to investigate the cause, he could see that it was Protos and a lady dog engaged in an exhibition of intercourse in the middle of the intersection.

Indeed, Protos was indefatigable in his pursuit of bitches in season, and a couple of times a year would return after being AWOL, usually for a day and night, bloodied but triumphant. North Fitzroy and Carlton were like a village then, many people knew us, and reports would come in. Daisy was one bitch to remember, a girl who knew how to flaunt her charms when the season was upon her, and would trawl up and down Brunswick Street with a chain of slavering, snarling and brawling would-be lovers behind her. It was winner takes all with Daisy!

One Sunday afternoon we visited Peter Freeman and Rosemary, who had a pretty Afghan bitch, Poppy, just coming into heat. They lived in North Melbourne, about 3 kilometres from Carlton Street, and when the time came to leave, Protos was reluctant. He must have thought about it during the night, for the next morning, when I was loading the van, he bolted towards North Melbourne. I got into the Mini and the race was on, dog versus car through the morning traffic to the Freemans' house. I had barely parked the car outside the house when Protos rounded the corner from the other direction, bright eyed, bushy tailed and hot to trot. 'Hello, sailor,' I said and opened the door of the car to a very unwilling passenger.

It was the same car he was sleeping in, on the back seat, when Sue lent it to her brother-in-law, Mick, to visit his daughter Anna at school in Geelong. He didn't know the dog was in the back seat until Protos got up, stretched and placed his massive head beside Mick's, to look out the windscreen. Mick naturally thought there was a gorilla in the car with him and died a thousand deaths before regaining control of the car without hitting anything. Protos was unperturbed and looking forward to the rest of the trip—he hadn't been to Geelong for a while.

He also had that extra sense that some dogs have, enabling them to anticipate arrivals or events. Twice, when I returned from Tasmania, I was surprised to find Protos on the front doormat. In both cases he had inexplicably broken out, in both cases somehow scaling 6- to 7-foot high corrugated iron fences, in both cases leaving his minders bewildered but very relieved when I rang them and informed them of his whereabouts. One was my brother Greg, at the time living about 10 kilometres away from Carlton in Reservoir, a place Protos had never visited but where he had happily stayed for nine days until deciding that Daddy was coming home tonight, which even Greg didn't know.

So Protos had a few adventures before he got to Kingower, where his greatest sport was chasing kangaroos, which he would overtake and push over with his shoulder whenever he was able. He would then stand back, wait for them to regain their footing and head off, whereupon he would pursue them again and attempt to repeat the performance. I watched it once in the Little Desert, and that's how we know.

His love affair was eventually consummated with Poppy the Afghan, which was a mistake as he should have been crossed back with a poodle. The resulting pups were all beautiful, but had a little too much of the Afghan in them for their own good. One of them, Amy, came to Passing Clouds with Protos and us, but she fell into bad company, killed sheep and was shot.

He'd had a few adventures and was loved by many before he grew old and a tumour appeared on his rump. It was deemed incurable by the vet, who said after a preliminary operation that it would grow more quickly now that the air had got to it. It did, and I was weeding the garden one day when Protos came up and nudged me with his nose and whimpered, something he'd never done before. I put him in the car, rang the vet to organise an injection to allow him a painless and dignified death, then drove him to St Arnaud, Protos looking out the rear window of the car at what he was leaving, another thing that he'd never done before. He died in my arms and was taken home to Kingower, to wait for his grave to be dug in the inhospitable soil beside the creek; angry sparks flew from my crowbar and pick in the enveloping darkness.

Mister Blue

I can't remember where Mister Blue came from; Sue would have known. He was a blue heeler and we got him as a pup in about 1998. He showed a facility for climbing so we arranged a series of boxes and ladders and things and, with the aid of meaty-bite rewards, he would scale these things and get onto the water tank. This was in the really early days when there was no electric pump, just gravity-fed tanks, so they were on stands and quite high. It was fun for us all and an adventure for him.

His name came about from our neighbour at Kingower, now unfortunately deceased, and because this story could arouse old unreasonable prejudices it was never explained to anyone. Only our neighbour John Sendy, his wife Dawn, Sue and I were in on the joke, which ran thus.

In 1950 John was a member and, I believe, an official of the Communist Party when Prime Minister Robert Menzies' Communist Party Dissolution Bill was passed, and he was advised (as all members of the party were) that he had better get his bum out of Melbourne or go to jail. The party sent John to South Australia, gave him a modest sum of money, and told him to go to a hotel somewhere and keep his head down. What he hadn't considered was an alias, so when the hotel clerk asked for his name, he panicked, knew that he mustn't say anything that sounded like red, and blurted out: 'Blue! Mister Blue!' An irresistible name for a heeler.

I wrote a song for Mister Blue and we'd sing it around the campfire:

> I've got the blues, I've got the Queensland blues.
> My mother she was a heeler, my father he was a heel
> too
> Because my mother was a heeler
> I've just got the blues.
> I got the blues,
> I got the Queensland blues.

Some folks are hooked on cocaine,
Some folks are hooked on booze,
Because my mother was a heeler
I'm just hooked on shoes.
I've got the blues,
I got the Queensland blues.

You folks may loom above me,
But we both walk the same street,
You folks are chasing money,
I'm just chasing feet.
I've got the blues,
I've got the Queensland blues.

Mister Blue was a great little mate—and an absolute pest. Any rope, any string, any electrical lead he'd play with behind your back, and take away and tangle. It was an hour's work to get the simplest project underway, for as soon as you'd untangled the lead he'd have the hammer down at the creek, where he'd be fighting it, and then when you got the hammer back you couldn't find the screwdriver that might reveal itself in the broken ground that was to be its grave. And by that time he'd be tugging and jerking and growling at the lead and drill, so you'd have to attend to that while he searched for a new game. Or we would feed the chooks, place the mash on the ground to open the gate and away would go Mister Blue with yesterday's sheep shank in his mouth and the mash trailing along behind it.

One night, having followed my car up the road, our little buddy died violently but quickly when he was about a year old. I was going to perform in a concert at Wedderburn. I made the point to one of the children who was staying with us that the dog should be kept inside so that he wouldn't try to follow me. But Mister Blue accidently got loose. He followed the scent of my car and was killed by somebody who was actually going to see the concert at which I was performing. It was Sally the 'topless cricketer', a friend of Ross Reading's, who was driving to the show. (During one of the 'Kingower versus the rest of the world' cricket matches Ross had organised, Sally had dispensed with all garments above her waist.) After consultation with Ross, they wisely decided not to tell me of the accident until after my performance.

So my poor little mate Mister Blue went to god. The next morning how I wished he was there to make me angry at his puppy bad behaviour. I fed the chooks with tears in my eyes and misery in my soul.

Bridgewater

Bridgewater came to us from Ian Roberts during a time when he was thinking of growing some grapes and asked my advice on the scheme. I should have advised him against it, and perhaps I did, but he grew them anyway, and later on we made wine from them. Ian had a fantasy about having a few vines and a little shed in the vineyard from which he could sell a few bottles to passers-by on the Calder Highway. He had tractors and things, all heavy-duty stuff, but he couldn't spray his grapes, so I would spray them.

At this stage the battery of the Ferguson tractor had been kaput for a couple of years so I would start it by rolling it down into the dry creek bed. I would spray my vines and, with the tractor still idling, put it on the trailer and drive it to Bridgewater to 'Misery Farm' as I called it then, for Ian was a man of melancholy disposition and visage. Ian lived 15 kilometres from Passing Clouds and now I don't quite know why I did it. I suppose it was my irrepressible desire to experiment, to make wines from different areas that drove me.

Ian had been to New Zealand and been so impressed with the abilities of the huntaway breed of dog in rounding up sheep that he bought a pair, planning to breed them and corner the huntaway market in Australia. He explained to me that the huntaway was bred basically from Australian sheepdogs crossed with Scottish staghounds. This bit of genetic engineering was arranged because standard sheepdogs wouldn't leave their master and cast away to retrieve straying sheep during a round-up. They needed to be crossed with another breed whose job it was to go further, to go beyond the call of its master, to contain and retrieve the sheep for its master's purposes. So what better dogs than staghounds, whose job it had traditionally been to round up the wild deer and head them towards the hunter? In New Zealand the precipitous mountaintops provided refuge for the sheep but no access to the farmer, no matter how stout or bold his mount. To see these dogs head off on those rugged hills and return with the mob in hand brings tears to my eyes, tears of admiration for these magnificent animals.

However, one of Ian's breeders escaped and disappeared. It was the male and it was deemed too hard to get another one, so the female bred with Ian's farm Queensland heeler and they had a lovely litter of pups. I wanted a pup, or Sue did, and I went to inspect them. I put them all into a convenient ditch and chose the one that displayed the most determination to make its way out and took him home. And that's how Bridgewater came to Passing Clouds.

I never could see much huntaway in him; he looked like a kelpie–heeler cross. But later, in New Zealand, I was introduced to a pack of huntaways. Some looked like staghounds, some like blue heelers, and some like border collies, but they were all called huntaways—maybe it's a generic New Zealand term for 'dog'.

That pack of dogs was in the back of the utility truck in which my new friend Barry and I were about to cross the enthusiastically flowing Wilberforce River in the Rakia Valley in New Zealand's South Island. I thought it significant that he unbuckled the dogs from their chains and leads before the crossing. Then I realised that the crossing was going to be challenging and unpleasant images of the vehicle being swept downstream, with the dogs still chained to it, flashed through my mind. It was an interesting crossing, with water up to the door handles of the ute, the tyres side-slipping on the ball-bearing-like stones that comprised the riverbed. Indeed, later, reading the book *A River Rules My Life,* I learned that over the years many men had died on that crossing, mostly shearers on horseback trying to get home to their families. I drove it several times after that with my friend Bob Stinson and it was always fascinating to wonder, as the ute proceeded at the rate of 3 feet forward and 1 foot downstream, whether we'd first reach the bank ahead or the rapids downstream—it was often disturbingly close. But the lure was that in a stream on the other side of the Wilberforce the trout were huge and challenging.

In any event, the huntaways did not have to swim on the day of that first crossing. In fact, one of them was a labrador, so it obviously crossed with no fear at all. Being fat and water loving it could have survived the coldest torrent and, I would have thought, was likely to have been more successful in the water than rounding up sheep on the mountains. However, it was still called a huntaway.

The young Bridgewater fitted in easily to life at Passing Clouds. It rained heavily not long after we got him, so that must have been in 1984 after the drought broke. Within hours the dry creek bed became a 30-metre wide torrent of big brown waves bearing all manner of sticks and branches and tree trunks upon their frothing bosoms, as well as old rusted-out petrol cans, broken plastic toys, sometimes a whole refrigerator—for the tradition had been long established then that when it rained enough for the creek to run, you chucked all unwanted items in the creek and they magically disappeared. The downside to this was that after the water subsided, it often revealed the dumped detritus from an upstream property, which lay in the creek bed outside your house until the next deluge. However, one man's rubbish is another man's treasure, I guess, and I once woke up to find a dead Simpson washing machine in the creek. Its wringer had a beautiful pair of rollers which I needed for the boat rack on the back of my ute. I can remember Bridgewater, a tiny pup, looking quizzically at all this flotsam going by.

He became a handsome dog, in appearance more Queensland heeler than anything else—a magnificent chest, the fur silkier than that of the normal heeler but displaying those trademark spots or stars, a legacy of the crossing of the heeler with the dalmatian.

He was intelligent, too, and I began playing a game with him at the cellar door when we were waiting for someone or other. The game was devised around three playthings: a stick, a ball and a discarded piece of radiator hose from the Ferguson tractor, called 'the rubber thing'. The idea of the game was that I would ask Bridgewater for one of the three objects and if he chose correctly I would then throw it for him. It only took about half an hour for him to discriminate between the three, for he wanted to retrieve whatever it was. It was an endearing sight to see him concentrating while his little doggy brain struggled with the problem posed by the three items, and so gratifying when he had it licked, as it were, and could select the appropriate thing to be thrown. I said to Sue: 'If he ever gets to write his autobiography it could be called *Sticks, Balls and Rubber Things*, and could sell well in some niche markets, or maybe become a popular dog blog.'

At this time Winifred was working with us. Four days a week she drove from Daylesford and worked ten-hour days. A ferociously independent and efficient Englishwoman, she worked tirelessly and seemed to survive only on white bread sandwiches. Bridgie would spend many hours in the vineyard with her and it was amusing to see her arm come up above the vines with almost metronomic regularity to throw yet another stick for him.

Winifred had a dog of her own, a female German shepherd, which she would sometimes bring to work, perhaps once a week. Working together and having meal breaks together in the small kitchen at Passing Clouds meant we were often in close physical proximity to each other and the dog appeared to be friendly enough. I used to pat her, although I had lost any respect I might have had for the breed many years before. One attacked Protos when he was a pup for no apparent reason, and I had a quite terrifying fifteen seconds or so as I beat the snarling biting beast off with the closest thing I had to a weapon at my disposal, a rolled-up newspaper. But I was very surprised, frightened and physically hurt as I was approaching the tasting room where Winifred was working, and her bloody dog came up silently behind me and bit me savagely on the upper leg! I can only assume that some latent need to protect its mistress stirred in its hunnish soul at the time, but I have had difficulty in being close to one ever since, and I know what the reason is—fear!

As Bridgewater grew older and more tired, he spent more and more time close to Sue, in front of her pot-bellied stove with her in winter, or lying outside her door in the sun, until he died of old age and another grave had to be dug beside the creek.

Argen

Then there was Argen, apparently so named after a child's attempted pronunciation of the word 'dog', which came out something like 'argen dargen'. When she came to us in 1977 Argen was getting on in years and had apparently endured a turbulent past. She was a scruffy little black terrier of some sort, stubborn, with a big heart, and she fitted into the domestic scene very well. Her background was obscure to us, but it was impossible to ignore the fact that when two children were fighting, usually playfully, she would always attack the larger child as if defending the smaller. It was also noted that if someone picked up a piece of electrical wire she would bolt with her tail between her legs. The irresistible conclusion was that she had lived in a situation of domestic violence, and had been beaten with a piece of electrical flex, probably when she went to the support of the female victim.

After a couple of years the woman who had once been Argen's owner rang to ask if she could visit and see her old dog. Of course she was welcome. When the woman and I were alone I suggested to her that her ex had physically abused her and had beaten the dog with electrical flex if it became involved.

The woman's face went white and she asked me, incredulously, 'Who told you that?'

'The dog did,' I replied, and explained how Argen had transmitted that knowledge. The woman agreed that such had been the case.

During the last year or so of her life Argen began cracking the tough nectarine seeds which lay in abundance around the place and eating the kernels within. A year later apricot kernels were being promoted as a cure for cancer by a doctor in Queensland—maybe she was keeping cancer at bay!

When Argen finally succumbed to doggy dementia she was gently eased into the next world by the vet. Another grave was dug by the creek. But when she was fit and well she was very much part of the action, much loved by Ondine and Sebastian. Once when Ondine was working in Melbourne, I mocked up the following letter and sent it to her:

Dear Oni,

It's been such a long time since I've seen you, I
thought I might take a little spell (and heaven knows,
a girl doesn't get a chance to take many) and put paw
to paper as it were, to let you know how I'm getting
on at Passing Clouds. As you know, Oni, the idea
was for me to have a holiday up here for a spell while
my new accommodation was being sorted out in
Melbourne, but it's not been exactly a holiday, I can
tell you—there's so much that a girl has to *do* here.
To be perfectly honest, I have *no idea* how they got
on without me before this so-called holiday. I mean,
getting-up time until bedtime it's practically all go;
and of course, a girl's not getting any younger!
   I'll describe a typical working day, and you'll get
some idea of what's involved. Straight after breakfast
it's usually a good solid meal of 'Good O' rings.
At first they tried me on some of that bulk Water
Wheel dog pellet stuff that country dogs eat, but I
soon let them know what I thought about that, I can
tell you! I mean, there's little enough glamour in a

girl's life here, and I think apart from the fact that
Good O rings are advertised on television there is
something very attractive about a full-colour box and
a cellophane wrapping, don't you?

Well, as I was saying, breakfast is hardly finished
when it's time for driving supervision, and I've got
to hop straight into the car and make sure we get
Sebastian into the bus safely and on time. First, they
expected me to sit on the carpet in the back of the
wagon, which as you can understand isn't exactly
luxurious. I've got a proper eiderdown in there
now—it's surprising how quickly a few tufts of black
hair discreetly left on the new car carpet made them
see reason! And my goodness, it's just as well I'm
there to supervise—you know, the only morning I
overslept, didn't they hit a kangaroo? I really don't
know what sorts of trouble they must have got into
before I got here.

Anyway, as soon as we get back from Inglewood
it's chook feeding and discipline time. These fowls
were so spoiled and arrogant when I first got here,
you really wouldn't believe it. Sue is not tough
enough with them, and after she goes back to the
house I usually have to return and knock them into
shape. I find that it's a good idea to go through their
mash at the same time; it's surprising what people
will throw out to fowls at times, perfectly good chop
and soup bones, often with meat on them. Sometimes
there are so many that I've got to put them into one
of what I call my 'bank accounts'. I've got one behind
the tank, another in the geraniums, and quite a large
one in the creek. Oni, I always think it's best to have
something put away for a rainy day, don't you?

Then of course I've always got to be ready to
mediate in goose squabbles; you just never know
when they're going to start a fight and Graeme and
Sue don't seem to be able to sort things out. A jolly

good nip on the back of the neck does the geese the world of good and quietens them down, I can tell you!

Well, by the time I've dealt with all of that and done my banking, it's time for a lie-down. I usually take a little nap on the pink chair; well, it used to be pink, it's more of a browny colour now. They should have it cleaned, really—heaven knows, it would be little enough trouble to put it in the car and take it to the dry cleaners! It might seem hard to believe, but I often don't even get a decent nap. Sometimes it seems I've hardly closed my eyes and a strange car will arrive.

There is a constant stream of potential burglars here; people who say they want to buy wine, that shifty-looking man who delivers the petrol, and some of those so-called friends. I wouldn't trust any of them, so I give them all a jolly good barking at! Then of course there's always Graeme to be helped with tractor cultivation; those tractors are dangerous things so I try to make a point of running up and down beside him, barking—you know, just in case anything does go wrong. Winemaking keeps a girl on her toes, I can tell you.

Twice now I have found a stray cat in the winery and what pandemonium has there been then! The cat trying to get away over all the barrels with me after it, Graeme yelling and forgetting to turn the pump off, test tubes and things getting broken, and wine flooding out of the barrel while the cat goes round and round the winery with me in pursuit. Honestly, Oni, if you could see the look on your father's face and hear him yelling and swearing, you'd laugh yourself almost hysterical!

After something strenuous like winemaking and tractor work, I usually go into the kitchen and get a spot of lunch from Sue—you know, just the ends of

gravy beef or something light like that. Then it's off
for a little snooze in the car. I must say that there's
been a bit of trouble about that, but as I was saying
to Bonny Sendy the other day, how is a girl going to
get into a car window without scratching the duco?
Especially if a girl has a tiny little weight problem?
So that's been a bone of contention. But still, if they
won't leave the car door open, they'll get scratches on
the paint, as far as I'm concerned. It's not as if it's a
black car where the scratches would show, in any case.
I think they're just neurotic because it's new; they'll
probably settle down when it gets a bit older. Come to
think of it, it doesn't really look new now, especially
around the windows.

Well, after a little snooze in the car I find it's a
good time to check up on Una, over-the-road's cat.
You should see it lying there in the sun! Well, it's got
no chance of getting sunstroke when I'm around, I
can tell you; it's in the shade under the house before
you can say Dick Whittington. When I'm over at
Una's I usually check out the rubbish heap; the silly
old dear throws good meaty bones away, too! Well,
she's always running out of the house and flapping
her arms round and complaining about the paper
blowing around, but how is a girl supposed to get
the bones without spreading a bit of paper about? It
would be so much simpler if she didn't wrap them
up; these country people are a bit thick, I can tell you.

Well, before I know it the afternoon's gone and
it's time to pick Sebastian up. I usually like to have a
stroll around Inglewood in the afternoons so I just
nip out of the car for a minute or two while we're
waiting for the bus. Sue gets furious if I don't get back
on time—I often hear her and Sebastian yelling but I
don't take the slightest bit of notice. They always wait
until I turn up in my own good time, they know what
a lot of extra work and worry there'd be at Passing

Clouds if I weren't there! Then of course it's almost dinnertime as soon as we get back to Kingower.

After dinner I usually watch Graeme split the wood and light the fires. I especially watch him lighting my potbelly and make sure he does it properly. I mean, a stove is only good if it's well stoked, I say. Would you believe that the other night he forgot to stoke it right up before he went to bed? I woke up freezing at five o'clock *in the morning.* Luckily, there was Graeme's Aquascutum crombie lambswool sports coat on the back of my couch and I was able to tug it down on top of me, so between it and the feather eiderdown I survived the rest of the night somehow. But really! I mean, a girl needs all the sleep she can get with a workload like mine, wouldn't you agree, Oni?

Look, Oni, I must dash, I can smell peanuts; Graeme is obviously raiding my packet out there in the kitchen again, I'd better go out there and get my share; *Days of Our Lives* isn't much good today anyhow. All the very best to you, my dear Ondine, look after yourself. I don't know if I'll see you next in Melbourne or up here at Passing Clouds. I really don't think I can leave them to their own devices up here; I mean, without a girl to look after them, where would they be?

All the best, dear.

Auntie Argen.

Bruno

Our next winery dog, Bruno, was a golden retriever. He'd been given to Cameron for Christmas, I think in 1997. Cameron and I had returned from a hiking and fly-fishing trip to Tasmania to find a beribboned box on the floor and a card 'To Cameron from Mum and Dad', and inside a lovely little six-week-old pup. In fact, Dad knew nothing about it. Youngest son Jesse and their mum, Julien, had cooked it up between them.

A few names were suggested. There was a schmaltzy film showing at the time about a golden retriever named Napoleon, and I could see that, or maybe Goldie, coming up as the name, so commented that the pup was darker in colour than many others of his kind, that indeed he had a touch of brown to him, and so he was named Bruno. He now has the perfect wheaten colour that the breed is supposed to have, and the name Bruno suits him admirably, and one doesn't mind yelling out 'Here, Bruno!', whereas to yell 'Here, Napoleon!', or 'Here, Goldie!', would demand a greater resistance to embarrassment than the master could muster.

After the Christmas holidays when the boys were back at school and the wife to work, I would be alone with Bruno. On the days we'd stay in Daylesford I'd go to the gym early and we'd then take that beautiful, magical walk down from the lake, past the waterfall beside the creek to Twin Bridges, then cross the creek redolent of mint and mineral water, where you could see the trout and eat the blackberries in season, then return along the opposite bank, surely one of the best little walks in the world. With Bruno as my companion and Greg Bennett looking after the wine at Kingower, I was a happy man, indeed.

Sometimes we'd go to Kingower, to Passing Clouds, sometimes to Melbourne, and sometimes to Musk where I was establishing the new vineyard and where there were all manner of things to bark at. There were rabbits and birds; cows were a particular favourite for they would come up to the fence from curiosity and if the dog made a concerted rush at the fence they could actually be pressured into running a few paces away, a very satisfactory result. The jet planes overhead were always worth a bark. As was the Sunday tourist train, a diesel electric modernistic space-age 'Buck Rogers' machine when I was a teenager, now a reconstituted vintage curiosity—how long life really is from that point of view! But the best thing of all was the rail trolley that just revealed the upper torsos of the riders as they chugged along behind the shrubbery at the lower boundary of the vineyard—the sight of that would send Bruno into a barking fit.

At one point it became apparent to me that some rabbits would have to be eliminated from the Musk vineyard, for they were damaging the young vines—the Lagrein (which in retrospect I wish they had, indeed, eaten for they never performed well at Musk). But lacking the wisdom of hindsight, I put the rifle into the ute with Bruno in his customary place on the back seat and we headed off to Musk in the gloaming. I shot a 'sitter' right away and in a flash Bruno was out of the ute window and with a quick snap of his teeth delivered the *coup de grâce* to the doomed creature. He then sat there with the rabbit in his jaws, looking slightly surprised at this sudden turn of events, having conformed to his destiny and connected with the purpose for which he was bred, instinctively and unknowingly.

From that moment on, it was not possible to touch a gun or rifle without sending him into a frenzy of excitement. He could be asleep two rooms away yet the tiny click of a safety catch going off would have him at your feet in an instant, panting and barking with anticipation. He once destroyed a door that was in his way when he realised that I was out shooting kangaroos, leaving him imprisoned—but not for long! To the surprise of people taking photographs at the cellar door, the telephoto lens on their cameras would elicit the same response from Bruno, and I never managed to train it out of him—but then, I didn't try too hard, either.

At Daylesford he was never chained, and it was a joy to see him spot a rabbit or fox from our balcony above the lake, to see him cover that 200 metres or so of rough country to the shore of the lake within seconds. But as a young dog he was constantly escaping, on weekdays over the road and up the hill from the house to the school, where his presence would be indicated by a rising swell of shrieks and screams from the children at play as Bruno joined in the game, offering his own variations to the activity—quite embarrassingly at times.

On weekends he'd scent the food being cooked along the main street of Daylesford and if any gate or garage door was open he'd be off. When we noticed he was missing, it was a race to retrieve him before some smarty with a mobile phone rang the shire council and the dogcatcher was alerted. There were some close calls, and once the dogcatcher beat me to the criminal. But usually a short drive up the main street would reveal Bruno's presence by that magnificent tail waving above the lattes as he was petted and fed by adoring ladies. Sometimes when people at the tasting room say, 'Hasn't he got a wonderful nature?' the response from me is, 'Well, if every second person you met in life said you were beautiful you'd probably find it not too hard to have a good nature.'

Once on a beach holiday I was surprised that Jesse and his mate were always wanting to take Bruno for a walk; being teenagers, they were generally disinclined to show much consideration for other humans or animals. But when they'd return Bruno and head off with pretty girls, it was obvious—retrievers are the best chick magnets ever! I recalled the time I'd taken Bruno as a pup to the beach and was mobbed by nubile surfie chicks desperate to touch him. When he heard children at the cellar door he'd be over as quick as he could, although in the last few years it was women's voices that attracted him most and he unashamedly lay on his back with his legs in the air, hoping for a tickle, which he usually got, for he was as much a chick magnet as ever. And this despite his arthritis, which we kept at bay by adding to his food a magical preparation made from shark cartilage and green-lipped mussel.

Postscript: Bruno went the way of all flesh in 2012, at the grand age of fifteen years. As I write this I'm still grappling with how much it hurts.

Nillo

Cameron has recently become the master of a kelpie pup, so it appears that Nillo will become the next Passing Clouds dog.

He is a lot like Susie's dog, Bob the kelpie, who used to come to work with her at Kingower. Nillo and Bruno became great mates but caused us much consternation, for at one stage they were disappearing for four or five hours at a time. There were no sheep nearby so we had no worries on that score but we never found out where they went—secret dog's business, we can only assume! Nillo doesn't seem to be a wanderer; he doesn't stray far from his tennis balls for which he has a passion bordering on the obsessive. The young Nillo and the ageing Bruno became good friends at Musk when I would go there to work, Nillo very keen to play but Bruno increasingly more inclined to rest.

Recently Nillo had a near-death experience after eating some fermented grape pressings that were toxic to him, causing him kidney failure. The agonising wait for the outcome reinforced for all of us how much human beings can love dogs.

Glossary of terms

Acetification The production of acetic acid in a wine that is caused by *acetobacter*. It can be prevented by good cellar hygiene and the use of inert gas and sulphur dioxide.

Acetobacter Basically, the bacteria that turn sound wine into vinegar.

Acid An essential component of wine. The main naturally occurring acids in grapes are tartaric and malic but there are many more, from caffeic and chlorogenic to shikimic and succinic— if one wants to get pedantic. Generally, if the must is found to be deficient in acid, it is added as tartaric, the principal acid of ripe grapes and no other fruit. Acidity (fixed) is the acidity of the combined acids—that is, malic, tartaric, citric, etc. which is measured by titration. Acidity (real) is the degree or intensity of a must's or a wine's acidity which is measured as pH. Acidity (total) is the overall acidity of a wine from combined and volatile acids.

Acidification The increase of acidity in a must or wine either by the addition of acids, or by infection from spoilage micro-organisms.

Aldehydic Wine that has succumbed to the influence of a group of chemical compounds, products of the partial oxidation of alcohol. There are various forms, many of which have their own odour, ranging from the pleasant to the very unpleasant.

(In) Balance In must, where all the components—acid, sugar and tannin—are in the right proportions to produce a harmonious wine; in a finished wine, where the alcohol, tannins, acids and flavours combine harmoniously.

Barrels Wooden casks for the maturation of wine. They come in an almost bewildering range of timbers from different forests from different parts of the world. The sizes are traditional, the most common being barriques of 220 litres, hogsheads of 300 litres and puncheons of almost 500 litres. They can be 'toasted' to various degrees by the application of flame to the interior. Thus the permutations are many and varied, and the winemaker chooses the type they consider appropriate for the wine being made.

Baumé It was French pharmacist Antoine Baumé who in 1768 gave his name to the scale that measures the total dissolved solids in grape juice, which gives an approximate concentration of grape sugar content, which in turn gives an indication of the end alcohol level of a wine if it is fermented to dryness. Thus, for example, 12 degrees baumé in a must fermented to complete dryness would produce 12 per cent alcohol by volume.

Bentonite A clay consisting mainly of montmorillonite (hydrated silicate of magnesium). It has an unusual ability to combine with unstable proteins and precipitate them from the wine, as well as tremendous swelling properties that serves it well in its role of fining and protein-stabilising wines.

Blister mite Otherwise known as erinose mite, it lives in colonies in the grape vine leaf, causing lumps or blisters on its surface. These are unsightly and if unchecked can debilitate the vine. The normal sulphur sprays used to combat powdery mildew are usually sufficient to control it, but if systemic sprays are used rather than the traditional sulphur the colonies can become invasive and require the use of miticides, an unpleasant option.

Brettanomyces One of the yeast genera sometimes found on grapes and in wines. It is usually seen as a spoilage product as it produces off flavours in wines, but at low levels it can sometimes be seen to enhance the flavours of red wine. It is considered an undesirable resident in the cellar and scrupulous hygiene seems to be its enemy. When it inhabits the barrels in a winery the only cure might be to replace the entire barrel storage with new wood.

Budburst That time of the year in spring when the overwintered buds burst forth into leaf, heralding the new vintage.

Burgundy (red) A dry, full-bodied table wine of superb colour, with an alcohol content usually around 12–13 per cent. The grape variety is almost invariably pinot noir. The tannins are not harsh and the wines are usually ready to drink in about five years, but in many cases will last much longer than this. As with the chardonnays, they seem to mature better if the grapes have sufficient natural acid, so that no additions have to be made. This is largely the reason for the Passing Clouds Musk vineyard being located where it is. In France, quite often the grapes don't ripen enough for them to ferment to an acceptable level of alcohol, so sugar is progressively added to the ferments.

Burgundy (white) A dry, full-bodied, firm, even flinty table wine that is a pale to medium straw colour, in which there is often a touch of green. It is usually ready for drinking after two or three years in cask and bottle. The finest wines are of superb character and individuality and easily earn their title as the best white wines in the world. They are made only from chardonnay grapes and seem to benefit from a climate that is only *just* warm enough to ripen them fully.

Cap When pulp is present in a must that is fermenting, the gas forms in bubbles around the solid matter and lifts it to the top of the fermentation. There it forms into a solid layer that floats on the top of the liquid with a large proportion above the surface. This layer of pulp is known as the 'cap'. It is essential that this cap be frequently plunged and broken up so that the pulp is submerged in order to (among other things) obtain the maximum extraction and to prevent the growth of contaminants. Of those few wineries that do hand-plunge, most do it at least twice daily, and that is what we consider appropriate at Passing Clouds with our shiraz and cabernets.

Carbon dioxide (CO_2) The gas given off during fermentation is carbon dioxide or CO_2. Of any given quantity of sugar, approximately 47 per cent is converted into CO_2 during fermentation and 48 per cent into alcohol. Although CO_2 promotes plant growth, it is now generally held to be an evil and villainous thing, and it is quite possible that one day soon people will come to our vineyards with CO_2 meters and calculators to establish how much tax we will have to pay for our CO_2 emissions! Then, logically, they'd have to be followed by yet more officials wielding oxygen meters and calculators to establish how much oxygen was being returned to the atmosphere from our growing vines . . .

Clone Vegetatively reproduced plants from one superior parent plant, selected to grow fruit with better flavours, larger crops, greater resistance to disease, etc.

Cork taint An unfortunate odour derived from cork 2,4,6-Trichloroanisole, which taints wine that has been bottled with it.

Destemmed The stems removed from a bunch of grapes, almost invariably with the use of a machine that employs an Archimedian screw to fling the stems out the end, leaving behind the (usually) crushed grapes.

Diam A manufactured cork product, cleansed of 2,4,6-Trichloroanisole, a substitute for natural cork.

Diammonium phosphate Common nitrogen-rich yeast nutrient that is often added to must during fermentation to avoid the production of hydrogen sulphide.

Downy mildew Debilitating mildew is always associated with tropical-type weather. A rough rule of thumb is 10 millilitres rain, a minimum of 10 degrees Celsius, with wet leaves for 24 hours, all of which provide ideal conditions for primary infection. Downy mildew can virtually destroy a crop in 24 hours. A preventative spray is copper or one of many systemics.

Drosophila The vinegar fly, or *Drosophila*, presents a challenge to the winemaker because of its habit of feeding on rotting fruit and subsequently transporting vinegar bacteria into the winery. If good housekeeping is observed, they should not become a problem, but if wine or fruit detritus is left about, they can breed at an astonishing rate due to their average egg-hatching time of 24 hours.

Erinose *See* **Blister mite**

Eutypa disease A fungal disease that attacks the woody parts of a vine. Sometimes called dead arm, it can be very destructive.

Ferment The process by which grape juice is turned into wine. Either introduced or naturally occurring yeasts cause the sugars in the must to convert to heat, carbon dioxide and alcohol.

Fining Fining has been practised since early Roman times but it is only fairly recently that its workings have been understood. There are two forms of fining. The most common is the clarification of wine by an agent that causes precipitation (physical fining). The other is purification by use of an agent (chemical fining). Egg whites, blood, casein, bentonite, gelatin, isinglass and milk are all traditional fining agents that are still used today to clarify or purify wine, and increase its organoleptical properties (or, in other words, remove unpleasant properties from the wine).

Foot-stomp A traditional means of crushing grapes by treading with bare feet, considered to be the gentlest means of crushing.

Grappa A spirit distilled from fermented grape material, especially marc, the solid residue of a ferment.

H_2S Hydrogen sulphide, a by-product of fermentation. Excessive amounts can cause wine spoilage.

Isinglass A gelatinous material made from the swim bladder of fish, especially the sturgeon. It is used for clarifying wines, especially white wines.

Lees Sedimentary matter that collects at the bottom of a vessel after fermentation or maturation. Wine is usually drawn off the lees, but in some cases may remain and be periodically stirred through the maturing wine.

Malo-lactic fermentation Malic acid is a natural acid of grapes and is quite sharp. Most wines benefit from the 'malo', as the bacterial action that occurs changes the malic acid into the softer lactic acid. If the desirable bacteria does not exist in the winery, or a different strain is desired, the winemaker can purchase the desired strain, either frozen or dried, and introduce it to the wine.

Marc Marc is the residue or by-product of the production of wine, comprising the leftover pips and skins.

Mouthfeel When all the components of a wine are in good balance the wine should feel good in the mouth.

Muscadet One of France's dry white commercial wines, muscadet can be very ordinary, but at its best compliments sea food, particularly that of the North Atlantic coast, very well.

Must The crushed grapes in the winemaking process.

Nose The smell, or bouquet of a wine.

pH values This is the measure of the active acidity/alkalinity of a wine, as opposed to the total acidity of the wine. The optimum range for ferments is between 3.1 and 3.4. The lower the pH value, the more acidic the wine.

Phylloxera A parasitic aphid on the roots of vines that in many cases causes the death of the vine. At the turn of the century a phylloxera outbreak devastated European vineyards, and the vines had to be grafted onto American rootstocks. Some phylloxera still exists in parts of Australia and many vineyards use grafted rootlings.

Rootlings Vine cuttings that have sprouted roots, usually planted out into the field as one-year-old dormant vines.

Spacings These vary tremendously. Depending on the whim of the grower, they can be as close as 1 metre by 1 metre or as far apart as you like. For practical purposes spacings of, say, 3 metres by 2 metres make sense.

Veraison This occurs when the berries begin to accumulate sugars and the colour of the pinot berries changes from green to red.

Vintage Winemaking, or vinification, is the production of wine, starting with 'vintage', the selection and harvesting of wine grapes, and ending with bottling the finished wine.

Volatile acids The main volatile acids are acetic acid and ethyl acetate. Small amounts of acetic acid are formed during alcoholic fermentation and are not deleterious, but careless handling can result in unacceptable amounts being produced, with consequent spoilage.

Yeast cells Yeast is a unicellular fungus and one of the lowest forms of life. The cells are tiny (7 to 8 microns) and they reproduce by budding. It is estimated that there are about 500 million cells in 250 millilitres of an active ferment.